MODERN HISTORY
OF
INDIAN PRESS

MODERN HISTORY OF INDIAN PRESS

By
Sunit Ghosh

Cosmo Publications
1998 India

All rights reserved. No part of this publication may be reproduced, or stored in retrival system, or transmitted in any form or by any means without the prior permission of Cosmo Publications.

First Published 1998

ISBN 81-7020-697-9

MODERN HISTORY OF INDIAN PRESS
© Sunit Ghosh

Published by :
MRS. RANI KAPOOR
for COSMO PUBLICATIONS Div. of
GENESIS PUBLISHING PVT. LTD.
24-B, Ansari Road,
Darya Ganj,
New Delhi-110002, INDIA

Typeset at :
Cosmo Publications

Printed at :
Mehra Offset Press

TO MY MOTHER

CONTENTS

Preface
Prologue
1. The Beginnings — 1
2. New Ventures — 13
3. Struggle For Liberal Environments — 37
4. Newspapers In Indian Languages — 61
5. The Liberation Of The Press — 95
6. Press And The First War Of Independence — 117
7. Repressive Measures — 137
8. New Era Of "Swadeshi" — 161
9. Press And World War I — 181

10.	Gandhian Era	193
11.	World War II And "Quit India"	225
12.	Independence And After	267

Epilogue 315

Appendices 325

    I. "Aeropagitica" Of Indian Press

    II. P.R.B. Act (Relevant Expracts)

    III. News Agencies In India

    IV. Guidelines For Journalists

    V. Chronology Of Events

    VI. Select Bibliography

Index

PREFACE

The history of the Indian press can broadly be divided into four parts— the first, from 1700 to 1817 when newspapers and journals were all in English language published and edited by the Britishers; the second covering roughly 66 years from 1818 to 1884 when the Indian language Press became the organ of expression of the masses; the third extending from 1885 to 1947 when the Indian Press, both English and language, was the ally of the freedom fighters and the fourth covering the period following independence in 1947. In the past various authors dealt with this subject but a comprehensive work was done by Margarita Barns whose **"The Indian Press"** gives a fairly authoritative account of the growth of public opinion in Indian from 1780 to 1930. This book has been the principal source of information for other later-day authors on this subject. Though faithful accounts of post-1930 developments in India's newspaper world are available not much convincing effort has been made to look beyond 1947.

In the early sixties I wrote a book on this subject in Bengali. Since then I have been contemplating to write a book in English, covering both the pre and post independence periods, in order to tie the loose ends and join the missing links of the glorious history of the Indian Press. A couple of years ago some students of Journalism narrated to me the difficulties they face in studying the history of Indian Journalism in the absence of adequate written accounts. This rekindled my interest and the upshot is this book which, I think, will provide a coherent history from 1780 to April 1997 and fill in the gaps left by others.

Though information culled from various sources has been checked and re-checked blemishes cannot be ruled out altogether. Suggestions from discerning readers will be most welcome.

I thank all those who encouraged me to write this book. I shall feel amply rewarded if the book proves to be useful to students and others interested in the subject.

My special thanks are due to my wife Shankari, who shared my labour in various ways.

Sunit Ghosh

PROLOGUE

Man communicate with his fellow-beings because he cannot live without this fundamental need which is as important as his physical requirements for food and shelter. The urge for communication is not only a primal one but also a necessity for survival in our contemporary society. Simply defined, communication is the art of transmitting information, ideas and attitudes from one person to another. Where it is not possible to communicate directly men have recourse to other indirect methods. The cave dwellers used to communicate among themselves through oral signals, sounds and signs. Maybe, they had their other methods of communication also. Even today, tribals to communicate certain types of messages, especially when one tribe declares war against another.

In the Bastar district of Madhya Pradesh, the tribes communicate important messages by circulating a mango leaf among fellowmen

In ancient times, conchshells and trumpets were used to send signals of war. The eternal teachings of the Vedas and Upanishad were passed on by the Rishis and Seers from one generation to another by word of mouth. The Bhagavad Gita was the outcome of the direct communication through dialogue between Lord Krishna and Arjuna.

With the change of time, the method of communication has also undergone change. As man learnt how to write the art of communication acquired may forms and dimensions. One of these forms was the "newsletter" written by hired writers which eventually took the shape of newspapers through a process of evolution.

During the Roman empire "Acta Diurna" (notes of daily activities) were posted in public places for information of the public. These notices used to carry information collected by "newswriters" posted at various courts. In course of time, these "newswriters" laid the foundation of the profession of journalism. During the reign of Queen Elizabeth Newswriter was an important factor. In India kings and emperors used to appoint a newswriter or Wakianavis in each district. These writers used to send reports of the important events. On the basis of these reports decisions were taken and policies formulated.

However, there were newswriters who would give false reports for pecuniary or other, considerations and kept the administration in the dark about the goings-on in the country. Accounts of Francis Bernier and the Venetian traveller Niccola Manuchi, who lived in Aurangzeb's Court for some years, give a vivid picture of the functions of *Wakianavis* and *Khufianavis* (the public and secret newswriter of the emperor) during the reigns of Shajahan and Aurangzeb. John Fryer, a doctor who had served in India during the reign of Aurangzeb, writes in his "travels" that the Emperor's failure in the Deccan, despite his formidable army, "was partly due to false reports sent by his newswriters".

"While the Generals and newswriters" he writes, "consult to deceive the Emperor on whom he depended for a true state of things, it can never be otherwise but that must be misrepresented, when the judgement he makes must be a false perspective: whereby it is apparent on what bases these kingdoms are supported".

Prologue

About corruptibility of the newswriters, another reference was found in "Rambles and Recollections" by Major General Sir William Sleeman who served the Indian Army. Referring to the kingdom of Oudh and defeat of a certain Ghulam Hussain Sleeman wrote: "Ghulam Hussain was so ashamed of the drubbing he got that he bribed all the newswriters within twenty miles of the place to say nothing bout it in their reports to court, and he never made any report of it himself. Sleeman in his "Journey through the Kingdom of Oude" has recorded that the King of Oude had on his pay-roll 660 newswriters. They were paid on an average between four and five rupees each per month. "Such are the reporters of the circumstances in all the cases on which the sovereign and his ministers have to pass orders every day in Oude."

In Bengal in the first half of eighteenth century it was a practice with the factors of East Indian Company to avail themselves of the services of newswriters to acquaint the Indian courts of items of intelligence. The Indian rulers were fully aware of the need of extensive channels of information and that the newsletters were of importance, as witness the publicity desired in them by the factors of the East Indian Company. "Another interesting fact is that considerable freedom of discussion was allowed in the Moghul Akhbars; an example which was certainly not always followed by their English successors", writes Margarita Barns in her "The Indian Press".

Though the art of printing was too slow to develop in India the concept of journalism was not unknown. According to S.S. Sanial, an authority on Indian journalism in Hindu and Mohammedan times, "The earliest distinct mention of ante-typographic newspapers is to be found in the Muntakhabat-al-Lubab of Khafi Khan where we find the death news of Raja Ram, of the House of Sivaji, brought to the Imperial Camp by the newspapers. The great historian also gives us clearly to understand that the common soldiers in Aurangzeb's time were supplied with their newspapers. Aurangzeb allows great liberty to the Press in the matter of news ..... During the declining period of the Mughol Empire the Manuscript Press continued their circulation. Thus we find British popular historians noticing that in the summer of 1792 the public newspapers of Delhi stated that the Emperor had expressed to Madhaji Scindhia and the Peshwa his hope that they enable him to recover the imperial tribute from the Bengal provinces .... I wish to mention two famous men who were connected with journalism in the eighteenth Century. One was Asaf Jha's Minister, Azim-Ul-Omrah. He was originally a gentleman of the Press but rose in time to be the Prime Minister of Asaf Jha. The other was Mirza Ali Beg —— the Imperial Gazetteer (*waganegaur*)—— the doyen of journalists throughout the empire. The officer was in constant attendance upon his Majesty. In his time the official Intellegencer in Guzerat was Abdul Jaleel, a Syed of Belgram, who was also paymaster of the forces in that important province."

Although there was a sizeable European community in Calcutta in the eighteenth century no English newspaper had been established in India till 1780. The European community depended entirely on newspapers sent from England —— received often, nine months or a year after publication. The East Indian Company certainly had printing presses. A printing press was in operation in Madras in 1772 and in 1779 an official printing press was established in Calcutta. The Calcutta press was under the management of Charles Wilkins who became known as the father of native typography in Bengal. In 1778 he had made the types for Nathaniel Brassey Halhed's Grammar of the Bengali Language and he taught the craft of type cutting to an Indian blacksmith Panchanan. Printing presses were also there in the northern India. When the British captured Agra Fort in 1803 a printing press was among the valuable property confiscated.

"The explanation of the delay in the introduction of

Prologue

English newspapers in India probably lies in the act that the majority of the English residents were either covenanted servants of the Company or were connected with the Company in some other way as, for example, surgeons, lawyers, professional men of various kinds. It would naturally be their duty to keep the authorities informed of any information in their possession and, the community being a small one, news quickly spread by word of mouth. There was, of course, considerable interest in European events, but this was to some extent satisfied by the receipt, though delayed, of newspapers from England. As, however, the community gradually increased by the addition of "interlopers" identity of interest gave way to differences of opinion" (The Indian Press). And desirability of newspapers to give vent to "these differences of opinion" was the motive force that laid the foundation of the heritage of the Indian Press, a brief history of which unfolds in the chapters following.

> *"Give me the liberty to knwo, to utter, and to argue freely according to conscience. above all liberties".*
>
> *John Milton, Areopagitica*

1
THE BEGINNINGS

On a certain day in 1766 the Calcuttans -- both sahibs and the baboos ---- were surprised to see a notice affixed to the door of the Council House and several other public places in the city. The notice read as follows:

"TO THE PUBLIC

Mr. Bolts takes this method of informing the public that the want of a printing press in the city being of great disadvantage in business and making extremely difficult to communicate such intelligence to the community, as is of the utmost importance to every British subject, he is ready to give the best encouragement to any person or persons who are versed in the business of printing, to manage a press, the types and utensils of which he can produce. In the meantime, he begs leave to inform the public that having in manuscript many things to communicate, which most intimately concern every individual, any person who may be induced by curiosity or other laudable motives, will be permitted at Mr Bolt's house to read or take copies of the same. A person will give due attendance at the house from ten to twelve in the morning."

It was not difficult to identify Bolts whose first name was William, a Dutch merchant employed by the East India Company. He resigned in 1766 on being censured by the Court of Directors for his private trading under the Company's authority.

The intention Mr Bolts was obvious. He was planning to bring out a newspaper to ventilate his personal grievances against the company bosses and also to keep "every British subject" informed of the goings-on in the high society of Calcutta which was dominated by the Company Directors and employees, foreign and native merchants, the `banias' and the `mutsuddis'.

He may have other laudable motives too. At that time there was no English newspaper in India. The European community had to depend entirely on newspapers from England which used to reach the Indian shores nine to ten months, sometimes a year, after their publication. They carried more news about developments at "home" but very little about the European society in India which was steeped in all sorts of vices and corruption. Many saucy stories were doing the rounds about the life-style of the ordinary "writers" of the company who started their career in India with a meagre salary of five pounds a year but lived lavishly and made a fortune before retirement. So anxious were youngmen to become "writers" in the service of the Company that contemporary newspapers contained advertisements from aspiring candidates offering to pay premium if such positions could be assured. "The secret was that the Company permitted its employees to engage in trade on their account by turning a blind eye on their activities. Many fortunes were created in this way and so, indeed, were a number of unenviable reputation for corruption and coercion," (Barns, The Indian Press, 1.43)

If this was happening in the lower strata of the European society what was going on in the upper strata was pure and simple "loot". When Lord Clive returned

The Beginnings

to England in 1760, only three years after his victory in "the battle of Plassey, his income was estimated at $ 40,000 per year. His contemporary Richard Barwell, who was known as "Nawab Barwell" because of his prince—like life—style, had made a pile of $ 8,00,000 All this caused unrest and indignation not only among the less fortunate Europeans in India but also in England.

In such a state of the society the communicator in Bolts must have felt the urge from within to share the intelligence he had with other and also to bring to light the increasing differences in the European Community whose ranks swelled by the addition of interlopers. It is also quite likely that the notice issued by Bolts drew inquisitive people to his house to browse the manuscripts that probably revealed a lot of interesting information hitherto kept from them by the company. However, the company authorities promptly took note of the potential threat to their vested interests from Bolt's move to bring out a newspaper. They put their foot down before he had proceeded further and on April 18, 1767 promulgated :

"That Mr. Bolts, having on this and many other occasions, endeavoured to utter an odium upon the administration and to promote faction and discontent in the settlement, has rendered himself unworthy of any further indulgence from the company and of the company's protection. That therefore, he be directed to quit Bengal and proceed to Madras on the first ship that was to sail from that Presidency in the month of July next in order to take his passage from there to Europe in September."

It was not possible for Bolts to challenge the order. One fine morning in July 1767 he boarded the Madras—bound ship on way to Europe carrying with him his unfulfilled desire to start a newspaper in India.

HICKY'S GAZETTE :

What William Bolts could not achieve James Augustus

Hicky did, about twelve years after the deportation of the former on January 29, 1780, this somewhat nondescript Briton introduced himself as "the late printer to the honourable company" published the *Bengal Gazette* or *Calcutta General Advertiser* which was literally the first newspaper in India and "the first child of British journalism in the subcontinent". Apparently a determined person, Hicky got off to his job in a rather planned way. In 1778, two years before he embarked on his journalisitic venture, Hicky had, with two thousand rupees, set up a printing press in Calcutta after having spent some time in jail for non—payment of his debt. He was not a well—off person by any standard. But he had a mission. Once explaining the reason for taking to journalism, Hicky said: "I have no particular passion no propensity. I was not bred to slavish life of hard work, yet I take pleasure in enslaving my body in order to purchase freedom for my mind and soul."

Hicky's *Gazette* appeared at a time when the British Press was bravely asserting its freedom invoking the great words in Milton's *Aeropagitica* (1644):

"Give me my liberty to know, to write and to argue freely according to conscience, above all liberties."

This spirit reappeared in the England of 1760s when John Wilkies quoted in his North Briton the words of Dryden "freedom is the English subjects prerogative."

But that "prerogative" was denied to the English subjects in India because a free press would be dangerous to a colonial administration precariously controlled by Lord North's Regulating Act of 1773. There were rancour among individuals in the Supreme Council in Calcutta. There were many things to hide from one another and from public in Calcutta and in London.

Hicky's initiative to publish the *Gazette* was, therefore, an 'adventure' which was frowned upon by the rulers. The reasons were not far to seek. If a newspaper was a nuisance with the government within ten years of

The Beginnings

Plassey it would be a greater nuisance in the year that saw the descent of Haidar Ali's forces on the plains of Carnataka. So when Hicky's paper made its appearance in Calcutta the Company bosses were jittery.

The *Gazette* which described itself as "a Weekly Political and commercial Paper Open to all parties, but influenced by none" consisted only of two sheets, about twelve inches by eight. Advertisements apart, which took much of its space, the paper devoted considerable space to comments on private lives of the people, including the Governor-General, Warren Hastings, and his wife. Many of the insinuations were made in an allegorical form, but it was not difficult to know to whom the statements were referred. Since Hicky was not a very cultured and accomplished person, it was suspected that Sir Philip Francis, Warren Hastings' sworn enemy, was behind these attacks. Gifted with a facile pen, Francis had already established himself as a powerful columnist through his famous *Letters* of *Junius* in the *London Daily Post*, the leading daily of London in the middle of the eighteenth century. In 1774, he came to India to serve under Warren Hastings in the newly constituted Supreme Council of Bengal and became the Governor-General's *bete noire*. It did not escape notice of keen observers that Francis--- whose record gave many opportunities --- was never the target of Hicky's attack. Even the great newsy event of the time --- the famous duel between Hastings and Francis which took place on August 17, 1780 --- was not carried by the Gazette.

Gossips about European residents of Calcutta figured prominently in the newspapers of those days. During this period the European society in India was generally composed of extremely unscrupulous men and women who had no regard for character, honesty, decency and decorum. The number of women was smaller than that of men. The heads of society were then men like Lord Clive and Warren Hastings. If Clive had amassed a fabulous fortune, Warren Hastings lived in open adultery with the wife of a Russian Painter, Imhoff. He also managed to get a political murder committed of Maharaja Nand Kumar in order to escape exposure about his real plunders, illegal monetary transactions and heavy bribes. "Drunkenness, gambling and profane swearing were almost universally practised; Europeans of all ranks ordinarily made Christian festivities a plea for absolute drunkenness and obscenity of conversations." This state of affairs more or less continued so long as the "Government servants freely contributed to the newspapers and sometimes became both editors as well as proprietors."

This "two clumsy sheets" of Hicky's *Gazette* unmasked the Great Moghul, Warren Hastings, and the new "Nobobs" --- the company's ruling clique. The exposure unnerved them because at that time, the rising industrial capitalists in England were waging a relentless war against the right of monopoly of trade in India enjoyed by the East India Company. It was determined to introduce the policy to make India the agricultural colony of British capitalism, supplying raw materials and buying manufactured goods'. The East India Company was often criticised in the House of Commons and Hicky's Gazette and other newspapers, subsequently published by the Britishers in India, supplied materials for such criticisms. That was among the reasons why the officers of the Company were opposed to the publication of newspapers. They were undoubtedly intolerant of criticisms but they were more afraid of criticisms reaching the hands of Directors of the Company and their hostile critics in England. That was why Hastings and his colleagues became nervous after publication of Hicky's Gazette.

Although Hastings received complaints from several quarters against Hicky's *Gazette* he took serious exceptions to the scurrilous allusions to Mrs. Hastings and promulgated the following Order on November 14, 1780. "Public notice is hereby given that as a weekly newspaper called the Bengal Gazette or Calcutta General Advertiser printed by J.A. Hicky, has lately been found to contain several improper paragraphs tending to villify private characters and to disturb the peace of the settlement, it is no longer permitted to be circulated through the channel of the General Post Office". Hicky sharply reacted to the Governor General's action and declared that the order is the "strongest proof of arbitrary power and influence that can be given."

Among other objects of Hicky's gibes were one Simeon Droz, Colonel Thomas Dean, Pearse, and a Swedish missionary, John Zachariah Kiernander. Simon Droz incurred Hicky's wrath as he allegedly encouraged a paper opposed to the *Bengal Gazette*. Hicky was angry with Kiernander as he had sold types to a rival newspaper, *India Gazette*, which had come up by that time. But he ventilated his anger by making a fictitious complaint that Kiernander was contemplating the sale of the Main Church. This was too much for the Swedish missionery. Eventually, he sued Hicky for libel. Hicky was sentenced to four months imprisonment until the sum was paid. This, however, did not deter him from carrying on his tirade. His favourite method of ridiculing those he disliked was to publish a programme of an imaginary play or concert and to assign to his enemies parts which would make them objects of public laughter. Their real names were not given but it was not difficult for the readers to identify them. This was the main reason why his paper was popular with those opposed to the people in power. As Government's hostility increased, Hicky became more abusive and bitterly attacked Warren Hastings and Sir Elijah Impey, the Chief Justice. In defence of his paper, he wrote:

"Mr. Hicky considers the liberty of the Press, to be essential to the very existence of an Englishman, and a free Government. The subject should have full liberty to declare his principles, and opinions, and every act which tends to coerce that liberty is tyrannical and injurious to the community."

But the Government was hell-bent to teach him a

lesson. In June 1781, an armed band of some 400 persons led by Europeans and some sepoys raided Hicky's press in order to effect his arrest. He met force with force, but soon after undertook to appear before the court on being shown the warrant of arrest. But the court had risen for the day before he arrived and he was imprisoned until the next morning when he appeared before the Supreme Court. He was remanded in jail as he was unable to pay the Rs 80,000 bail.

Hicky, however, continued to edit his paper while in prison without even changing the tone. In January 1782 Hastings returned to Calcutta after being absent in the north-western provinces for some months and the case against Hicky was heard. It resulted in his being sentenced to one year's imprisonment and a fine of Rs 2,000. On the second indictment, the Chief Justice awarded Hastings damages to the extent of Rs 5,000 which, however, the Governor—General waived. Undeterred by all these setbacks, Hicky continued his writings but was gradually reduced to penury which eventually broke him. The ruthless company even deprived him of the money which was due to him on account of a job work which involved the printing of the proceedings of the council. He was paid less than one-fifth of the sum he demanded 16 years after he undertook the job.

The main charge against Hicky was that he was vulgar, for he encouraged publication of insinuations which could only have been inserted in order to excite the lowest forms of interest. The frequent references to certain human frailties make curious reading when contrasted with the moral tone he was apt to affect.

Nevertheless, Hicky possessed a doggedness and a persistence in the face of all calamities which spoke well for the trader-printer-turned journalist. Hicky was indeed the Wilkes of the Indian Press and he compared himself with the editor of North Briton in one of the

The Beginnings

issues of the *Gazette*. The case of Hicky was exactly similar to that of Wilkes; the one standing up for the liberty of the Press, the other that of the subject.

Hicky fought bravely and his paper could be stopped when the types were seized. His paper asserted liberty of expression even when he was in jail and was unable to take care of his wife and children. Hastings and Impey did not just destroy the freedom of the Press; they were determined to destroy the undaunted spokesman of that freedom by putting him in jail and by taking away all his types.

And as one reflects on what he suffered for the sake of a free press one remembers the words of Danial Defoe, the editor of the Review:" If I might give a short hint to a public writer, it would be to tell him his fate. If he regards truth, let him expect martyrdom on both sides, and then he may go on fearless, and this is the course I take myself."

Hicky took the same course and he was so fearless because he was ready to suffer for a great cause. Despite his shortcomings, Hicky deserves to be remembered as the pioneer of the Indian Press who fought an uncompromising fight for the liberty of the Press and died of great poverty, but with his head high.

2
NEW VENTURES

Hicky's *Gazette* was both a failure and a success. Commercially it was a failure, though a great success as a source of inspiration for others who had discovered great potentiality of the Press in India for commercial purpose and as a moulder of public opinion. When Hicky was fighting for Press freedom with the Company, B. Messink and Peter Reed set up in November 1780 the *India Gazette*, country's second English newspaper. Messink was associated with theatre companies and Reed was a salt trader. Unlike Hicky, these two were very cautious in their approach. They first obtained the consent of the Governor-General and then addressed him in writing for postal concessions assuring him that they would abide by the regulations he may lay down. They also wanted to be appointed the printers to the Company at Calcutta.

Annoyed by Hicky, the Company authorities also needed the support of a compliant newspaper. The publisher got the permission quite readily. In the meantime, the authorities were also thinking in terms of having their own mouthpiece, and in February 1784 came out with the *Calcutta Gazette* under the official patronage. *Bengal Journal* was published in February

1785 and the *Oriental Magazine* or Calcutta Amusement, a monthly paper, in April the same year. Then in January *Calcutta Chronicle* came into being. Thus five newspapers --- four weekly and one monthly ---- appeared in Calcutta within six years of Hicky's pioneering venture. The new editors did not try to cross swords with the company bosses. *The India Gazette* editor had already given an undertaking and *Calcutta Gazette* was an official publication. *The Bengal Journal* proprietor Thomas Jones offered to publish all Government advertisements free of charge. Very little is known of the fate of *Calcutta Chronicle* beyond the fact that issues of the paper are to be found in the National Library, Calcutta (between 1782 and 1794) and in the British Museum Library (between 1787 and 1790).

The administration was now realising the utility of newspapers. On October 14, 1786, James Hatley, Secretary at Bombay, writes to Secretary Bruere at Fort William stating, among other things, that the President-in-Council had directed him to desire that he (Bruere) would request the Governor-General-in-Council to order the printers of *Bengal Gazette* (the official publication) to send those papers to them regularly "by such opportunities as may offer by land or sea from the time the Governor-General-in-Council first published the orders of their Government in those papers." (Barns, The Indian Press p.57)

The newspapers were securing the resolutions and minutes of the Council and getting them printed without the permission of the authority. This was not to the liking of the Council. On April 21, 1785 the editors of various newspapers were called upon to explain to the Board by what authorities they published the Orders and Resolutions. They were further told to desist from publishing these documents, else step would be taken to put an end to this practice. It appears that these newspapers conducted themselves without an incident till 1791.

New Ventures

Madras was the second city in India to have a newspaper. On October 12, 1785 the *Madras Courier* was established by Richard Johnston, the Government's printer. This paper was officially recognised and the Government notifications, which had previously been pasted at the Sea Gate, were now published in the Courier. The relevant order said, "all advertisements which appear under the official signature of either of the Secretary of this Government, or any other officer of the Government properly authorised to publish them, in the *Madras Courier* are meant and must be deemed to convey officially and sufficient notification of the Board's orders and resolutions in the same manner as if they were particularly specified to any servants of the Company or others to whom such orders and resolutions have a reference." The four-page weekly used to publish extracts from English papers, letters to the editor, poetry and advertisement. The paper was allowed to circulate through the postal system free of charge within the presidency. The price was one rupee per copy. The Government continued its approval of the paper and in March 1786 recommended that the new presses, types and materials, which Richard Johnstone had ordered from England, should be permitted by the Court of Directors to be transmitted to India free of duty. Hugh Boyd, the editor of the paper in 1789, was suspected by some of being the author of the *Letters of Junious*. Boyd, who served the Company as Master Attendant, resigned from the Courier in 1791 and started the *Hurkaru* two years later. But the paper ceased publication a year later when he died.

The early Madras newspapers were, however, not free from trouble. On October 12, 1791 the Directors of the Danish East India Company complained to the Madras Government against the *Courier* for an item which placed their Company in a very prejudicial light to the people and requested that the offensive item might be contradicted under the authority of the Government. On inquiry it was found that the item in question was an extract from British newspapers and it had not originated with the Courier. The complainant Danes were asked to issue a counter statement which the Courier had to bring out. About this time Landon, a Civil Servant of the Company at Madras, brought a libel for an item published in the Courier. The Company took note of it immediately and asked the newspaper to explain. The editor James Stuart Hall denied any intention of casting any aspersion on Landon and consequently apologised.

The *Madras Courier* carried on without a competitor till 1795 when R. Williams started the *Madras Gazette* followed a few months later (April 12, 1795) by the India Herald. This newspaper was published without the authority of the Government by one Humphreys who did not hold the Company's licence. In September 1794, he had written to the Company seeking permission to publish a paper. But permission was refused, and the result was the unauthorised paper. The Government which soon found "several gross libels on the Government and the Prince of Wales" decided to arrest Humphreys and send him to England. But soon after the arrest he escaped from the ship on which he was embarked. Nothing was heard of him since then.

Thereafter, the Government introduced censorship, for the first time in India, and on December 12, 1795 the editor of the *Madras Gazette* was directed to submit all general orders of the Government for inspection of the Military Secretary. Four years later, on June, 29, 1799, all the editors were directed to submit their newspapers for officials scrutiny before their publication. About the same time, the free postage facilities were withdrawn from the newspapers. But on the proprietors of both newspapers protesting the pre-payment of postage, it was decided to impose the levy of the prescribed fees on delivery.

PRESS IN BOMBAY

History says that Bombay came under English

domination in 1661 (much earlier than either Bengal or Madras) when the island was ceded by Alphonso VI of Portugal as part of dowry of his sister, catherine of Braganza on her marriage to Charles II. But the first newspaper *The Bombay Herald*, a weekly, appeared in Bombay in 1789, that is nine years after Hicky's pioneering effort. The *Bombay Courier*, founded by Luke Ashburner, an Alderman of the Mayor's Court of Bombay, came out in 1790. The Courier, which was the ancestor of the Times of India, published advertisements in Gujerati printed from the founts moulded by a Parsee printer, Mobed Jijibhai Behramji Chapgar. The following year appeared the *Bombay Gazette* in which *Bombay Herald* was merged in 1792.

Newspapers in the early period in Bombay and Madras was somewhat docile. They were more anxious to earn official recognition and to enjoy official favour than to uphold press freedom. In fact, the proprietor of the Madras Courier Richard Johnson, secured new presses, types and material free of duty through the good offices of the government.

In Bombay, the *Bombay Gazette* editor gave an undertaking to respect any government order. Once he was hauled up for commenting on the conduct of the police. But he promptly apologised for the lapse and readily agreed to submit proofsheets of his paper to the Government before publication. Later, he sought "exclusive patronage" of the Government on the plea that he had incurred heavy expenses to make the paper "subservient to the purposes of the Government." The Government agreed and the *Gazette* became known as the Government paper.

Its allergy for the Press notwithstanding, the government also soon discovered that the newspapers were quite useful for record purpose. On July 13, 1793 John Morris, Secretary at Bombay Castle, wrote to Secretary Hay at Fort William forwarding two copies of the *Bombay Courier*. He stated that the paper would be regularly transmitted and "as it may be very useful to have a set of Government newspapers from Bengal, the Hon'ble President-in-Council had directed me to apply to you for the same to be sent hither weekly by the post" (Barns, The Indian Press No. 60). The Bombay authorities were already receiving the official *Gazette* of the Bengal Government.

In those days news gathering facilities were extremely limited. Yet, the early newspapers made remarkable effort to cater news on various aspects which were good sources for the Government. News of debates in the House of Commons used to take pride of place though discussions but were not reported for some six months after they had occurred. As soon as the mail ships signalled their arrival representatives of the rival newspapers would row to the ships as fast as they could to secure the latest intelligence from London and the continent for publication in their respective papers.

Parliamentary reports apart, there were editorials on subjects of interest to the 'Sahibs'; on events in England; on the army ; and on the reported plans of Indian rulers. The papers also carried news letters and reports from Paris, Stockholm, Vienna, Madrid, China, Rio de Janeiro and other centres of interest. Indeed, most of the features which made today's papers lively were to be found in those newspapers of the 18th century. There were letters to the editors, Government notices, social news, "Poets' Corner" and even fashion notes.

The social news included lists of arrival and departures in the British community and announcements of births, deaths and marriages. Special mention was made of the number of children who seemed to die in infancy and the fact that the average age of death of Europeans appeared to be between twenty and thirty years. This was not entirely the result of climatic conditions as Lord Curzon testified. In his work "British Government in India" Curzon remarked.:

"Cornwallis did, however, both by perception and

New Ventures

example, bring about one very desirable change in the moral standards of the time. Before his day there was very little dancing after supper, because the gentlemen were usually intoxicated to stand upright. Indeed, Hicky's and all contemporary memoirs reveal a universal habit of drinking which would be deemed inconceivable now, and which must have accounted in large measure for the sudden or premature deaths that were then so common. However, under Lord Cornwallis the Indian newspapers remarked that the young bloods who had previously remained at the supper table returned to the ball room, so that the ladies had all due respects. There was also a great diminuation in gambling, and a consequent falling off in the number of duels and suicides in the British community."

Advertisements covered a wide field, from lotteries, house for sale, choice wines to " several dozens of blackwood chairs of very handsome pattern". An issue of the *Bombay Courier* contained an appeal for subscriptions towards the publication of a new edition of Shakespeare's works. Another announcement reported the opening of a school in the Garrison for the education of children where "the greatest care will be taken of them and strictest attention paid to their morals."

Supplements were published when the reports from London were too long for the usual four pages. Supplements were issued for Parliament debates on the Quebec Bill and on the debate for the Impeachment of Warren Hastings. These newspapers, however, paid scant attention to the problems of the people of India. The reason was that the English Press at that time was a vehicle of comments on the British administration by those who were outside the privileged circle of the Company's higher office. Though the authorities were not favourably disposed to the Press they used to take note of the writings and tried to sort out the problems. For instance, Bengal Journal of May 29, 1789, carried a report that a mariner took on board at Tullah 150 children whom he had purchased in Bengal. The children were transported under British flag to Colombo where they were sold as slaves. The Dutch Governor refused to permit their being landed : but the mariner slave-dealer eluded the vigilance of the Governor and found a market for the children. The news caused a sensation. The authorities got the complaint fully probed and took suitable measures against the captain of the ship. That the Press even in those formative days was quite powerful was borne out by the episode.

DUANE'S EXPERIENCE:

The hazards press proprietors had to experience were quite considerable. William Duane's is a typical case. A native of north America of Irish ancestry, Duane came to Bengal in 1787 as a private in the service of East India Company. A printer by profession, Duane was employed in the Revenue department of Calcutta between 1788 and 1791. Leaving the job in 1791, he entered into partnership with two lawyers, Messrs Dimkin and Cassan, and became the editor of Bengal Journal. It was the period when Mahratta War was on. The Governor-General, Lord Cornwallis, was campaigning in the war. For some months, there was no news about the Governor-General. A rumour was afloat that Cornwallis had died. Duane not only published the rumour but attributed it to an eminent Frenchman. The Commandant of the affairs of the French Nation in India, Col de Canaple, wrote in protest to the Bengal Government assuming that the reference must have been to him. When the Government discovered the writer, Duane was asked to make reparation to the French Colonel. The latter demanded an unqualified apology and withdrawal of the news item. But Duane was willing to carry a contradiction only. He sent a precis of the interview he had had with the Colonel and his agent to the Government who took a serious view of the matter.

Lord Cornwallis was the First Governor General to be sent from England. The problems awaiting him for solution were vast. Apart from consolidating the Company's conquest, he had to undertake administrative reform in such a manner that it would no longer be held in suspicion and contempt. He was not willing to tolerate any person whose actions might create any unnecessary friction with the French. He consulted the law officers on his power to deport Duane and subsequently ordered his arrest and transportation. Duane filed an application to the Supreme Court for a writ of habeas corpus which was granted though the Supreme Court unanimously recognised the right of deportation asserted by the Government. Duane was, however, saved by the timely intervention of the French Agent M. Fumeron, who informed the Bengal Government that as the Colonel had died, no further action against the editor, who had already been punished enough, seemed to be called for. Duane was saved from deportation but could not evidently continue as editor of the Bengal journal. He subsequently started another paper, the Indian World which prospered steadily in the next three years.

After three years, he again ran into trouble. On March 10, 1794, he wrote to J. Addison, a clerk to the Court of requests, stating that a constable from the Court raided his house that morning with two warrants. He did not resist though the warrants were in the names of parties whose claims he had already partly paid and which he intended to go on paying. Duane attributed the outrage to the disclosures in his paper. But worse was yet to befall Duane. On March 14, 1794, a group of persons armed with clubs and headed by a European took him by force. The European dragged him out of his house by the hair and along the street to the Court of Requests. From that place, he wrote to the Secretary Hay requesting him to inform the Governor General of his plight. He declared that the alibi for the outrage was a debt, with costs, which he agreed to pay. But the real cause, in his opinion, was 'personal' pique for matters that had appeared in my paper relative to enormous abuses and peculations of the Court". The

Government deeply resented Duane's journalistic activities and would have gladly seen the demise of his paper. It put all kinds of pressures on subscribers, traders and advertisers and military personnel to dissociate themselves completely with Duane and his paper. He wrote: "Subscribers to my paper apologised for withdrawing their names, the alternative had been given to them of relinquishing that or the goodwill of persons in power.

Tradesmen attached to me by personal regards, were compelled to withhold their advertisement. They were told that to advertise with me would be to ensure the loss of custom of the same persons and all their friends; the military, where my most numerous attachments lay, were in like manner attempted but not with the same effect .... ". On June 2, 1794, a body of armed sepoys raided his house. He had, in the meantime, filed a complaint in the Supreme Court and wanted to know the cause of its resentment against him. Instead of any reply he received an order to quit India and proceed to Europe on ship

Nothing, however, happened during the tenure of Lord Cornwallis. But Sir John Shore, who had succeeded Cornwallis was determined to deport Duane. One day Duane sought an audience with Sir John Shore and threatened that 'if he were not granted an audience he would publish his case, copies of which had already been printed.'

The Governor General perused his application and decided to act expeditiously. Duane was asked to call at the Government House. On arrival he was met by the Governor General's private secretary and after heated exchanges, was seized by armed guards and detained in the Fort William for two days. He was then put aboard the armed 'Indiaman'. Three orphan children, of whom he was the guardian, were allowed to accompany him to England. He had left property worth about Rs 30,000 for which he got no compensation. After his liberation in England he protested:

in vain to the Court of Directors of the Company. Afterwards, Duane went to America and at Philadelphia became the editor of the Aurora. Under his editorship the paper pursued an anti—British policy which was but natural.

Explaining his action in a private and secret letter to Rt. Hon'ble Henry Dundas on December 31, 1794, Sir John Shore worte:

"Our newspapers in Calcutta have, of late, assumed licentiousness too dangerous to be permitted in this country. I have ordered one of the editors to be sent to Europe. His name is William Duane and I think, you will agree with me, that his conduct did not entitle him to the protection of the Company."

The Supreme Court upheld the Government's order setting a precedent for expulsion of journalists for press offences.

Duane's was not the only instance of the official's vindictive attitude towards the journalists. In 1796 Holt Mckenly, the editor of the *Telegraph*, drew the ire of the authorities by publishing an article alleging that a gentleman in office had extorted excessive discount (batta) on the exchange of gold mohurs for silver. He was hauled up to explain the grounds of his allegations, which he did. In the same year, Horsely, the editor of the *Calcutta Gazette*, was censured for having referred to certain communications which had passed between the Court of Directors and the French Republic. The matter was, however, shelved after the editor had asked for pardon promising to refrain from publishing such articles in future. In 1798, the founder—editor of *Bengal Harkaru*, Charles Maclean, had a series of clashes, first with the Post Master General for detaining certain letters addressed to Maclean and later with the government for contributing a signed letter to the *'Telegraph'*, commenting on the conduct of Rider, the Magistrate of Gazipore. The *Telegraph* editor Mckenly apologised but Maclean politely refused to do so. He was immediately arrested, manhandled and ultimately deported to England. Maclean had, on a previous occasion, came into conflict with the authorities for leaving the ship to which he was attached as surgeon and remaining in India without permission.

Lord Wellesley explained his action against Maclean saying that he and the editor had "assumed the privilege of animadverting through the medium of a public print, upon the proceedings of a Court of Justice, and of censuring the conduct of a public officer for acts done in his official capacity". On his return to England, Maclean played an important part in the campaign against Wellesley. He wrote a pamphlet called, "the affairs of Asia", in which he described Wellesley's action as "the *ne plus ultra*" of human despotism.

(R.R. Pearce, Wellesley's Memoirs, Vol. pp 45, 108)

His effective campaign against Wellesly eventually compelled the Governor General to quit in 1805. Leicester Stanhope, a champion of freedom of the Press, wrote in his History and Influence of the Press in British India — "On Lord Wellesley's return to England Maclean published his case and no man throughout ever behaved with greater prudence and firmness." In brief, between 1791 and 1798, editors of different newspapers were pulled up for various lapses and they apologised to avoid stringent punishment.

Wellesley took over as the Governor General of India in 1798. It was a period when Britain's hold on India was being threatened by Napolean from outside and by Tippoo Sultan from within and when the Government felt that it could ill—afford to have its actions and policies publicly discussed and criticised in press. He was determined not to allow public criticism of official actions. "I am resolved," he declared, "to encounter the task of effecting a thorough reform in private manners here, without which the time is not distant when the Europeans settled at Calcutta will control the government, if they do not over turn it. My temper and character are now perfectly understood, and while I remain, no man will venture *miscere vocem* who has not made up his mind to grapple instantly with the whole force of the government." (Historical Mss. commission manuscript of J.B Fortescue, vol IV).

Strong words these were, indeed, to be followed by strong action. Wellesley at that time was in Madras engaged in the final struggle with Tippoo Sultan. He became furious when Bruce, the editor of the Asiatic Mirror, published some conjectures on the relative strength of the Europeans and native population. Wellesley considered the article "mischievous". He was determined to stop what he considered intolerable interference. In April 1799, he wrote to Sir Alured Clarke, the Commander-in Chief, "I shall take an early opportunity of transmitting rules for the conduct of the whole tribe of editors. In the meantime if you cannot tranquilise the editors of this and other mischievous publications, be so good as to suppress their papers by force, and send their persons to Europe."

He meant what he had said. On May 13, 1799, the following regulations were issued from Fort William for the control and guidance of the proprietors of the newspapers published in Calcutta.

1. Every printer of newspaper to print his name at the bottom of a paper;
2. Every editor and proprietor of a paper to deliver in his name and place of abode to the Secretary of the Government;
3. No paper to be published on Sunday;
4. No newspaper to be published at all until it shall have been previously inspected by the Secretary to the government, or by a person authorised by him for that purpose;
5. The penalty for offending against any of the above regulations to be immediate embarkation for Europe.

Besides, the following rules were promulgated for the guidance of the Secretary who was to act as censor.

1. To prevent the publication of all observations of the state of public credit or the revenues, or the finances of the company;
2. All observations respecting the embarkation of troops, Stores or Specie or respecting any naval or military preparations whatever;
3. All intelligence respecting the destination of any ship or the expectations of any, whether belonging to the company or to individual;
4. All observations with respect to the conduct of the government or any of its officers, civil or military, marine, commercial or judicial;
5. All private scandals or libels on individuals;
6. All statements with regard to the probability of war or peace between the Company and any of the native powers;
7. All observations tending to convey information to an enemy or to excite alarm or commotion within the Company's territories;
8. The publication of such passages from the European newspapers as may tend to affect the influence and credit of the British power with the native States;

In harshness and severity, these measures, in the words of Wellesley's biographer, R.R. Pearce, "vary in no material from the ordinances promulgated by the Star Chamber in A.D. 1585."

Strangely enough, the seven newspapers in Calcutta complied without demur. William Hunter, proprietor-editor of *Bengal Harkaru*, Archibald Thompson, Paul Ferriss, Morley Greenway, proprietor and editors of *Morning Post*; Holt Mckenly and H.D Wilson, proprietor and editor of *Telegraph*; Thomas Hollingbery and

New Ventures

Robert Khellen, proprietor of *Calcutta Courier*; Richard Fleming, proprietor and editor of *Oriental Star*; William Morris, William Farrlie and J.D. Williams, proprietors of *India Gazette*, Charles Bruce and John Schoolbred, proprietor and editor of *Asiatic Mirror* wrote to the government agreeing to comply with the new rules.

Lord Wellesley did not allow Baptist Missioneries to start a press in Calcutta. He proposed to start a newspaper by government itself; but his proposal was turned down by the court of directors because of financial constrainsts.

Violations of the rules and regulations started coming to light in no time. Newspapers were not submitting to pre-censorship with any regularity, that military information was being published and that books and pamphlets were being printed and published in the presses containing information which it was forbidden to publish in the newspapers. Prohibitory instructions were sent to six out of the seven newspapers.

Another source of great anxiety to the authorities was the publication of military information. On August 4, 1801, the editor of the *Calcutta Gazette* was prohibited from printing any military orders issued either by the Governor-General-in-Council or by the Commander-in-Chief, except such as may be sent for publication under the signature of one of the Secretaries of the Government. The editor was also prohibited from printing and publishing "any army list, book or pamphlet, or in any shape whatever, an account of the numbers or strength of the Civil Corps of the Army, or of the disposition or situation of corps, unless he shall have obtained the particular permission of Government for so doing."

Much to the chagrin of the Government, some newspapers continued to publish news about movement of Company's ships during the second Mahratta War (1802—1804). Annoyed, the Governor-General himself wrote on October 18, 1803 to the editors of the newspapers asking them not to "publish any article of intelligence respecting the departure of ships from any part of India during the war or any information from which a knowledge may be obtained by the enemy of the situation or strength of any part of His Majesty's Naval Force in the Indian seas."

Four months later on February 15, 1804 the proprietors of seven newspapers were reminded that "during the present war, you will not publish in your paper any naval or shipping intelligence whatsoever excepting such as may appear in the first instance in the *Calcutta Gazette* under the sanction of Government." The Company was, indeed, very averse to the publication of any information or the dissemination of views not acceptable to it. Restrictions were also put on public meetings.

A notice issued by the Public Department at Fort William on April 9, 1807 said:

"The following extract from a general letter from the Hon'ble Court of Directors, dated 23rd of July 1806, is published for general information;

"We direct on receipt of this despatch that public notice be issued, forbidding, under pain of our high displeasure, any public assemblage either of our own servants or of private merchants, traders or other inhabitants whatever, without first obtaining the sanction of the Government through the medium of the Sheriff for the time being; and we further direct that with the application for holding such meetings the subjects intended to be taken into consideration be also submitted to your previous consideration, in order that you may have it in your power to judge of the propriety of allowing the questions that may be proposed to be agitated, and on no consideration whatever is the Sheriff, or the officers presiding at such meetings, to allow any subject to be considered that has not been previously submitted for your consideration. We have full confidence, however, that our Governments in India will not preclude our servants or other European inhabitants from meeting for the purpose of expressing

New Ventures

their sentiments, whenever proper subjects are submitted for their deliberation.

Published by Order of Hon'ble Governor-General in Council."

It was clear from all these restrictions that the Company was not concerned with the rights of free speech and it reserved to itself all the functions of the judiciary and the executive.

In July 1805, Lord Cornwallis began his second term of office as Governor General, but he died soon after. He was succeeded by Sir George Barlow, the then Secretary. During Barlow's temporary rule and during the regime of his successor Lord Minto (1807—13) many editors of newspapers were warned for their "lapses". In 1811 the Government decided to establish a new rule requiring the name of the printer uniformly affixed to all publications. This was done primarily to check some of the objectionable activities of the Baptist missioneries of Serampore who, in their proselytising zeal, frequently published statements casting aspersions on the religious beliefs of Hindus and Muslims. Lord Minto, who had earlier seen the effect of circulation of similar pamphlets had in preparing the ground for the Vellore mutiny, was apprehensive about the consequences of the activities of the Serampore missioneries. He promptly directed that the missionery press should be transferred from Serampore to Calcutta where it would function under the strict vigil of the government. The order, however, did not come into effect as the missioneries promised to withhold all future publications until they had received the prior approval of the government. But since the practice of publishing anonymous pamphlets, casting aspersions on the individuals showed no sign of decline the Government at last on December 21, 1810 decided to take action which would cover this offence and also that of Serampore missioneries.

The Madras Government had gone a step further. It received in August 1807 from Sir Henry Guillim, a

Judge of the Supreme Court, a printed copy of a charge which he had delivered to the Grand Jury containing an attack on the government. The then governor of Madras, thirty-three-year old Lord William Bentinck, recorded a minute in which he strongly pleaded for keeping the Press under "rigid control". He said, "It matters not from what pen the dangerous matter may issue. The higher the authority, the greater the mischief.

We cannot prevent the judge of the Supreme Court from uttering in open court opinions, however mischievous, but it is in our power, and it is in our duty, to prohibit them from being circulated through the country by means of the press. Entertaining strongly this sentiment I would recommend that the order of the government may be given to all proprietors of printing presses, forbidding them, upon the pain of utmost displeasure of the governor-in-Council, to print any paper whatever without the previous sanction by the Chief secretary. The paper in question had been printed by Madras Gazette at the request of the Grand Jury. The Governor's orders were carried out and the printing presses were forbidden to publish any book or paper without the previous permission of the government. The censorship in Madras was more severe than that in Calcutta or Bombay. Curiously, this was the person who was later to develop a much more liberal outlook.

About this time there was a furore in the British Parliament over the curbs on freedom of the Press in India. In March 21, 1811 Lord Hamilton wanted to know the directives issued on the press in India since 1797 and questioned the authority of the Company to impose such restrictions. "If the Press was to be prevented from publishing on these heads (economy, movement of ship, war and peace etc) I am at a loss to know what subject was left open to it", he asked. But H. Dundas, President of the Board of Control of the Company, opposed Hamilton. "There could be no doubt that the very government would be shaken to its foundation if unlicensed publications were allowed to circulate over the continent of Hindustan" he said. But it was left to Sir Thomas Turton to expose the hypocrisy of the British authorities. In a sarcastic speech he said that he was aware that in the barren land of autocracy it was difficult to grow a tender plant like press liberty. "Why should you give Indians the advantage of knowledge? You would only thereby be giving them the means of detecting your own injustice. You have ransacked their country, you have despoiled their people, you have murdered their princes and of course, for your protection you must keep them deluded, deceived and ignorant. You might as well tell me of the liberty of the Press in Morocco and Algiers as under your Government in India. According to the Right Hon. gentlemen, the people of India are considered as nothing. If such is your principle, to keep them ignorant is as much your policy as to put them enslaved has been your crime," he said caustically. These strong words, however, fell on deaf ears of the authorities, for the time being at least. Hamilton's proposal for lifting press restrictions was voted out.

In October 1813, Lord Minto was succeeded by Lord Moira (afterwards Lord Hastings), a Governor General whose influence on the Indian Press and public opinion was to be extensive. After arriving in Calcutta the Governor General, who was also Commander in Chief, enforced on October 16, 1813 the following new rules for the control of the printing offices.

First, that the proof sheets of all newspapers including the supplements and all extra publications be previously sent to the Chief Secretary for his revision;

Secondly, that all notices, handbills and other ephemeral publications, be in like manner previously transmitted to the Chief Secretary for his revision;

Thirdly, that the titles of all original works, proposed to be published, be also sent to the Chief Secretary for his information who will, thereupon, either sanction the publication of them or require the work itself for his inspection, as may appear proper.

The order made it clear that the rules of 1799 and the order of 1801 would remain in force except in so far as their operation was modified by the instructions enumerated above. Lord Hasting's order was generally interpreted by the Press as a measure relaxing the earlier restrictions. Later events showed they were not very wrong in their assessment of the Governor-General's intentions.

Meanwhile Dr James Bryce, the first Presbyterian Minister in India, acquired the *Asiatic Mirror* in 1814 and became its editor. Soon he had a brush with John Adam, the Chief Secretary, who was also the Censor. In 1817 Bryce complained against Adam for having "overstepped the powers of his office" as Censor in striking out of the proof sheets a critique on a historical, political and metaphysical work. Adam held that he considered the article" to be written in a tone of sarcasm and bantering, likely to produce irritation and to have occasioned an angry discussion in the newspapers." Though Hastings was personally averse to the manner in which the Government tried to thwart the legitimate activities of the Press he did not entertain the complaint of Bryce because of personal dislike for the man

Another incident happened involving Heatley, the proprietor-editor of *Morning Post*. Heatley's father was a European but his mother was an Indian. When he was asked by the Censor to delete certain passages from an article, written for his paper and submitted for precensorship, he refused to do so. When Heatley was threatened with action he submitted that no action could be taken against him as he was a native of India. The Press Censor represented to the Governor-General that he was "powerless in dealing with an editor who was Indian-born".

Repeated representations by Bryce and Heatley's courageous stand had their effect on Hastings who

New Ventures

wanted to follow somewhat liberal policy towards the press. He wanted to put the onus of selecting matters of publications in their papers on editors themselves. He abolished the post of Censor and promulgated the following regulations prohibiting editors from publishing any matter coming under the following head:

1. Animadversions on the measures and proceedings of Court of Directors or other public authorities in England connected with the Government of India, or disquisitions on political transactions of the local administration or offensive remarks levelled at the public conduct of the members of the Council, the judges of the Supreme Court or of the Lord Bishop of Calcutta;

II. Discussions having a tendency to create alrm or suspicion among the native population of any intended interference with their religious opinions or observances;

III. The republication from English or other newspapers of passages coming under any of the above heads otherwise calculated to affect the British power or reputation in India;

IV. Private scandal and personal remarks on individuals to excite dissension in society.

Thus, though the censorship was abolished vigilance over the press was not relaxed.

3
STRUGGLE FOR LIBERAL ENVIRONMENT

About this time, two eminent personalities appeared in the field of journalism in Calcutta. They were James Silk Buckingham, an Englishman and Raja Rammohan Roy. Both fought energetically against any bureaucratic encroachment on freedom of the Press and suffered for it but left the impress of their vision and character on contemporary journalism. Both played a significant part for the freedom of the Press. Both attracted the staunchest supporters from among their countrymen and at the same time provoked bitterest antagonism. Ties of friendship and mutual admiration brought them closer and they waged relentless fights for the right of the press simultaneously in England and in India. Here we will first deal with Buckingham and then with Rammohan.

Buckingham was born in 1784 near Cornwall in England. Son of Christopher Buckingham, his was a chequered career — as a jailor, printer, book-seller, mariner and editor. In 1813 he offered his services to the Pasha of Egypt to explore the Isthmus of the Suez to trace as far as possible the course of ancient canal. Thereafter he was given a commission by the Pasha to establish a trade between India and Egypt. But the venture did not succeed owing to unwillingness of the Bombay merchants. In June 1818 he was commanding the "Humayoon Shah" when he was asked to sail to Madagasacar coast for the purpose of giving convoy to some ships carrying slaves. Rather than embark on such an obnoxious quest, he surrendered his command. This gesture, widely applauded in Calcutta, did not escape the notice of the Company authorities and other leaders of the society in Calcutta. It inspired the public to read the journal in which he had recorded some impressions of his travel in Palestine. His literary ability caught the imagination of John Palmer, head of the well-known mercantile house of that name. Palmer felt that the merchants of the city should have their own paper to air their problems. He requested Buckingham to accept the editorship of the paper. Buckingham gave his consent. On September 22, 1818 Buckingham published a prospectus of a new newspaper to be entitled "*the Calcutta Journal or Political or Literary Gazette*".

The prospectus announced: "The state of the Press has been a subject of surprise, of disappointment, and of regret to all strangers on their first arrival in India; and the impression of its imperfections gradually loses its force after a long residence in the country, yet some of its ablest apologists and most zealous supporters acknowledged its reform to be desideratum."

Referring rather critically to the nine newspapers which were then in circulation in the city of Calcutta Buckingham said, "that though each of them offered itself as the organ of public sentiments, each of them professed to have the earliest intelligence of great events and each of them promised their portion of original disquisition, these journals, with the exception of two or three at most, are found, however, to have no sentiment, either of public or of their own."

The '*Calcutta Journal*', he declared, would bound its claim on public patronage on an exemption from the defects, and as a gurantee that it would be able to discharge its obligations the publishers announced. The management has been placed in the hands of a gentleman who possesses a general knowledge of the duties of an editor and a particular acquaintance with some of the branches of information proposed to be treated in their columns, besides considerable experience of most of the subjects which compose the essence of our public Prints."

The Calcutta Journal appeared as a bi-weekly with eight pages on October 2, 1818. The first issue came out with a quotation from Bacon in bold letters, which was declared to be the motto of the paper. It stated, "A forward retention of custom is as turbulent a thing as innovation and they that reverence too much old times are but a scorn to the new."The paper presented a wide selection of news and drew the attention of the people and the authorities to such prevailing grievances as the inefficient state of the police and the allegation that certain persons in European dress were making the streets of Calcutta unsafe at night. The correspondence columns were thrown open to any who had grievances to air.

As an editor, Buckingham said, he considered it his "Sacred right to admonish Governors of their duties, to warn them furiously of their faults and to tell disagreeable truths." He courageously faced all odds, followed the motto scrupulously and performed his duties fearlessly. The paper was a success from its very first issue. Speaking about the paper Rev. Dr John Marshman said: "a knot of youngmen of the public services, of brilliant talents, headed by Henry Meredith Parker, ranged themselves round the paper and contributed by their poignant articles to its extraordinary success and popularity. Parker used to contribute to the journal under the signature of Bernard Wycliffe and Lawson under that of Cytheron. The editor, availing himself of the liberty granted to the Press by Hastings, commented on public measures with great boldness. But the great offence of the Journal constituted in the freedom of its remarks on some of the leading members of the government. Nursed in the lap of despotism, the company officials were rudely disturbed by the sarcasms inflicted upon them. Madras, as a rule, had been unfortunate in its Governors; no fewer than six of them had been recalled, one of them unjustly, and with the exception of three or four, the rest had been second rate men. One of these, Hugh Elliot then filled the chair, to the regret of the public; and (Buckingham's) *Journal* affirmed that he had obtained an extension of his term of office which was announced to the community in an inset with a black border. This was considered a great offence by the paper. But Buckingham was unconcerned. Pooh-poohing the red eyes of the bureaucrats who used to wear green coats, he called them the "gangrene of the State."

The paper, "well conducted," "independent" and "clever," became the talk of the town in no time. Buckingham was a whig and most of his reprints from the British papers were in condemnation of the Tories. Buckingham also gave a proof of his literary bent of mind by introducing Byron's "Childe Harold" and "Don Juan" and Scott's "Ivanhoe" to Calcutta readers. As a sailor he was interested in the development of new means of communication. He drew attention in his columns to the North—west passage, the Red Sea route, steam navigation, and the possibility of a voyage by air from Bombay to London in a gas-filled leather bag stretched over a cane frame and propelled by oars and bellows. A champion of free trade, Buckingham campaigned for the abolition of the East India Company's monopoly. In his view the whole continent of Asia should be opened to the unrestricted competition of whoever was willing to risk his health and fortune. The Government and the papers which he criticised in his "Prospectus" now joined hands to crush him. Undaunted, Buckingham soon converted his bi-weekly into the "first daily of Calcutta" on May 1, 1819 "under all the disadvantages of a combined opposition.

Referring to this Buckingham wrote: " A reference to the manner in which this journal had been hitherto conducted under all the disadvantages of a combined opposition, over which it has ultimately triumphed, and the dependence on casual supplies of friends for information, now attainable through direct and regular channels, will give the most accurate idea of what may be hoped from it, when such obstacles are removed".

Quite expectedly, the existing newspapers in Calcutta received this newspaper with violent opposition. Rev. Samuel James Bryce, who owned the Asiatic Mirror, openly cast doubts on the moral standard of the new editor. His allegations were based on the fact that Buckingham had demonstrated the steps of a quadrille on Sunday — apparently a heinous offence against Bryce's ideas of Sabbath.

In reply to these charges Buckingham pointed out that Bryce did not hesitate to publish his Asiatic Mirror on the Lord's Day. The exchanges eventually increased the popularity of the journal and led to the death of the Mirror. The financial success of the journal enabled it to have its own building constructed, a new improved Columbian press imported from England together with English, Greek, Hebrew and Arabic founts. The value of the enterprise in 1822 was estimated at 40,000 pounds, three-fourth of which belonged to the editor, the remainder being owned by a hundred purchasers of 100 pound shares. According to Margarita Barns, "At that time the annual profits were stated to be in the neighbourhood of thirty per cent on the investment and Buckingham's yearly income was about eight thousand pounds, he may be called one of the leading pioneers of modern journalism in India" (the Indian Press). (Barns, The Indian Press, p 96)

In May 1819 Buckingham came into conflict with the authorities over his adverse comment on the appointment of Hugh Elliot as the Governor of Madras. "It is regarded in Madras as a public calamity, and we fear it will be viewed in no other light throughout India, generally", he wrote. An infuriated Elliot asked the Calcutta authorities to punish the editor. Elliot himself censored the Madras press and compelled newspapers to be submitted twice for censorship before they were published. The Government at Fort William sent a warning to the editor with which was enclosed a copy of the Press Rules of 1818. In his reply, Buckingham expressed regret at "having caused his Lordship—in Council to express his displeasures" and calling attention to the fact that other newspapers had violated rules relating to "personal slander" — almost all of which was directed against himself. In the words of Dr Turner, "the episode disclosed the policy both of the government and of the editor. On the part of the former the policy was to reprimand but not to punish; with the latter it was to regret but not to comply."

Unrelenting, Buckingham carried on his tirade and spared none in his attacks. Not even the Chief Justice, the Governor of Madras or the Lord Bishop of Calcutta. His latest attack was directed against the Bishop of Calcutta. The article in question, published in the Journal of July 10, 1821, criticised the Bishop for allowing Chaplains to leave their local duties in order to perform ceremonies elsewhere. Buckingham was asked to divulge the name of the writer. He evaded the question and expressed the hope that the publication must be productive of good.

Unconvinced, the Government of Lord Hastings issued the following sharp rejoinder:

"When certain irksome restraints, which had long existed upon the Press in Bengal, were withdrawn, the prospect was indulged that diffusion of various information, with able comments which it would call forth, might be extremely useful to all classes of our countrymen in public employment. A paper conducted with temper and ability, on the principle professed by you at the outset of your undertaking, was eminently calculated to forward this view. The just expectations of the Government have not been answered. Whatsoever advantages have been attained, they have been overbalanced by the mischief of acrimonious dissensions, spread through the medium of your journal. Complaint upon complaint is constantly harassing Government, regarding the impeachment which your loose publications cause to be inferred against individuals. As far as could be reconciled with duty, government has endeavoured to shut its eyes on what it wished to consider thoughtless aberrations, though perfectly sensible of the public .... I am thence, Sir, instructed to give you this information; should Government observe that you persevere in acting on the principle which you have now asserted, there will be no previous discussion of any case in which you may be judged to have violated those laws of moral candour and essential justice, which are equally binding on all descriptions of the community. You will at once be apprised that your licence to reside in India is annulled, and you will be required to furnish security for your quitting the country by the earliest convenient opportunity."

Replying in his characteristic style on July 27, 1821 Buckingham stated that the concluding portion would give the friends of the freedom of the press considerable pain because it really reduced the freedom of opinion to a more perilous and uncertain state than it was under the existence of censorship. He must now consider the letter as establishing a new criterion in lieu of the former, more safe, because more clearly defined, guides for publications.

Buckingham wrote, "If so severe a punishment as banishment and ruin is to be inflicted on a supposed violation of laws of Moral Candour and Essential Justice, of which I know not where to look for any definite standard, I fear that my best determination will be of no avail. My path will be so beset with danger that I know of no way in which I can escape the risk of such supposed violations when those who are at once to be both judges of the law and the fact may at the same moment make the accusations, pronounce the sentence, and carry it into execution --- except by relinquishing entirely an occupation thus environed with perils from which no human prudence could escape."

From this time onwards, Buckingham had many encounters with the authorities. This was a blessing in disguise for his paper whose circulation went up by leaps and bounds. His rivals faded into background. This left the "old Tories" without a mouthpiece. So on June 3, 1821 the employees of the company brought out" John Bull in the East" to uphold the "principles of civil and social order". It was obviously intended as an answer to the *Calcutta Journal* and Buckingham's old adversary James Bryce was appointed editor. The newspapers engaged themselves in lively controversies. As a Whig Buckingham gave his full support to popular demands and *John Bull* championed the traditional Tory cause. On one occasion Buckingham, turning to Indian affairs wrote, "if no wrongs are to be redressed, or suggested improvements listened to, except those which go through secretaries and public officers to the government, none will be redressed or listened to but those whom they favour ....". John Adam, a senior member of the Governor General's Council, who was looking for an opportunity to teach Buckingham a lesson, at last found one for action. Adam inspired a criminal libel suit against Buckingham. The prosecution failed but it cost Buckingham 600 pounds. A few months later the *Journal* was again in trouble over a letter, published in his paper, from a military correspondent who referred to the question of promotion in the Army. He ended with the following postscript:

"I congratulate the natives from the bottom of my heart at the good you (Buckingham) have already done them; and I hope to see the time when it will no longer be in the power of those who are supposed to protect them from fraud and violence to harass them even in legal courts, and under rules and regulations."

Struggle For Liberal Environment

The Government immediately demanded the name of the author of the letter. The *Journal* editor revealed the source after communicating with the correspondent. It was Lt. Col. Robison of His Majesty's Twenty—fourth Regiment of Foot at Nagpur. On receipt of this information the Government resolved that unless the Colonel could disapprove the charge made against him it was inexpedient for him to be placed in any situation where an important trust might devolve upon him, and this opinion was communicated to the Commander-in-Chief. Renewing his campaign against Buckingham, Adam proposed that Robison be removed from the Command of the Regiment and Buckingham be deported. He was supported by two other Council members — Fendell and Bayley. Again Hastings stood in the way. Liberal as he was in his outlook, Hastings, in his Minute dated June 1, 1822, wrote," In this country (India) many discussions are objectionable which would be indifferent in Europe. But this is distinctly seen only by us who from our situation have a more extensive view than can be attained by an editor. Certainly when reproved for aberrations, Mr Buckingham has shown a petulant forwardness from imitation of the affected independence of newspaper publishers at home. Still the question will recur, is it not more just to chasten with moderation than to overwhelm? It is asserted that chastening is ineffectual. I see no grounds for thinking so. Till within these few days past, we have used nothing but menace. I acknowledge that it has proved unavailing. Yet I suspect that it has been so from a persuasion that although we threatened we should not apply the lash". Hastings concluded by saying," I still wish to forbear resorting to a severity so extreme as that which is urged upon me and I must decline assenting to the proposition of the Board".

Buckingham was saved but the hapless Colonel was ordered to march off. However, before leaving the shores of India Robison in a spirited and sarcastic letter to the Governor-General expressed his surprise that an officer should be turned out of their country on twenty-four hours' notice for daring to publish a single comment or sentiment upon public affairs displeasing to the Government. Robison died on his way to England.

"No matter what motives actuated him, if the Government fancy it contains the least offensive matter the writer shall be turned out of his house and quarters like a dog with the mange on the point of the bayonet, and left sick or well, ready or not ready, to march off and embark for Europe if the sea coast be seven hundred miles distant.

Oh my Lord, if you had accompanied your precious gift of a Free Press to the people of India, as the prudent Vicar of Wakefield accompanied his gift of a guinea to each of his children with the solemn admonition to look as much as they pleased at the gift, but never to make use of it, I certainly should not be found a transgressor in the present instance. In short, had I not felt myself invited by Lord Hastings' own noble sentiments so publicity and triumphantly expressed on the Freedom of the Press, to speak and write freely whatsoever I thought upon public events passing before me I should naturally have reserved what I was desirous of drawing public attention to for publication in England.

At his Lordship's hands I lay my death should that dreaded event happen and let him thank those merciless, corrupt and ignorant Counsellors."

Unfortunately, his premonition came true. He died on his way to England.

Robison's letter had its instant impact on the authorities who were deeply concerned about the effect of the open discussion of military matter --- both on the lower ranks of the army and on Indian readers. The Robison episode, therefore, was subject of open debate among military personnel. Taking note of the fall out the Commander-in-Chief on June 8, 1822, issued an order prohibiting officers from sending anonymous letters to the newspapers and threatened that they will be penalised and suspended from duties while a solicitation was being made to the Hon'ble Court for their entire removal from the service.

Meanwhile, Adam continued to carry on his campaign against Buckingham. In a minute dated June 13 he says that his propositions regarding Buckingham having been negatived by the decisions of the Governor—General, he has only to bow to his decision and to express his earnest hope that His Lordship's anticipation of an improved line of conduct on the part of the editor would be confirmed by events.

Adam agreed that deportation would have been a very heavy punishment but added that the interest of the public was of greater importance to him, and his compassion for the object of punishment must yield to his sense of what was necessary for the public good.

Shortly after the Robison episode Adam got another opportunity to vent his spleen on the *Journal* editor. In July 1822 the Government appointed one Dr Jameson as the Superintendent of the Medical School for Indians. But Dr Jameson was already holding the offices of the Secretary of the Medical Board, Clerk to the Committee for controlling the Expenditure of the Stationery and Surgeon of the Free School. This was a case of sheer favouritism. Commenting on this Buckingham doubted Dr Jameson's fitness for the new appointment as he did not possess the qualifications which appeared requisite though he must be" no mean public character or he could never have attained the eminence from which he now looks down on so many of his fellow servants far above him in years and length of service." The Government took exception to this comment, which, in its opinion," substantially charges the Supreme Government with a violation of its duty and reflects upon its proceedings in a manner neither consistent with decency nor truth". The bureaucrats headed by Adam demanded Buckingham's immediate deportation but the Governor-General politely turned it down. But Buckingham could not save himself from Jameson's wrath. Both of them fought a pistol duel at the Race Course on July 6, 1822 to decide on the point of honour. Both, however, came out unhurt. It was a draw. This was the first and last instance when an editor had to fight a duel to vindicate his honour.

Despite heavy odds Buckingham had so long held aloft his ideal of Press freedom. But his fortune suffered a jolt after Hastings' regime came to an end. By an irony of fate, George Canning, who was to have succeeded Hastings, had to take over as the Foreign Secretary of England. Owing to a delay in choosing the new Governor-General, John Adam became the officiating Governor-General on January 13, 1823. The tide had turned against Buckingham.

Adam's first task was to appoint his friend Samuel Bryce, the editor of John Bull, as Clerk of the Stationery at a salary of 600 pounds per annum. In a broadside against this jobbery Buckingham said that though at first sight the information which should be within the knowledge of a Clerk of the Stationery "many seem to be incompatible with the theological education, yet we know that the country abound with surprising instances of that kind of genius which fits a man in a moment for any post to which he may be appointed". This was an ironical reference to the system of plurality which the Government was hardly likely to ignore.

For Buckingham the die was cast. His licence to stay in India was revoked. In the "Statement of facts relating to the Removal from India of Mr Buckingham" Adam explained his action. "The document" writes Margarita Barns, "is of importance not only because it gives a concise summary of Buckingham's misdemeanours from the point of view of the administration, but also it discloses the very wide gap in the conceptions of the newspapers on the part of the Government and journalists themselves". According to Adam, if Buckingham's references to Government appointments were allowed to pass

Struggle For Liberal Environment

unquestioned, "they would establish at once the right to assail, by name, those who might incur their displeasure, and still more material right of passing judgement on specific measures of Governments, with the same freedom used in discussing such subjects in the English newspapers". (The Indian Press p. 108)

In the statement of facts Adam made it explicit that the objection was to the "assumption by an editor of a newspaper of the privilege of sitting in judgement on the Acts of the Government, and bringing public measures and the conduct of public men as well as private individuals, before the bar of what Mr Buckingham and his associates miscall public opinion. It must be quite unnecessary to disclaim any wish to conceal the real character of measures of the Government, or even their most secret springs, from the knowledge of those controlling authorities to which the law has subjected it, or of the great body of our countrymen, whom the spirit of the Constitution, and the practice of the Government at home, have rendered the ultimate judges of the conduct of every public functionary. No one entertains a more unfeigned deference for the constitutional control of public opinion, than the Governor—General; or is more solicitious of every public measure, in which he has been engaged, submitted to that tribunal, which, in the end, will always do justice to upright intentions and honest endeavours in the public service. With equal readiness does he acknowledge the utility of this species of control, in rendering public men circumspect in the performance of their duties, and checking every propensity to abuse the power, influence and authority derived from public station. But he protests against the assumption of this right of control over the Government and its officers, by a community constituted like the European Society of India. He denies the existence of such a right in that body, and he maintains that it never can be exercised with efficiency for the professed purpose, or with any other consequence, than weakening the just and necessary authority of the Government, and introducing the worst spirit of party animosity and violence into this limited society, through the agency of a licentious press. The latter result has already been produced in a considerable degree, and if the former is not yet perceptible as injuriously affecting public measures, it must not be supposed, that the perpetual assaults on the character and respectability of the Government, contemptible as they frequently are, are not calculated to shake greatly that salutary confidence in its justice and integrity, and that habitual deference for its authority and judgment which, with advertence to the anomalous structure of our power in this country, it is so essential to preserve unimpaired". (John Adam, Statement of Facts pp 51—52)

In a statement to his readers Buckingham announced that he expected to return to India in near future. He said, "the Governor General has, in his supreme wisdom and unimpeachable judgement, though fit to distinguish his brief but happy elevation, by an act without parallel in the history of India during the whole of the preceeding administration. I contend that it (power of deportation) ought not to be used against anyone, unless an urgent case of danger to the State could be made out; and even then, not without a hearing and a defence granted to the accused, instead of his being subject to a caprice which makes a Governor at once Accuser, Witness, Judge, Jury and even Executioner. Such a subjection to the arbitrary will of the best man that ever breathed is monstrous and every Englishman ought to raise his voice in reprobation of it, from principle as well as self-preservation".

He declared that he would lose no time in directing "all his exertions in another and higher quarter to obtain for his countrymen in India that freedom and independence of mind which was not denied to the most abject individual of Indian birth." "While," he said, the power of banishment without trial existed, "no Englishman could hope to enjoy independence of mind in the performance of his public duties, or the promulgation of his opinions in that quarter of the British Empire". Then, avowing that he felt malice towards none, Buckingham concluded, "I can safely lay my hand upon my heart and say, I leave the shores of India in peace with all mankind". Though Buckingham left after auctioning his personal possessions the Journal continued under the editorship of Mr Sandys, who having been born in India, could not be deported. He was assisted by Sandford Arnot and James Sutherland.

In England Buckingham failed in most of his attempts to secure compensation for the damage he had suffered. All his appeals to the authorities fell on deaf ears. He sought to draw public sympathy through his column in *"Oriental Herald"*, a monthly periodical he first published in January 1824. But he was not without friends among the public, in the Court of Directors, in Parliament and elsewhere. They strongly felt that Buckingham had made significant contribution to political life. Indeed, Leicester Stanhope declared, "with the exception of Edmund Burke, Lord Cornwallis, Lord Hastings and Mr Mill no man had conferred greater benefits on the people of India ... than this said persecuted Buckingham". Moreover, Lord Hastings also let it be known that he did not approve of Buckingham's deportation.

With unflagging zeal Buckingham started in January 1826 the "Athenaeum". Its object was to bring serious literary criticism to bear on the masses of books which were being turned out for the printing presses partly as a result of wider education and partly owing to increase in wealth as a consequence of industrial expansion. Shortly after its inception Buckingham handed the paper over to others while he concentrated on his demand that the Company's Charter should not be renewed, and the Eastern trade should be free and open to all. In this campaign he was supported by the merchants who were against East India Company's monopoly. Later Buckingham joined politics. His public meetings had established for him a reputation as an orator and his advocacy of radical measures led his supporters to look upon him as an ideal parliamentary representative. On December 14, 1832 he was elected to the first Reformed Parliament from Sheffield. When the question of renewal of the Company's Charter came up before Parliament Buckingham opposed the measure on various grounds, the chief being that it failed to recognise the political rights of the people who were being held in subjection. At that time, he pointed out, any purchaser in England of 500 pounds of the Company's stock had more influence on the Government of India than the most able Indian". "Buckingham," wrote Margarita Barns, "was advocating a point which was far in advance of his age and almost beyond the comprehension of the members of the old school of thought".

Buckingham, however, continued to be a subject of debate in the Calcutta Press though he was not in India. His critics dwelt on his past career, repeated their accusation of literary piracy and returned to the question of Press freedom. The *Calcutta Journal*, naturally, defended the absent editor against the attacks of John Bull only to find itself in trouble. Since Sandys, the editor, could not be deported as he was an Anglo-Indian, Sandfort Arnot who was living in India without a licence from the Company, was chosen for the deportation. Under the authority of Lord Amherst, Chief Secretary Bailey wrote to the proprietors of the Journal ordering the immediate deportation of Arnot, the Assistant Editor:

Gentlemen,

1. After the official communication made to you in my letter of the 18th July last and the recent assurances on the part of the conductors of the Calcutta Journal conveyed in Mr Sandys' letter to your address of the 29th of that month, the Right Hon'ble the Governor—General in Council has noticed with surprise certain passages contained in the Calcutta Journal of the 30th ultimo, page 833.

2. The renewed discussion in the *Calcutta Journal*

of the question of Mr Buckingham's removal from India, after the correspondence which has so recently passd, is in itself disrespectful to the Government, and a violation of the rules prescribed for the guidance of the editors, and the offence is greatly aggravated by the mode of treating the subject and by the manner in which the motives of the Government in removing Mr Buckingham are grossly and wilfully perverted.

3. The passages in question marked by a double line which clearly impugn the motives of the Government in removing Mr Buckingham from India would warrant the immediate recall of the licence under which the *Calcutta Journal* is published; but notwithstanding the just cause of displeasure afforded on this occasion, the Governor—General in Council is still unwilling from the considerations connected with the interests of those who share in the property, to have recourse to so extreme a measure, while it can be avoided.

4. His Lordship in Council cannot, however pass over the present insult offered to Government with the mere expression of his displeasure, and he has resolved to adopt the following course.

5. The article containing the offensive passages above quoted is professedly an editorial article for which Mr Sandys and Mr Arnot, the avowed conductors of the paper, are clearly and personally responsible.

6. Mr Sandys cannot be subjected to any direct mark of displeasure of Government suitable to the occasion and to the nature of the offence, which would not equally injure the interests of the shareres in the property : But Mr Sandfort Arnot is a native of Great Britain residing in India, without any licence from the Hon'ble the Court of Directors or other legal authority. The Governor—General in Council has accordingly

resolved that Mr Arnot be sent to England and that immediate orders be issued to give effect to the forgoing resolution.

7. The Governor—General in Council trusts that this measure will be sufficient to prevent any further violation by the conductors of the Calcutta Journal of the respect due to Government, and of the rules prescribed for the regulation of the periodical Press, and will render it unnecessary to have recourse to the ultimate measure of withdrawing the licence under which the Calcutta Journal is now published.

General Department.   **W.B. Bayley**

23rd September, 1823   (Chief Secretary to Government)

(Source : Home Miscellaneous Series No 533)

Buckingham, by this time, had started a paper in England called the *Oriental Herald*. Extracts of the paper were reprinted in the *Calcutta Journal*. The paper also published passages from Leichester Stanhope's "Sketch of the history and Influence of the Press in British India". Since these passages referred to the question of the freedom of the press the Government took umbrage and slapped the following letter on the proprietors revoking the licence of the journal.

To Mr John Palmer and Mr George Ballard

Gentlemen,

You were apprised by my official letters of the 18th July and 23rd September last of the sentiments entertained by the Governor-General in Council, with regard to the repeated violation on the part of the conductors of the Calcutta Journal of the rules established by Government for the regulation of the periodical press. The editor of the *Calcutta Journal*, notwithstanding these communications, has since, by the republication in successive numbers of that newspaper of numerous extracts from a pamphlet published in England, revived the discussion of topics which had before been officially prohibited, and has maintained and enforced opinions and principles which, as applicable to the state of the country, the Governor-General in Council has repeatedly discouraged and reprobated, the extracts themselves so published, containing numerous passages which are in direct violation of the rules prescribed by Government under the date the 5th April last.

The Right Hon'ble the Governor—General in Council has, in consequence, this day, been pleased to resolve that the licence granted by Government on the 18th of April 1823 authorising and empowering John Francis Sandys and Peter Stone de Rozario to print and publish in Calcutta a newspaper called *The Calcutta Journal* of Politics and General Literature and supplement thereto, issued on Sundays, entitled and called *New Weekly Register* and *General Advertiser of the Interior* with heads of the latest intelligence, published as a supplement to the country edition of the *Calcutta Journal*, shall be revoked and recalled, and you are hereby and respectively required to take notice that the said licence is resumed, revoked and recalled accordingly.

Council Chamber   I am & Ca,

10th November, 1823   **W.B. Bailey**

                           Chief Secretary to Government.

In an act of extreme vindictiveness the authorities prevented Arnot from depositing the necessary security, arrested and locked him in the military prison. He, however, secured his release by a writ of habeas corpus and took shelter in the French territory of Chandernagore. In due course he was deported to England for not having any licence to stay. The publication of the Calcutta Journal had been suspended. The proprietors were given to understand that a new licence would not be granted so long as Buckigham was, in any way, connected with the paper. The proprietors then offered the editorship of the Journal to Dr Muston, a son-in-law of Harrington, a member of the Governor-General's Council. The authorities objected to this appointment on teo counts; first, since Muston was already working as a Presidency surgeon his duties would suffer and secondly, as Buckingham still held a share in the concern, Muston, it was feared, would be "constantly exposed to his influence" although proprietors assured the Government that they had already ascertained from the Medical Board that Muston could, without prejudice to his medical duties, take on the editorship, the licence was not given.

In London the Court of Directors approved of Buckingham's deportation and agreed with the contention of the Bengal Government that "he (Buckingham) was resolved to bring the matter to issue and that further toleration would have been a virtual acknowledgement of the inability of the Government to curb him". But they characterised the appointment of Bryce as Stationery Clerk as "grossly improper" and annulled the appointment despite Adam's explanation. They similarly disapproved of Muston acting as a Presidency surgeon. But the Court of Directors regretted the deportation of Sandford Arnot after he had promised to have no connection with any newspaper and had also presented a memorial from a number of Indians praying that he be allowed to remain to teach English. Later they were satisfied with the explanation given by Lord Amherst and his Council for deporting Arnot who had to pursue his case in London.

Muston was a clever man. Since the authorities were determined not to grant him a licence, whether for the *Calcutta Journal* or the British Lion (as he proposed at one time to call the paper) so long as Buckingham might be even remotely connected with the project. Eventually, on February 12, 1824, Muston was granted a licence as editor and sole proprietor of a newspaper to be called *The Scotsman of the East* which was, in the words of Buckingham," printed with my types, published

Struggle For Liberal Environment 59

at my premises and supported by my subscribers but the profit wholly his (Muston's)." The latter did not pay "a singe shilling" to Buckingham who held a half share in the property. There were seventy co—proprietors and they each received free copy of the new paper as part of the rent charge which was Rs 2500 per month for the use of the printing materials and the house. But Buckingham did not even receive this much though, as he said, his labour and capital had built up the concern. Muston, on the other hand was paid a fixed salary of Rs 600 per month with a share in any profits. But Muston could not run the paper for long. Eventually, he sold the paper to the proprietors of *Bengal Hurkaru* and the materials were sold by public auction. The three thousand pounds which Buckingham left to maintain the paper had been spent for maintenance of the staff during the protracted negotiation with the Government for a new licence and the proceeds of the auction were absorbed by the debts which had by now accumulated; with the result that instead of having a credit, Buckingham now owed about Rs 27,000.

In suppressing newspapers Bombay also did not lag behind. The editor of the *Bombay Gazette*, C.J. Fair was ordered to furnish a security of Rs 20,000 with two sureties of Rs 10,000 each for his comments on the Supreme Court. Having failed to deposit the money Fair had to leave India in 1824. But Fair was not the last English editor to be deported from India. Decades later, B.G. Hoirniman, editor of *Bombay Chronicle*, was deported because he raised his voice against the inhuman oppression of the British Government during the Martial Law regime in the Punjab in 1919.

4
NEWSPAPERS IN INDIAN LANGUAGES

In the history of the Indian Press 1818 was a landmark year. So long the newspapers were all in English language and they were owned and also edited by Englishmen. A new trend was set in with the public appearance of *Vangal Gazette, Dig Darshan* and *Samachar Darpan*. Both *Dig Darshan* and *Samachar Darpan*, though started by the Serampore missioneries, were the first Journals published in Bengali. While *Dig Darshan* came out in April 1818, the first copy of *Samachar Darpan* rolled out of the printing press on May 23. In between, the Baptist missioneries also started on April 30 the monthly periodical, The *Friend of India* which was later merged with the *Statesman*. The principal aim of *Dig Darshan* and *Samachar Darpan* was to carry on tirade against the prevailing religious faiths in India in order to popularise Christian ideas.

Samachar Darpan avoided comments on contemporary political issues but had arrangements for gathering and printing elaborate social and other news from about 60 stations in the districts of Bengal. Hastings believed in the utility of the language press. At his instance *Samachar Darpan* was allowed concession in postal rates. His successor, Lord Amherst, subscribed one hundred copies which were distributed to Government offices. It was widely patronised by the leading functioneries of the Government and chief civilians of the mufussil. The subscribed to it for the valuable information it carried about their districts, information which could not be obtained through official channels. Indians who contributed to the journal did so because of its official circulation.

Ganga Kishore Bhattacharya's *Vangal Gazette* marked a new era in Indian journalism. A teacher having progressive reformist ideas, Bhattacharya started the first Bengali weekly paper, assisted in his efforts by Hara Chandra Roy, a close associate and member of Raja Rammohun Roy's "Atmiya Sabha". The *Gazette* represented progressive views of the day. Rammohun's first Bengali tract on "Sati" was printed on the pages of the *Gazette*.

There is a controversy over the date of publication of "Vangal Gazette". According to Margarita Barns, the paper was established by Gangadhar Bhattacharya in 1816. "Its existence was a short one but it was the pioneer of hundreds of Indian-owned newspapers," she writes. J. Natarajan. (History of Indian Journalism) was not sure about the date. He simply says that the paper lived for one year only. In his "A History of the Press in India" S. Natarajan writes, " The most significant development in public life was the launching of the first Indian newspaper in English, the weekly *Bengali Gazette*, by Gangadhar Bhattacharya, a teacher who was greatly influenced by Raja Rammohun Roy." All the facts seem to be incorrect. J.K. Majumdar in his, "Raja Rammohun Roy and Progressive Movements in India" maintains that the weekly continued till 1820. It was published in Bengali language but sometimes it published articles in English and Hindi also. The '*Friend of India*' claimed *Samachar Darpan* to be the first weekly paper in Bengali language. But Bhowani Chanran Banerji, editor of *Samachar Chandrika*, and Iswar Chandra Gupta, editor, *Sambad Prabhakar*, claimed that honour for *Vangal Gazette*. Brajendra Nath Bandyopadhya, in his "*Bangla Samayik Patro*" supported the view of Rev. J. Long that the *Gazette* was preceded by *Samachar Darpan*. However, the incontrovertible fact that came out of the conflicting views is that the *Gazette* was the first Bengali newspaper published by a Bengali.

RAMMOHUN'S CONTRIBUTION

But the Indian who left his indelible imprint on the Press of the day was Raja Rammohun Roy.

Of Rammohun one hears mostly as a social reformer and little as a journalist. No doubt the Father of Indian renaissance who, to quote Rabindranath Tagore, "inaugurated the modern age in India," was a social reformer, having spent every ounce of his energy on activities pertaining to social reform. When he took to journalism it was society he sought to serve in as much as the Press has close relation with the society. Impact of one on the other has always been great and the Indian Press is no exception. Any Press leader in the country is invariably regarded as a social leader and the Press mirrors stirs and changes in the social structure.

Quest for truth was Rammohun's mission; his torch, reason. And he would not swerve from the path once he believed it was the right one. Indeed, this quest was the mainspring of all his activities. It inspired him to defend Hinduism from the onslaught of the Christian missioneries, reform the religion by doing away with idolatry and polytheism; to start three papers viz, (1) *Sambad Kaumudi* (Bengali weekly) 2, *Meerut—ul—Akhbar* (Persian weekly) and 3. *Brahminical Magazine* (English weekly) -- all these to hold aloft the truth he realised.

Indian journalism started on its course with Rammohun Roy as the leader of the movement. Peculiarly enough, the stalwarts of the time who toiled so hard to bring about social reforms in our country had receded to the background; No appreciable effort had been made either to make their contribution popular or to place before the reading public the journals of the day. The reason, of course, is not far to seek. Documents and records badly needed for research work are wanting. They have mostly been lost or not been properly preserved. Without casting any reflection on the authorities concerned it might be said that while there are enough materials on the life and activities of our former feudal chiefs and national heroes the first issue of a particular newspaper, now defunct, might not be available in our libraries and archives. We are, nevertheless, grateful to those persevering scholars who have dug out a lot of materials by diving deep into the past and handed down the fruits of their labour to their successors for further study and research.

As to the actual birthdate of *Sambad Kaumudi* opinion differs. Margarita Barns says that the paper was founded in December 1820 by Bhowani Charan Banerji and later taken over by Rammohun Roy. Rev. J. Long, in a note submitted to the Government in 1859 on the 'Past Condition and Future Prospects of the Vernacular Press' said that the weekly was established in 1819 by the Raja and Banerji was the editor. This seems to be more authentic.

While Rammohun was pioneering all kinds of social reforms, editor Banerji, conservative in his outlook, was against all such moves. It was, therefore, practically impossible for these two personalities to sail in the same boat for long. They clashed sharply on the '*Sutti*' issue and the editor gave up the job after the 13th issue of the paper had come out. From now on Bhowanicharan's role was one of active hostility to the Kaumudi. He started another weekly *Samachar Chandrika*, all on his own, only to counter Rammohun's reform activities. Fortunately for him, the wind was in his sail for the time being. The progressive *Kaumudi* had to cease publication at the impact of the conservative *Chandrika*. But it was a brief spell. The *Kaumudi* was revived by the Raja and Rev. Long records that it "lasted to see the abolition of "Sutti" by Lord Bentinck, the actual carrying out of which was in no small degree owing to the *Kaumudi* and similar papers preparing the native mind for the abolition".

In a catalogue of Bengali newspapers and periodicals prepared by him and submitted to the Government in 1855 Rev. Long shows the *Sambad Kaumudi*' as having been first published in 1819, having continued for thirty—three years and as edited by Babu Tarachand Dutt and Babu Bhowanicharan Bandopadhya. The next paper shown is the *Samachar Chandrika*' as still in existence in 1855 and edited by Bhowanicharan Banerji. In his 1859 review Long described the *Chandrika* as the oldest of the existing newspapers and an advocate of old Hindu regime. He adds: "The editor of *Chandrika* for 25 years was Bhowani Banerji, an able Sanskrit and Bengali scholar, the leader of the Dharma Sabha of which *Chandrika* was the organ. The *Chandrika* occasionally barks now, but it is toothless; the body of the Hindu reformers is too strong for it."

In official quarters *Kaumudi* was feared more than any other paper, for when the paper ceased publication for a period because of its desertion by its editor, Bhawani Charan Banerji, Buckingham commented on its demise in the *Calcutta Journal* as follows:

"The paper which was considered so fraught with danger, and likely to explode over all India like a spark thrown into a barrel of gunpowder, has long since fallen to the ground for want of support; chiefly we understand because it offended the native community, by opposing some of their customs, and particularly the burning of Hindoo widows. The innocent *Sambad Kaumudi*, the object of so much unnecessary alarm, was originally established in the month of December, 1821, and relinquished by the original proprietor for want of encouragement in May 1822, after which it was kept alive by another native till the September following, when about the commencement of the Doorga Pooja holidays, it was first suspended and then fell to rise no more."

Rammohun's second venture was a Persian weekly — *Meerut-ul-Akhbar*. It's motto, according to Rammohun, was truth. The paper, he said, would cling to what is true. It would communicate to the rulers a knowledge of the real situation of their subjects and make the subjects acquainted with the established law and customs of their rulers. That the rulers may more readily find an opportunity of granting relief to the people and the people may be put in possession of the means of obtaining protection and redress from the rulers". The criticism and discussions which had then appeared were always constructive in approach and restrained in language. The subjects dealt with covered a wide range -- from the administrative and social problems of the day to the issues connected with British diplomacy in India and Ireland.

Meerut-ul-Akhbar, it has to be mentioned, was not the first Persian newspaper published in India. Indeed, some were published towards the end of the 18th century but there are no records of them. The Meerut was followed by two other Persian newspapers -- *Jam-i-Jahan—Numa* and the *Shams-ul-Akhbar*.

Meanwhile, the Press in India was coming under many rigorous rules. As had already been mentioned, Buckingham was deported for his strong attacks on the British administration. The influence of the Raja's paper as well as critical writings of several other newspapers annoyed the rulers. William Butterworth Bailey, the Chief secretary to the Government, made a catalogue of "objectionable passages" in newspapers and submitted a lengthy minute on October 10, 1822 in which he concentrated his main attack on *Meerut-ul-Akhbar*. About the Press in India, Bailey frankly confessed, "The liberty of the Press, however essential to natives of a free State, is not, in my judgment, consistent with the character of our institutions in this country and with the extraordinary nature of their interests."

The immediate fall-out of the report was the notorious ordinance which the acting Governor General Adam promulgated. Known as Adam's Gag, the Ordinance laid down: "Henceforth, no one should publish a newspaper or a periodicial without having obtained a licence from the Governor-General-in— Council, signed by the Chief Secretary. The application for licence should give the name or names of printer and publisher, of the proprietors, their place of residence, the location of the press and the title of the newspaper, magazine, register, pamphlet or other printed books or paper." The penalty for infringement was prescribed to be fine and imprisonment.

Before the ordinance could come in to force, the law required it to be put up in the Supreme Court for twenty days and, if not disallowed, it was registered. Accordingly, the regulation was entered on March 15, 1823 and read in public. Rammohun foresaw that the *Meerut-ul-Akhbar* would surely be a victim of these regulations as some of the writings in this paper were already taken note of by W.B. Bailey. The Raja also realised that these regulations would thwart the healthy growth of the Press in India. He and five other leaders of the then Bengali society—Sundar Kumar Tagore, Harachandra Ghosh, Dwarakanath Tagore, Gaur Charan Banerji and Prasanna Kumar Tagore --- put in a joint representation to the Chief Justice. They declared that the people of Calcutta were opposed to such extreme regulations. The petition which came to be known as "Areopagitica of the Indian Press" said that the rules will preclude Indians " from making the Government readily acquainted with the errors and injustice that may be committed by its executive officers in the various parts of their extensive country and it would also prevent the natives from communicating frankly and honestly to their Gracious Soverign in England and his Council, the real conditions of his Majesty's subjects in the distant part of his dominions and the treatment they experience from the local Government. (See Appendix 1)

Sir Francis MacNaghten, the judge who heard the

appeal, declared that there was no town, city or place on earth enjoying "more practical liberty" than Calcutta. He continued," if we are to give a free constitution, which we have not, let a Free Press follow, not precede it". Notwithstanding this judgement MacNaghten was not so authoritarian as his civilian colleagues, as the records show. The petition was rejected.

Without giving up the fight Rammohun appealed to the King-in-Council against the Press Regulations and compared the privileges enjoyed by the Hindus under the Moghul rule with their position under the British. He declared :

"Notwithstanding the despotic power of the Mogul Princes who formerly ruled over the country, and that their conduct was often cruel and arbitrary, yet the wise and virtuous among them always employed two intelligencers at the residence of their Nawabs or Lord Lieutenants, Akhbar—novees or news—writer who published an account of whatever happened, and a Khoofea navees, or confidential correspondent, who set a private and particular account of every occurence worthy of notice; and although these Lord Lieutenants were often particular friends or near relations to the Prince, he did not trust entirely to themselves for a faithful and impartial report of their administration, and degraded them when they appeared to deserve it, either for their own faults or for their negligence in not checking the delinquencies of their subordinate officer; which shews that even the Mogul Princes, although their form of Government admitted of nothing better, were convinced, that in a country so rich and so replete with temptations, a restraint of some kind was absolutely necessary, to prevent the abuses that are so liable to flow from the possession of power ----

In conclusion, your Majesty's faithful subjects humbly beseech your Majesty, first, to cause the Rule and Ordinance and Regulation before mentioned, which has ben registered by the Judge of your Majesty's Court, to be rescinded; and prohibit any authority in this country, from assuming the legislative power, or prerogatives of Your Majesty and the High Council of the Realm, to narrow the privileges and destroy the rights of Your Majesty's faithful subjects, who claim your protection, and are willing to submit to such laws, as your Majesty with the advice of your Council, shall be graciously pleased to enact.

Secondly, your Majesty's faithful subjects humbly pray, that your Majesty will be pleased to confirm to them the privilege, they have so long enjoyed, of expressing their sentiments through the medium of the Press, subject to such legal restraints as may be thought necessary or that your Majesty will be graciously pleased to appoint a Commission of intelligent and Independent Gentlemen to inquire into the real condition of the millions Providence has placed under your high protection.

Your Majesty's faithful subjects from the distance of almost half the globe, appeal to your Majesty's heart by the sympathy which forms a paternal tie between you and the lowest of your subjects, not to overlook their condition; they appeal to you by the honour of that great nation which under your Royal auspices has obtained the glorious title of Liberator of Europe, not to permit the possibility of millions of your subjects being wantonly trampled on and oppressed; they lastly appeal to you by the glory of your crown on which the eyes of the world are fixed, not to consign the natives of India, to perpetual oppression and degradation."

But the Privy Council rejected the appeal described as one of the noblest pieces of English to which Rammohun Roy ever put his hand. In sheer protest Rammohun stopped the publication of the paper. Adams Regulations were thus a forerunner of the Vernacular Press of 1878.

Incidentally, a reference to Rammohun's conception of freedom of the Press would not be out of place here.

When the Indian Press was practically in the craddle, Rammohun visualised that for the smooth functioning of the society the need for liberty of publication was utmost. It was essential, he knew, to ensure "the freedom to pursue the truth and to evolve a way of life proved by test of reason. "Every good ruler", observed Rammohun," who is convinced of the imperfection of human nature and reverences the eternal Governor of the world must be conscious of their great liability to error in managing the affairs of a vast empire; and, therefore, he will be anxious to afford every individual the readiest means of bringing to his notice whatever may require his interference. To secure this important object, the unrestricted liberty of publication is the effectual means that can be employed. And should it ever be abused, the established law of the land is very properly armed with sufficient powers to punish those who may be found guilty of misrepresenting the conduct or character of the Government, which are effectually guarded by the same laws to which individual must look for protection of their reputation and good manner."

One is still in doubt if the concept of the freedom of the Press has, in any way, been improved upon even now.

But the efforts of the bureaucracy not to allow Indian journals to function freely failed to check the wave of enthusiasm that time had brought about. Newspapers were started in Bombay, Madras and North-west provinces.

Fardoonji Murzeban, who started the Gujerat Printing Press in 1812 in Bombay, launched after ten years *Mumbaina Samachar*, weekly Gujarati paper, in 1822 as a commercial venture. The paper which later assumed the titile of *Bombay Samachar*, is still going strong.

Besides *Mumbaina Samachar* there were two English papers in Bombay — the *Daily Gazette* and the *Courier*.

In Madras there were two newspapers --- the *Government Gazette* and the *Madras Courier*.

In Cawnpore the first printing press was set up in 1822 and the *Cawnpore Advertiser* was published.

However, Bengal was ahead of other provinces. *John Bull*, which was published in 1821, subsequently converted itself into *Englishman* with the financial help from Prince Dwarakanath Tagore.

Besides *Sangbad Kaumudi*, *Samachar Chandrika* and *Samachar Darpan*, another Bengali weekly, *Sangbad Timir Nashak*, was published in October 1823. Three years later the first Hindi paper *OOdant Martand* was launched by Joogal Kishore Sookool on February 9, 1826. Sookool applied for a licence to publish a weekly newspaper "In Hindi language and Deo Nagri character to be entitled *OOdant Martand*. He was to be the publisher and Munnoo Thakur the printer. After the licence had been granted Jugal Kishore solicited that first eight numbers of the paper be allowed to pass from the General Post Office free of charge into the mufussil "where most of my countrymen reside in order that they may be informed of the existence in Calcutta of such a Nagri paper as *OOdant Martand*." He added," I will scrupulously attend to the regulations of the Government regarding the better conduct of the papers in Calcutta and it will be my prime object to instil into the minds of the readers a reverence for the reigning power in India." The authorities however, did not accede to the request to circulate eight issues free of postal charges, but authorised the Post Master—General to permit the first or any single number of the paper to pass free of charge to the stations in question. Jugal Kishore was not very well—off financially. Soon he found it difficult to bring out the paper regularly. Less than a year later he wrote to the Government stating that the pecuniary advantage derived from his paper hardly covered the expense of the establishment which he employed on a most economical scale for printing, much less to compensate him for the trouble as editor. An improvement in the circulation of the paper is by no means possible owing to there being but few persons in the city who read the language in which it was published. The upper provinces and the "countries remote from hence" were the places where his potential readers resided. But as the charge of postages were heavy, they were obliged to refrain from subscribing to the paper. He, therefore, took the liberty of bringing this subject to the notice of the Government in the hope that "should they liberally wish to promote the knowledge amongst their military officers and give publicity to their regulations amongst their subjects in the upper provinces, His Lordship in Council might perhaps deem it requisite to preserve the continuance of the paper by means of conferring on him the same indulgence which has been granted to the editor of the Bengali paper styled the *Samachar Durpan*, by allowing his paper to be distributed throughout the country free of postage as was the rule with other papers. He concludes that on his proposition being approved by His Lordship in Council, he would be ready to publish in the newspaper in question the translations of the regulations that might, in future from time to time be enacted by Government as also of the requisite general orders, and every week forward copies of them to the several Government offices and the military stations at the western provinces at the rate of *sicca* rupees two per month for each of the officers." The writer then lists two hundred and three Government officers to whom the paper might be sent. Unfortunately for the enterprising pioneer, the Governor—General turned down his request.

But Huree Hur Dutt, the proprietor of the Jam-i-Jehan-Numa was rather fortunate. Requesting that his publication be accorded the same postal facilities as the Serampore newspapers Dutt wrote the following "picturesque" letter of application.

From Huree Hur Dutt

To Simon Fraser, Esq.

Officiating Secretary to Government in the Persian Department

Sir,

Impressed with the strongest conviction of the benovolent and philanthropic disposition of the Government in the most humane, laudable an honorable exertions that have been made and are making under their favourable auspices for the intelectual and moral improvement of their Native subjects, and the lively interest that they so graciously take in the amelioration of the condition of those very subjects, I feel strongly assured that the solicitation which I am to submit respectfully through your kind recommendation to the liberal and benovolent consideration of his Lordship the Vice-President in Council, will most assuredly be granted, as it has the tendency and scope of promoting the interests of literature.

As the sole proprietor of the Persian and Oordu newspaper now published under the appellation of the *Jami Jehan Numa*, I beg leave most respectfully to present to you for the purpose of its being brought under the favourable notice of Government that the circulation of the above publication has been hitherto materially impeded and obstructed even in spite of my best exertions and efforts to extend it in consequence of its being liable to payment of full postage, which has indeed restrained many intending subscribers in the mofussil from patronizing the same newspaper; whereas the Bengali and Persian newspapers denominated the *Samachar Darpan* and *Ukhbara Seerampore* enjoy the privilege in common with English newspapers of paying one—fourth of the established postage demandable from the *Jami Jehan Numa*; a circumstance which has alone most essentially conducted to the augmentation of the very extensive circulation which those papers now respectively enjoy.

But as the Paper conducted by me is in no respect inferior to its above—named contemporaries, but, on the contrary, I may respectfully venture to affirm, without being guilty of exaggeration that it by far much superior to them in point of diction, matter, execution & ca. a fact which will easily be convinced by their gracious condescension in directing these several publications to be contrasted with each other, for which purpose, I beg leave to submit herewith a number of my newspaper, as you are an eminent scholar and consequently an excellent judge of oriental languages. I further leave to submit the point of superiority to be determined by your judgement you will therefore be graciously pleased to represent to Government whether my publication is or is not fit to be placed at least on equal footing with the *Samachar Durpan* and *Ukhbara Seerampore* in regard to payment of postage, and if you are of opinion that it is deserving of that distinction and privilege that you will be so obligingly kind as to recommend to Government to extend their liberal consideration to the *Jami Jehan Numa* by causing it to be put on the same footing as the above—named newspapers concerning their payment of postage and by this gracious and benovolent and liberal act of the government I feel persuaded the circulation of my paper will be much extended beyond its present obstructed and limited circle.

Calcutta Colootollah   I have etc,

The 13th October, 1826   Huree Hur Dutt

Unlike in the case of *Oodant Martand*, the Government promptly complied with his request and issued necessary order to the Post Master General to forward his paper at the same rate of postage as the other native newspapers". Yet another Persian-cum-Hindustani newspaper, *Shamsul Akhbar*, was published by Mothor Mohan Mitra.

These apart, the following English journals were in existence during the period between 1824 and 1830: The *Scotsman in the East, weekly Gleaner*, the *Columbia Press Gazette*, quarterly *Oriental Magazine, Keleidoscope, Calcutta Chronicle, Calcutta Gazette* and *Commercial Advertiser*.

Recognising the significance of the growth of Indian press the *Friend of India* wrote in December 1823

"How necessary a step this (the establishment of native press) was for the amelioration of the conditions of Natives, no person can be ignorant who had traced the effects of the press in other countries. The Natives soon availed themselves of this privilege; no less than four weekly newspapers in the Native language have now been established, and there are hopes, these efforts will contribute essentially to arouse the Native mind from its long lethergy of death; and while it excites them to inquire into what is going forward in a world, of which Asia forms so important a portion, and urge them to ascertain their own situation respecting that eternal world, which really communicates all the vigour and interest now so visible in Europeans. Nor has this liberty been abused by them in the least degree; yet these vehicles of intelligence have begun to be called for, from the very extremities of British India and the talents of the natives themselves, have not unfrequently been exerted in the production of essays, that would have done credit to our countrymen."

However, for the Serampore missionaries things were not going well. On May 23, 1828 the Government decided to discontinue subscriptions to their Persian and Bengali newspapers owing to financial constraints. But apparently the views of the Government had undergone a change. On April 25, 1828, the Secretary of the Persian Department, A Stirling, wrote that the Persian *Akhbar* is conducted in a very poor style and can be little valued by native readers of any class". It was also decided to discontinue subscription to *Jami Jehan Numa* and the editor concerned were informed that the measure was "founded on the necessity for the observance of the strictest economy during the existing pressure on the public finance."

Lord Amherst took a somewhat lenient attitude towards the press during the last years of his regime.

At first he was influenced by the Civil Service with tradition of autocratic rule. But when he left India he was complimented by the journals in Calcutta "on the liberality and even magnanimity with which he tolerated the free expression of public opinion on his own individual measures, when he had the power to silence them with a stroke of his pen", wrote J.C. Marshman. (Marshman, History of India, Vol II, p 411)

The Serampore missionaries tenaciously pursuded the matter when in 1828 Lord William Cavendish Bentinck took over as the Governor-General from William Butterworth Bailey who had succeeded Amherst for a brief period.

In a letter dated October 8,1828, Dr Marshman pointed out that their Bengali newspaper had been in existence for ten years and that for about two years the Government had patronised it by getting the Government regulations printed in it and by subscribing to the journal for the Government offices. Later the patronage was extended to the Persian newspaper also. But because of the Government's decision to withdraw the subscriptions they (the missionaries) had to abandon the Persian paper and a similar fate seemed to be in store for the Bengali version. Marshman emphasised that their object in these undertakings was not pecuniary profit. He wrote, "Many years must elapse, and a great revolution take place in the propensities of the Natives before such an undertaking can yield pecuniary advantage. But the publication weekly of intelligence from all parts of the world, interspersed with remarks calculated to correct error and abate prejudice, appears an object of such moment to the ultimate civilisation of these provinces, that we would cheerfully continue the undertaking, even at a trifling loss. Having enjoyed opportunities of ascertaining that the perusal of the papers has been silently aiding the cause of improvement, and that in many a little circle through the country a spirit of enquiry has been stirred up, we cannot admit the idea of relinquishing a plan which promises so rich a harvest of benefit without the greatest reluctance. Should your Lordship be pleased to sanction a subscription for the same number of copies at any reduced rate which may appear justifiable, we shall again be enabled to prosecute the undertaking with vigour.

"With reference to the editorial principle of the paper we can appeal with confidence to Your Lordship's colleagues for a testimony of the strict faith with which we have adhered to our original resolution of admitting nothing calculated to irritate the Native mind, and nothing on the subject of Indian politics which was not calculated to confirm the stability of the British sway."

Marshman repeated the suggestion that the "great advantage would be conferred on the Persian newspaper if the Government would allow it to circulate free of postage."

But the Government did not oblige the missionaries. It replied:

"The Governor-General in Council duly appreciates the importance and usefulness of your endeavours to excite a spirit of enquiry and to disseminate knowledge among the natives of India, through the medium of newspapers in the Persian and Bengalee languages; But the Government having deliberately come to a resolution of withdrawing its pecuniary support from those papers scarecely a month previous to His Lordship's arrival, His Lordship in Council feels precluded at the present moment from renewing the public subscription, under any modification which would answer your purpose: more especially as the grounds on which the above resolution was formed viz: the necessity of introducing rigid economy into every branch of the public expenditure, still exist in the fullest force.

The objections to allowing the Persian newspaper to circulate free of postage, although of a different character, are scarcely less weighty than those which oppose compliance with your application for direct assistance, and the Governor—General in Council regrets therefore that it is not in his power to extend encouragement to your undertaking in either of the modes suggested in your letter.

Fort William   I have & Ca,

29th November, 1828   A. Stirling

Meanwhile, the Bombay Government passed on January 1, 1827 a resolution" for restricting the establishment of printing presses and the circulation of printed books and papers". The regulation provided that printing presses could not be established without licences which could be recalled by the Government; that all printed works should contain the names of the printer and the place of printing; that any breach of these regulations should be punished by a fine not exceeding one thousand rupees which might be commuted to ordinary imprisonment for a period not exceeding six months. The Governor was also empowered to ban the public circulation, within the Bombay province, of any book or paper which violated certain conditions.

A TURNING POINT

When Lord William Bentinck was appointed the Governor-General of India the editors and owners of "native" journals were apprehensive. And not without a reason. Bentinck's image as the Governor of Madras was not better than that of Adam because of his rigid control of the press. But on assuming the topmost office Bentick became altogether a different person. A shrewd administrator, Bentinck could feel the wind of changes in the country and among the people in general, the middle class of Calcutta, in particular. It did not escape his notice that both the progressive and orthodox Hindu Press had welcomed the British rule as a "blessing" to India. Though at times they were critical of the administration they could not dream of its downfall. The Adam's Regulations were in the Statute book, hanging like the Sword of Democles over the heads of the editors. The Press itself took care not to walk into its trap and avoided comments, for a period of about seven years, on political matters which might irritate the bureaucracy and invite avoidable trouble.

In his report to the Court of Directors in London Bentinck said," I need hardly mention the increasing demands which almost all who possess the means evince for various articles of convcenience and luxury purely European; it is in many cases very remarkable. Even in the celebration of their sacred festivals a great change is said to be perceptible in Calcutta. Much of what used in old times to be distributed among beggars and Brahmins is now in many instances devoted to the ostentatious entertainment of Europeans". (Mohit Moitra, A History of Indian Journalism, p 85)

Bentinck fully made use of the situation. On the one hand, he backed the scheme of "colonisation" of Britishers in India, while on the other he approved of certain progressive social reforms. As regards the Press, Bentinck followed," in the interest of administration", a policy of "relaxation". In this he was, doubtless, influenced by his colleague in the Council, Sir Charles Metcalf, who sincerely believed in the concept of Press freedom. This encouraged the emergence of many new newspapers and periodicals, mostly vernacular, during his regime.

One of his first acts of several reforms was the abolition of "*Sutti*". He was aware that Raja Rammohun Roy, more than any other else, had prepared the ground for legislation. The orthodox Hindus made representation to the Governor-General on January 14, 1830 against the measure. The Government was warned against false interpretaions of Hindu religious feelings and thoughts by persons "who had apostatised from the religious of their forefathers and defiled themselves by eating and drinking forbidden things in the society of Europeans". The arguments in support of the petition were embodied in a separate note signed by 123 Pandits. The progressive section of the community led by Rammohun submitted a counter—petition in the form of an address to Lord Bentinck. This game of petition and counter—petition was repeated but ultimately the Privy Council rejected the orthodix petition and the controversy was set at rest. And with it died several newspapers who were supporting the orthodox.

Bentinck saw the obvious advantage of newspapers published in the Indian languages pursuing freely social controversies and of generally relaxing the restrictions imposed on all sections of the press in the interest of efficient administration. He instituted inquiries into the circulation and influence of newspapers, the findings of which were revealing. The figures were contained in an official minute dated September 24, 1828 and signed by Stockwell.

"Daily papers

Bengali Harkaru: Weekly: 1089. Average daily,

155 of which one is daily sent to the address of a native at Santipore.

John Bull

Weekly: 1432. Average daily, 204 of which one is sent to a Native Parsee at Bombay.

Government Gazetter:

Weekly: 595. Average daily 297 of which seven are sent to Natives, viz: one to Lucknow, Chandernagore, Burdwan, Cawnpopre, Santipore and Moorshedabad.

Calcutta Chronicle:

Weekly: 397. Daily 189, none of which is sent to natives.

Persian:

Issued every week: 26, of which nine are sent to natives, viz to Aurangabad, Rungpore, Benares, Futtehgurh and Gwalior one each to Lucknow and Delhi to each.

I have reason to believe that out of the five numbers

sent to W. Ainslie at Buldelcund, several are for Natives, the independent Rajhas perhaps who are under him as Political Agent."

A report from A. Sterling on the Indian Language Press reveals that between 1824 and 1826 there were six papers in all published in Calcutta (Bengali 3, Persian 2 and Hindi 1) in addition to 2 papers -- one in Persian and other in Bengali— published by the Serampore missioneries. The Serampore Persian papers ceased publication when Government subscription was withdrawn as a measure of retrenchment. The second Persian paper and the Hindi paper ceased publication in 1826. The Jam-i-Jehan Noome, existed on the patronage of a few English gentlemen, including Sterling himself, who attached importance to the circulation of these papers as a means of diffusing knowledge and exciting a spirit of enquiry and reflection among the natives of India.

Sterling drew the conclusion that newspapers in the Indian languages were a luxury for which there was no demand beyond Calcutta and that without Government's assistance they could not have any sales. He made an exception in the case of Bengali papers which "have always flourished because they find abundant supporters in that large class of Hindoo population of Calcutta who have become imbued, to a certain extent, with English tastes and notions, and amongst the rest a love of news, which is thus supplied to them in a cheap and accessible form".

To these observations may be added the point that the Adam Regulations killed many newspapers published in English and in the Indian languages and that interest in Bengali newspapers were greatly stimulated by the socio-religious controversies of the day.

With Bentinck's liberal attitude towards the Press becoming apparent a number of newspapers came into existence. The 16 Indian language newspapers and periodicals that existed in 1830 are listed as follows:

Daily —— *Prabhakar, Chandrodaya* and *Mahajan Darpan;*

Tri—weekly ——*Bhaskar;*

Weekly ——*Gyanadarpan, Banga Doot, Sadhuranjan, Gyan Sancharini, Rasasagar, Rangpur Bartabaha* and *Rasamudgar;*

Bi—monthly:—— *Nitya Dharmanaranjika* and *Durjan Daman Maha Nabam;*

Monthly; *Tatwa Bodhini;*

The number of English dailies and periodicals published in Bengal was 33 and the total number of subscribers to these newspapers were 2205. Significant additions during this period were the Bengal Herald or Weekly Intelligence established jointly by Robert Montgomery Martin and Neil Ruttan Halder, published in English, Bengali, Persian and Nagri characters and the weekly Banga Doot in which Martin, Dwarkanath Tagore, Prasanna Kumar Tagore and Raja Rammohun Roy were interested. This progress would have been maintained but for the financial crash of 1830, as a result of which several newspapers, particularly those published in the English language, were either closed down or changed hands.

Bombay newspapers were growing in influence during this period. The *Moombai Samachar*, to which a reference had already been made earlier, became a daily in 1832. The *Moombai Vartaman* was started in September 1880 by Naoroji Dorabji Chandaru and the following year, the Jam-e-Jamshed, was started by Pestonji Maneqji Motwala. Parsee journalism received a shot in the arm from a calendar controversy started by Dastur Mullah Firoz, who after a visit to Persia, expressed the view that the Bombay Parsee Calendar was inaccurate. As a result, the community split into two sects, the Shahanshaites who stood by the old calendar and the Kadmis Dastur Mulla Firoz's new calendar. The newspapers which took part in the controversy were short—lived, including a paper named "Iris published in English by J.H, Stocqueler whose express purpose was to ventilate current controversies. After closing down the "Iris" Stocqueler purchased *Bombay Courier* from Warden and Bell.

Like the controversy over the "*Sutee*" in Calcutta the Parsee calendar controversy also gave rise to a number of newspapers in Gujerati in Bombay. The Kadmis established the "*Ebtal-E-Kabiseh* while their opponents published the *Akhbar-E-Kabiseh*; These publications did not live long. The habit of discussion among the Parsees received an impetus and the community began to take deep interest in public affairs and the Press.

The periodicals of Bombay, at this time, also included the *Chronicle*, the *Commercial Advertiser* and the *Oriental Christian Spectator*, the last of which was established by Dr John Wilson. The Governor of Bombay, Sir John Malcolm, set up the *Bombay Government Gazette* in order to economise on the payment which was being made to the *Courier* for Government advetisements and the latter, in the words of Stocqueler, was "at once mulcted of four thousand pounds a year." It may be mentioned that this enterprising journalist later became the editor of *Bengal Harkaru* and afterwards the proprietor of *John Bull* which paper he renamed the *Englishman*.

Another field of journalism—— that of scientific interest was now opening up. The establishment of literary magazines— the *Mirror of the Press* and the *Political and Literary Register*——had already been noted. For some time the Asiatic society, founded in 1784 by Sir William Jones, had been publishing papers relating to zoology, botany, anthropology, mathematics, physics, chemistry, geology medicine etc.

While all these socio-religious controversies and growing clash of interests between the foreign traders and the rising Indian bourgeoisie were creating a spirit of resurgence in the country the time for the renewal of the Charter of the East India Company, granted in 1813 for twenty years only, approached near. A section of British industrialists and bourgeoisie launched a vigorous campaign in England against granting the Company any privilege for monopoly of trade in India any longer. But all this was not reflected in the then Indian Press.

Meanwhile, Raja Rammohan Roy, Prince Dwarakanath Tagore, Prosonna Kumar Tagore and others organised an agitation in the country to counter the effects of propaganda in Britain and to urge on the British Parliament to renew the Company's Charter for a further period of twenty years. On December 15, 1829 they held a meeting for this purpose in the Town Hall of Calcutta. In the meeting Raja Rammohan said;" From personal experience, I am impressed with the conviction that the greater our intercourse with European gentlemen, the greater will be our improvement in literary, social and political affairs, a fact which can be easily proved by comparing the conditions of those of our countrymen who have enjoyed this advantage with that of those who unfortunately have not had that opportunity; and a fact which, I could, to the best of my belief, declare on solemn oath before any assembly. As to indigo-planters, I beg to obsrve that I have travelled through several districts of Bengal and Bihar, and I found the natives residing in the neighbourhood of indigo plantations evidently better clothed and better-conditioned than those who lived at a distance from such stations. There may be some partial injury done by the indigo—planters; but on the whole, they have performed more good to the generality of the natives of this country than any other class of Europeans whether in or out of the service". (Royal Asiatic Journal, Vol. II. New series. May—August, 1830).

At the same meeting Prince Dwarkanath Tagore said: "I have several zemindaries in various districts and that I have found that cultivation of indigo, and residence of Europeans have considerably benefited the country and the community at large; the zemindars becoming wealthy and prosperous, the ryots materially improved in the condition, and possessing many more comforts than the generality of my countrymen where indigo cultivation and manufacture is not carried on their value of land in the vicinity to be considerably enhanced and cultivation rapidly progressing." (Ibid)

After this meeting a petition was presented by prominent Indian citizens to British Parliament requesting it to renew the Company's Charter and granting the privilege of "colonisation" and free trade scheme. While forwarding this Lord William Bentinck supported the schemes. But another section of zemindars of Bengal sent another petition to England opposing colonisation scheme. In that petition they said: "In the districts where the indigo planters and others have in a manner settled themselves the people are more injured and distressed than in other parts of the country, in consequence of such indigo taking possession of land by force, sowing indigo by destroying rice plant (which is the cause of diminution in the produce of rice and dearth of articles of consumption) detaining cattle of and extorting money from poor individuals, whose frequent complaints induce the Indian Government to pass Regulation VI, 1823; nevertheless, if they be permitted to hold any zemindary or landed property here, the native zemindars and their ryots must be unavoidably ruined .... natives of superior caste and higher rank— having no opportunity to secure public office ——have no other means to subsist on than their landed property .... Under these circumstances their real estates .... be allowed to be purchased by foreigners they should inevitably under great distress and dfficulty for the necessaries of life and for the preservation of their rank and character."

Prosunno Coomar Tagore's "*Reformer*" supported the scheme and wrote on January 1832:" India wants nothing but the application of European skill and enterprise to render her powerful, prosperous and happy .... The idea of the Natives of India suffering oppression from an additional member of European settlers, is equally absurb. They would be subject to the same laws and would enjoy no peculiar privileges whatever above the Natives".

Sir Charles T. Metcalfe, a member of the Governor General's Council, wrote in his minute of February 19, 1829: "I am further convinced that our possession of India must always be precarious unless we take root by having an influential portion of the population attached to our Government by common interests and sympathies. Every measure, therefore, which is calculated to facilitate the settlement of our countrymen in India and to remove the obstructions by which it is impeded must, I conceive, conduce to the stability of our rule."

Holt Machenzie, giving evidence before the Parliamentary Committee, said on February 23, 1832: "The European settlers in India would be very useful agents of the police. They would be centres of information we now want, and would have great influence over those connected with them. They would be bound to us by a common feeling."

Before the same Committee, Raja Rammohan Roy, who was then in England, pleaded for renewal of the Company's Charter and colonisation scheme but urged for the separation of judiciary and executive. Later on it was one of the main demands of the Indian National Congress but at that time none could probably conceive of the question of separation of executive and judiciary.

In 1833 the Company's Charter was renewed in which the scheme of colonisation and free trade were approved. Individual British citizens or Company was given the right to invest capital and settle here to start factories and plantations. The Charter further declared that no person by reason of his birth, creed or colour, should be disqualified from holding any office in the Company's service. Though this promise remained a dead letter the Indian leaders considered it as a great constitutional milestone for a long time to come.

Sambad Kaumudi' supported the agitation for renewal of the Charter but it painfully pointed out that due to cultivation of indigo the production of paddy had gone down.

The question of the freedom of the Press was again raised in 1830 when the Court of Directors, in order to meet the financial liabilities incurred in the first Burma War, decided to effect economy by reducing the allowance given to army officers. The order, known as "Half—Bhatta" Order, was the subject of prsistent criticism in the Press. Lord Bentinck regarded the order as extremely unwise and inexpedient, fraught with mischief, and unproductive of any good. "He was nevertheless, apprehensive of the effect of the agitation on the Army which recalled to him the circumstances which led to the mutiny of Madras officers in 1809. His minute embodying the decision to impose restrictions on the press, in this behalf, is interesting for the comparison he drew between the state of the Press in Madras in 1809 and 1830 as well as for the views he expressed that the Press is a "safety—valve for discontent."

"The order itself, so many years the topic of discussion and of contention between the authorities in England and in India, was quite sufficient to excite universal dissatisfaction, and it is quite as clear that it could only be set at rest by a definite resolution of the superior authority. The Adjutant—General of the Madras Army who was at the time at Calcutta, described the angry feeling and language so loudly expressed here, and all the signs of the times, to be precisely similar to those which prevailed before the Madras mutiny, and he anticipated a similar situation. Let it be remarked that liberty belonging to the press there, the communication and interchange of sentiment and concert was as general as if it had passed through the medium of a daily press, without the reserve which the responsibility of the editor more or less requires for his own security. My firm belief is that more good than harm was produced by the open and public declaration of the sentiments of the Army. There was vent to public feeling, and the mischief was open to public view; and the result is so far confirmatory of the opinion here given, that no over act took place."

Nevertheless Lord Bentinck drew a distinction between discussion of a proposal and clamour against and censure of a final decision given by the supreme authority, and favoured the imposition of a ban on all further discussion in the later case in the press. Bentinck was strongly supported by William Butterworth Bayley who maintained that "the unfettered liberty of the Press, as it exists in our native country (England) is totally unsuited to the present state of our dominion in the East". But Charles Metcalfe differed with both Bentinck and Bayley. He opposed restriction on the ground that freedom of discussion had had the good effect of providing an outlet for feelings strongly held against an unpopular measure; it gave an assurance to those who resented the order that their complaint had been made known. It was Metcalfe's contention that the worst had already been said, that the arguments had been exhausted and that the subject was worn out. He further held that any restrictions imposed on the Press at that stage would cause fresh irritation and provide a new grievance." I have for my own part, always advocated the liberty of the Press, believing its benefits to outweigh its michiefs; and I continue of the same opinion.

Metcalfe further said," Admitting that the liberty of the Press, like other liberties of the subject, may be suspended when the safety of the State requires such a sacrifice, I cannot, as a consequence, acknowledge that the present instance ought to be made an exception to the usual practice of the Government; for if there were danger to the State, either way, there would be more, I should think, in suppressing the publication of opinions, than in keeping the valve open, by which bad humours might evaporate. To prevent men from thinking and feeling is impossible; and I believe it to be wiser to let them give vent to their temporary anger, in anonymous letters in the newspapers, the writers of which letters remain unknown, than to make that anger permanent by forcing them to smother it within their own breasts, ever ready to burst out. It is no more necessary to take notice of such letters now than it was before.

"The Government which interferes at its pleasure with the Press becomes responsible for all that it permits to be published. We continually see in the Calcutta papers gross abuse of public authorities; and we answered to the complaint of one that this Government did not interfere with the Press or something to that effect. I think that we made a similar assertion in a communication to the governor of a foreign settlement. How can we say such things at one time, an at another interfere with the Press, as it is now proposed to do?

"If I could think it sound policy to shackle the Press I should prefer the steady operation of the censorship, or any fixed rule, to the occasional interference of the Government by its arbitrary will. Every letter addressed by the Government to the editor of a newspaper has always appeared to me to be derogatory to the government; and the Bengal Government has been exposed to more ridicule from this sort of correspondence than from any other cause. It is true that the power now exists of converting ridicule into terror by the destruction of the property, but who can desire to see a newspaper impertinence brought to such an end? Even punishment has sometimes proved a farce, the real offender soon reappearing in the field, with new honour as a pretended murderer.

"For all these reasons, I object to the measure proposed, considering it preferable on every account to leave to the Press the uninterrupted enjoyment of its supposed freedom, and to the public the means which it now practically possesses of expressing its sentiments on all subjects, without any other restriction than those of law and discretion".

6th September, 1830   C.T. Metcalfe

In 1834, Sir Federick Adam, the Governor of Madras, in a communication to the Governor General, submitted that a regulation should be enacted in the Madras Presidency requiring licensing of printing presses. But the Governor General advised that introductions of such regulations should be postponed in order to enable him to consult the members of the Law Commission on the subject.

A petition remarkable for its joint submission by the Indian and European journalalists in Calcutta, was presented to the Governor General on February 6, 1835. It was signed by William Adam, Dwarkanath Tagore, Russick Lal Mullick, E.M. Gordon, Rusamoy Dutt, L.L. Clerke, C. Hogg, T.H. Burkin, David Hare, T.E.M Turton, Young and J. Sutherland. The representation covered the entire ground of restriction imposed on the Press under the Adam Regulations of April 4, 1823 and the auxiliary regulation issued the same year for the control of printing presses. The points made in the petition were:

(1) That the restrictions imposed were not only useless but mischievous and degrading both to the Government and to the Press;

(2) That Englishmen who came to India outside the Company's service should not be considered as having been admitted on sufferance but as being as interested in the maintenance of national power and supremacy as the proprietors of the company and its servants and that coming to India could not deprive them of the rights enjoyed by them in England;

(3) That the publication of journals in English did

not constitute a danger to the supremacy of the ruling power because of the number of natives of India conversant with the language was deplorably small and confined to the limits of Calcutta;

(4) That danger to the supremacy of the ruling party from publication in the vernacular languages could not justify the prohibition of all printing or publishing in such languages without a licence;

(5) That there was greater danger of dissemination of libels and false intelligence among the native soldiery by written rather than by printed libels, and that periodical publications would dispel ignorance and correspondingly diminish the credulity of those towards whom such writings were directed with a view to mislead and subvert them. That prohibitions against the circulation of obnoxious native publications were uncalled for as the government could prevent the circulation of such publications by the imposition of stamp duties; it was pointed out that newspapers were still subjected to a heavy rate of postage.

In reply, the government assured the petitioners that a system would be established which, while giving security to every person engaged in the fair discussion of public measures, would effectually secure the government against sedition and individuals against calumny; that all classes of the community would have an opportunity to offer their comments and suggestions to such a measure before it was finally passed into a law and that the government had no intention of restricting the liberty the inhabitants of Calcutta were enjoying.

Shortly after these assurances had been given Bentick was compelled to resign owing to ill-health and Metcalfe, the senior-most member of the council, assumed the Governor-Generalship.

5
LIBERATION OF THE PRESS

instead of the original order... printed under old
law, which the Jail order made the Commander-
in-Chief objectionable to the government. The then
Governor of Madras, Bentinck, was about to sanction
Hamill's appeal... rule, to which he strongly
objected. Action on the part... judge... He
was of opinion that from violence the Inhabitants
had... may arise... danger... the military was
ready for the attack...

The Chief previous Judges of the Supreme Court
had no... over the Press, but powers if otherwise
... of those powers which it is our duty, to prohibit
them from being... within this country by
refusing to... tolerating strongly this statement...

... ... them, until the editor... at presence
... ... not to summon to emit any paper whatever
without the previous sanction of the Chief according to
... paper in question had been printed by Madras
... ... called up by the Grand Jury. The Governor's
... cautioned out... the printing presses were
... to permit his employer to print without the
previous permission of the government. The censorship
... ... was more severe than that in Calcutta or
Bombay. Curiously, none as the persons who was left
to decide... such matters of opinion...

About the Same time... future in the articles
Parliament over the rates of freedom of the Press in
India. In March 21, 1811 Lord Hamilton wished to
know the directive notice on the press in India since
1799, and questioned the authority of the Company to
impose such restrictions. "If the Press was to be
prevented from publishing on these heads (economy
movement of ship, war and peace etc.) I am at a loss to
know what subject was left open to it," he asked. But
R. Dundas, President of the Board of Control of the
Company opposed Hamilton. "There could be no doubt
that the very government would be shaken to its

Metcalfe was true to his word. He did what he had said. A firm believer in Press freedom, Metcalfe, in one go, removed whatever restrictions were there during the time of Bentinck. His earnestness was manifest during his meeting with a delegation of journalists when he said," We are not here in India to maintain order and collect taxes and make good the deficit; we are here for a higher and noble purpose, to pour into the east the knowledge, the culture and civilisation of the west." To translate his profession into practice Metcalfe invited Macaulay, the legislative member of the Supreme Council, to draft a Press Act to be incorporated in the Code which was being drawn up by the Law Commission.

Arguing in favour of the new Act Macaulay pointed out that the "licensing regulations were indefensible and should, therefore, be repealed. He contended that while the regulations were rigid and comprehensive, the Press in India was in practical effect a free Press. He opined that it was unwise of the Government to incur the odium of repressive press laws which in their application did not ensure the smallest accession of security or of power." "It seems to be acknowledged," Macaulay wrote, "that licences to print ought not to be refused or withdrawn except under very peculiar circumstances, and if peculiar circumstances should arise, there will not be smallest difficulty in providing measures adapted to the exigency. No government in the world is better provided with the means of meeting extraordinary dangers by extraordinary precautions. Five persons, who may be brought together in half an hour, whose deliberations are secret, who are not shocked by any of those forms which elsewhere delay legislative measures, can, in a single sitting, make a law for stopping every press in India. Possessing as we do the unquestionable power to interfere, whenever the safety of the State may require it, with overwhelming repidity and energy, we surely ought not, in quiet times, to be constantly keeping the offensive form and ceremonial of despotism before the eyes of those whom nevertheless we permit to enjoy the substance of freedom. It is acknowledged that in reality liberty is and ought to be general rule, and restraint the rare and temporary exception. Why then should not the form correspond with the reality? .... Drawing attention to the absence of any restriction on the press in Madras, Macaulay concluded, "The Act which I now propose is intended to remove both evils, and to establish a perfect uniformity in the laws regarding the Press throughout the Indian empire. Should it be adopted, every person who chooses will be at liberty to set up a newspaper without applying for a previous permission. But no person will be able to print or publish sedition or calumny without imminent risk of punishment."

Endorsing the views of Macaulay the Governor General wrote in his minute:

"The reason which induced me to propose to the Council the abolition of existing restrictions on the Press in India accord entirely with the sentiments expressed by Mr Macaulay in the minute accompanying the draft of an Act, which at our request, he has had the kindness to prepare, with a view to give effect to the unanimous resolution of the Council. These reasons were as follows: First, that the Press ought to be free, if consistently with the safety of the State it can be. In my opinion it may be so. I do not apprehend danger to the State from a Free Press; but if danger to the State should arise the Legislative Council has the power to apply a remedy. Secondly, that the Press is already practically free, and that the government has no intention to enforce the existing restrictions while we have all the odium of those restrictions, as if the Press were shackled. It is no argument in favour of the continuance of these unpopular restrictions that they may at any time be enforced instanter," Thirdly that the existing restrictions leave room for the exercise of caprice on the part of the governments in India. One Council or one Governor may be for leaving the Press free; another may be for restraining it. There is no certain law, and any one connected with the Press might be any day subjected to arbitrary and tyrannical power for any slight violation of rules, the total violation of which has been long tacitly sanctioned. Fourth, the different state of the law, or the want of any law, at the other presidencies, renders the enactment of some general law for all India indispensible. To extend the odious and useless restrictions which now exist is out of the question; and no law, in my opinion, could be devised with any good effect except the law making the Press free. We are much indebted to Mr Macaulay for the Act which he has had the goodness to prepare for us. The penal provisions which it contains have been partially discussed, and will come more fully under consideration at the next Council. They are, I conclude, unavoidable; but they show how much easier it is to rescind laws than to make them, for while the existing restrictions are got rid of in a few words, we are compelled to make a long enactment for the sole purpose of making printers and publishers accessible to the laws of the land.

Calcutta, April 17   C.T. Metcalfe

Metcalfe's proposal to frame a uniform law for both European and Indian newspapers all over India and to repeal the harsh Press law, was opposed by H.T. Prinsep and Lt. Col Morrison, two members of his Council as well as the Governors of Bombay and Madras. But Metcalfe brushed aside the objections. He persuaded his Council to accept the measure unanimously. In giving assent to the Act he wrote" ... we cannot prevent the progress of knowledge, and it is undoubtedly our duty to promote it whatever be the consequences."

Replying elaborately to an address presented to him Metcalf decalred the repeal justifiable on general principles. At the same time he thought that it had become "almost unavoidable for circumstances obtaining at that time."

"The (Indian) Press," said Sir Charles, "had been practically free for many years, including the whole period of the administration of the late Governor—General, Lord William Bentinck; and although laws of restriction existed in Bengal which gave awful power to the Government, they had ceased to operate for any practical purpose. They were extremely odious, they gave to the Government arbitrary power, which subjects in any part of the world would detest. No Government could now have carried them into effect, without setting universal opinion in defiance. After the liberty given by Lord William Bentinck's forbearance, no Government could have ventured to enforce those laws, unless it had been gifted with a most hard insensibility to ridicule and obloquy. Even supposing them to be good, they were utterly useless, and as they brought unnecessary odium on the Government it would have been absurd any longer to retain them."

Thus the year 1835 was a landmark in the history of journalism in India. The fight started in 1823 by Raja Rammohun Roy and five other respectable citizens, achieved notable success in 1835. All restrictions were withdrawn and the Press was liberated, for the time being at least.

The Metcalfe Act repealed the Adam Regulations of 1823, the Bombay Press regulations of 1825 and 1827

Liberation Of The Press

and censorship in Madras was extended to all the territories of the East India Company. It provided for a declaration by the printer and publisher of any newspaper or periodical giving a true and a precise account of the place of publication. Any change of address must be notified to the Government and the penalty for running a Press without declaration was fixed at a sum not exceeding Rs 5000/- and an imprisonment for a term of not exceeding two years. It was further required that every journal or book, printed in a press, must bear the name of the printer and publisher as well as the printing press and its address. The penalty for non-compliance was the same as that for not taking out a declaration.

For his magnanimous act of the liberation of the Press in India the citizens of Calcutta paid a homage to Sir Charles Metcalfe by presenting him and address and constructing a big hall, christened as "Metcalfe Hall" at the junction of Hare Street and Strand Road, which stand today" to perpetuate the name of the liberator." Describing the occasion Sir John Kaye wrote," It was a great day (September 15) which the people of Calcutta were eager to celebrate. So they subscribed together and they erected a noble building on the bank of the Hooghly to contain a public library and to be applied to other enlightening purposes, and they called it Metcalfe Hall. It was to bear an inscription declaring that the Press of India was liberated on the 15th of September 1835 by Sir Charles Metcalfe and the bust of the liberator was to be enclosed in the building". The Calcutta Public Library founded earlier by local citizens by raising subscriptions from the public was removed to the Metcalfe Hall to associate his name with efforts for spread of knowledge. The library was later taken over by the Government and renamed as Imperial Library. After Independence the library was renamed as National Library and removed to the Belvedere House at Alipore.

However, Metcalfe paid dearly for his convictions.

The Whig Ministry which came to power in Great Britain in 1835 appointed Lord Auckland as the Governor-General and proposed that Metcalfe should continue his service in India as Lt.— Governor of North—western Province, a proposal which he only accepted with utmost reluctance.

Worse was to come. The Dispatch of the Court of Directors on the removal of Press restrictions dated February 1, 1836, not only condemns Metalfe's action but insinuates that he was prompted by "an unwise desire for temporary praise". The Dispatch, inter alia, stated :

"This proceeding (removal of restrictions on the Press) is in all opposition to all our previous orders, to the solemn decisions both of the Supreme Court of Calcutta and His Majesty's Privy Council delivered in both cases, after full arguments on both sides of the question, to the recorded opinions of all preceding Government of Bengal, Madras and Bombay and more specially to the carefully considered measures of Lord William Bentinck and Sir Frederick Adam for extending the Licensing Regulations to Madras."

"We are compelled to observe," the Dispatch continued, "that this proceeding must be considered the most unjustifiable inasmuch as it has been adopted by a Government only provisional; and also when a commission for framing a Code of laws for the three presidencies was about to commence its important labours."

"The concluding paragraph of the Dispatch ran thus :

"We should then be prepared to avail ourselves of the power entrusted to us by Act of Parliament, and disallow your new law when passed, were we not aware that immediate repeal of such a law, however ill advised and uncalled for its enactment may have been, might be productive of mischievous results. We shall, therefore, wait for the deliberate advice of the Governor—General—

Liberation Of The Press

in—Council after arrival of Lord Auckland, your present Governor—General, before we communicate to you our final decision. But you are in possession of our sentiments, and we shall not be sorry to find by returning to the former system you have rendered our interference unnecessary."

Not content with the caustic Dispatch, the Court of Directors found another opportunity of slighting Metcalfe when, in 1836, he was passed over for the Governorship of Madras. Again he thought of resigning. In answer to his inquiry, one of the Company's Directors frankly informed him that his freeing of the Press was unforgiven.

Metcalfe eventually embarked for England on February 15, 1838, a man who had known the stimulas and responsibility of autocratic power, a man who had seen a vision of things to come. As one of his biographers, Edward Thompson, has said, he was " the last of the great men of the heroic age that had lingered so long as he was still in the lands." (Edward Thompson, Life of Metcalfe, p 330)

Metcalfe later became Governor of Jamaica and subsequently of Canada.

Lord Auckland who succeeded Metcalfe as the Governor-General was entirely in favour of his predecessor's policy regarding liberation of the Indian press. Relations between him and editors of various Calcutta newspapers were cordial. He tried to persuade the Company to withdraw ban on their servants being connected with the press since, as a number of Company's senior officers regularly contributing to newspapers, the order had become a dead letter.

The Company bosses were perhaps convinced of the logic of his stand. On June 28, 1841 a notice was issued from the Political Department of Fort William revoking "the existing prohibition against the connection of their servants with the public newspapers subject to the restraints from Military officers by the rules of the service."

Auckland asked John Clark Marshman (son of Dr Joshua Marshman of Serampore) in 1836 to make a survey of the press in Indian languages. The survey quoted the following circulation figures of a few selected newspapers. *Samachar Chandrika* had a circulation of 200 or 250; *Samachar Darpan* 398; *Banga Doot* less than 70 ; *Purnachandradaya*, about 100; *Gyananneshan*, between 150 and 200. Marshman's general finding was that not a single copy of any paper was read by the native officers or sepoys of the Army. *Sangbad* Rasaraj and *Sangbad Bhaskar* were founded in 1839 and made a mark in no time. In 1840 J.C. Marshman published, on July 2, the *Bengali Government Gazette* which aimed at explaining the proceedings of the government from a constitutional point of view.

Though English was the language of the courts, Persian continued to be used as the medium of conversation and the dissemination of information. At least five Persian newspaper were in existence at this time. They were : Jami-Jehan-Numa, Aina-i-Sikander, Sultan-ul-Akbar, Mah-i-Alam Afroz, Mihr-i-Munir.

Calcutta had, by 1839, twenty-six European newspapers (six of which were dailies) and nine Indian newspapers; Bombay had ten European journals and four Indian; Madras had nine European journals and Ludhiana, Delhi, Moulmein, Agra and Serampore had one newspaper each.

Let us have a look at the general situation. Three new factors emerged—— first, monopoly of the East India Company no longer existed; secondly, the administration had assumed some responsibility for education and thirdly, the English was being used as the medium of instruction.

Another development of great significance was the acceptance by the administration, of the principle of religious neutrality. The Government- aided schools were asked not to impart "religious knowledge" and

Liberation Of The Press

they were entirely secular. But the Muslims did not avail themselves of the opportunities offered to the same extent as the Hindus did. Moreover, Muslims were also displeased by the adoption of English in the courts in place of Persian. It was many years before the community changed its attitude. "As a result of their hostility to secular education", writes Margarita Barns," the Muslims were backward and consequently there was practically no Muslim press in English. It was due to work of two brothers that the Muslim attitude was reversed. Sir Syed Ahmad Khan, who will also be remembered as the founder of the Aligarh Muslim University, led the way in the field of education. His elder brother, Syed Mohammed Khan, led the way in journalism by founding *Sayyad-ul-Akhbar*, probably the first Urdu newspaper, which was published in Delhi in 1837. Unfortunately, the editor died while still in his prime and the paper was continued by Sir Syed Ahmad Khan who was compelled to suspend it as he was occupied with other works. In 1838, *Delhi Akhbar* appeared and this was followed by *Fawai-Nazarin* and *Quran-ul-Saadin*, the two latter being edited by Hindus" (The Indian Press, p 231)

The Government once again toyed with the idea of establishing an official organ. The Bombay Government wanted to have a mouthpiece of its own and the question arose Bengal should also have similar arrangement. A conference was held which was attended by number of officials and leading journalists. But Lord Auckland rejected the idea as the arguments were convincingly against establishment of a Government organ.

Lord Ellenborough became the Governor-General of India in February 1842 for a brief period. He was somewhat unconcerned about the views aired by the Press. Still he had passed an order which widened the breach between the officials and the newspapers. Colonel William Sleeman, then Assistant Agent to the Governor-General, had been criticised in *the Delhi Gazette* in August 1843 for his management of Bundelkhand and

Saugar territories. The Colonel refuted the charge made against him in a letter to *the Bombay Times* and supported his case by attaching translations of official documents which he had sent to the Governor-General. *The Bombay Times* brought out both the letters and the enclosure. Annoyed by this publicity of his own orders, Ellenborough passed on August 3o, 1843 an order prohibiting official documents and papers from being made public without the previous consent of the Government. The officer in possession of such documents and papers, the order said, "can only legitimately use them for the furterence of the public service in the discharge of his official duty; and it is to be understood that the same rule which applies to documents and papers applies to information of which officers may become possessed officially."

The effect of the order was to deprive government measures of any "authoritative defenders," a result which Sir Charles Trevelyan, who used to write frequently under the pen name "Indophilus" thought unfortunate. He wrote, "Freedom of the Press in British India is inevitable . We could not hold the country with advantage either to ourselves or to the natives, even if could hold it at all, unless Englishmen, not in the service of the Government, went thither in considerable numbers to trade and exercise their professions; and Englishmen are not disposed to embark their fortunes in a country in which they are debarred from the free expression of their opinions. They can bear the suspension of their Parliamentary privileges, but the freedom of discussion through the Press is as necessary to them as the air they breathe. It is a habit which they cannot cast off, and it is felt by them to be a practical security against abuse, and practical means of influencing public measures which goes a great way towards supplying the place even of a free Parliament.

"The freedom of the Press in British India is also, on the whole, *highly beneficial.* In the absence of a Representative Assembly, for which India is at present

Liberation Of The Press

totally unfit, there is no other medium through which abuses can be brought to light and the sense of the community be taken on matters of general interest. There cannot be greater evil than that public officers should be exempted from the control of public opinion. In Lord William Bentinck's, Lord Metclafe's and Lord Auckland's time the press was held in wholesome respect by the public functionaries, even at the most remote stations, and it acted as a sort of moral preventive police, furnishing in a fair degree, in reference to the whole governing body, an answer to question "*Quis custodiet ipsos Custodes*? .... (Trevelyon, The Letters of Indoppilus, pp 44—45)

As a matter of fact, many editors felt that Ellenborough was "unfriendly" to the Press. The editors were used to receive from his predecessor an outline of the intelligence which arrived almost daily in Calcutta from the vicinity of Afghanistan. Ellenborough stopped that useful supply of information for no conceivable reason. Narrating his personal experience J.H. Stocquelar wrote: " I called at Government House, and in an interview vouchsafed by the autocrat, remonstrated with him on what was at least a piece of bad policy. He admitted the weight of the arguments advance, and directed Captain Henry Durand, his Secretary, afterwards the distinguished and much lamented lieutenant-Governor of Punjab, to continue the supply of the requisite budget of news. In a week or two, Lord E. capricously revoked the order, and of course the public were left entirely in the dark as to the fate of their captive friends, or the intended policy of retribution. Falsehoods naturally found their way into the public papers, and no means were nor left of contradicting rumours or refuting calumnies." (Stocquelar, Memoirs of a Journalist, p 122)

Stocquelar who left India about the same time as Ellenborough made the following interesting comments in his `Memoirs'.

"I found that the (press) of western India in 1823 in a childish condition, that of Bengal essentially weakened by commercial failure and gubernatorial persecution. I remained long enough, with the exception of two brief visits to England, to see it reach a healthy maturity, and to become, literally, the organ of public sentiment, and a useful auxiliary of the Government."

However, the "old Tories" carried on their hostility towards the expansion of liberal ideas in India. Both the House of Lords and the House of Commons were accustomed to such sentiments as those of the Duke of Wellington who, addressing his fellow Peers on March 9, 1843 declared:

"The state of things in that country (India) is one of much greater difficulty than when I was there, because there is now established in India what is called a free Press, but which I should make free to call a most licentious press; and by referring to these papers your Lordships will see that the mischievous influence of the press is repeatedly complained of. For my own part I must own I do not see how the operations of war can be carried on in a satisfactory manner in India, with such a press constantly exercising its influence, and connected through its correspondents with every cantonment of the army."

Lord Hardinge succeeded Ellenborough as the Governor-General. Primarily a soldier, he used to keep himself busy with his own affairs and no events affecting the Press took place during his tenure.

GOLDEN ERA

The removal of Press restrictions and repeal of the repressive laws gave a fillip to the growth of newspapers. The Christian missionaries took the lead in casting moving types in Bengali, Hindi, Marathi, Tamil, Telegu and Malayalam languages mainly for printing pamphlets to preach christianity. As a result, printing presses came up in different parts of the country with moving types. The introduction of lithography in 1837 gave a boost to the growth of Urdu journalism in Delhi and North-west province.

For the Press it was sort of a "golden era". Since the time of Lord William Bentinck the Press in India remained, more or less, free for a period of about 28 years. The Brahmo Samaj, founded in 1828 and other socio—religious movements during the period were but expressions of national awakening. The division of the Hindu society into orthodox and progressive groups was reflected on the newspapers over the question of social reform. After the liberation the number of Bengali newspapers rose to 19, the combined circulation of which exceeded 8000 copies. *Sambad Kaumudi, Banga Doot* and *Gyananeswan* were for social reforms while *Samachar Chandrika, Sambad Prabhakar, Purnochandroday, Sambad Timir Nasak* etc. supported the orthodox cause.

Pandit Iswar Chandra Vidyasagar's efforts to legalise widow remarriage created a stir in the country. He wrote several pamphlets to drive home the truth that widow remarriage was quite in order and enjoyed the support of scriptures. The orthodox Hindus of Bengal, Bihar, Orissa and Madras burst out in protest against any measure validating widow remarriage. To counter this Vidyasagar also submitted a petition to the Government with signatures of more than a thousand Hindus demanding immediate legislation on and widow remarriage bill was passed into law in 1856. The progressive newspapers stood by Vidyasagar. Within five months of the passing of the Act, the first widow remarriage took place and in the next five years 25 such marriages were solemnised.

The question of widow remarriage apart, the Press was divided on many other issues, like the inheritance of property by the Hindus who had embraced Christianity, use of Bengali language in Courts of law, the helpless condition of ryots under the Permanent Settlement. The reformers pursued their cause through forcefully written pamphlets and plays. Rev. J. long who gave details about individual newspapers and journals wrote: "The taste of the Hindus for dramatic performance has been employed to speed the cause of widow remarriage. Several ably-written Bengali dramas have been published which in caustic and cutting language expose the evils that arise from widow's celibacy. Some of these dramas have been acted on the stage by natives to crowded audience both in Calcutta and Hooghly, to the intense disgust of the old school of Hindus. A drama has lately been published holding up to scorn spirit drinking and ganja smoking. Babu P.C Mitter, the Librarian of Calcutta Public Library, has with a powerful and satirical pen, pointed out the various social evils that exist among our countrymen and has a work in the press advocating by tales, anecdotes, biography etc. the cause of female education. The outrages and oppresions of indigo planters have called forth songs and pamphlets. 'Kulinism' (Kulin Brahmins were in the habit of marrying many wives, in some cases running to 20) and caste have been vigorously attacked and in a number of pamphlets social reform has been powerfully advocated". (J. Natarajan, History of Indian Journalism pp 45-46).

Meanwhile, technical advances made and rapidity of communication development of postal and telegraph facilities during the rule of Lord Dalhousie brought about a significant change in the hitherto archaic methods of collection and transmission of news as well as distribution of newspapers. The British capitalists started investing more and more money on textile and jute mills, coal mines and plantations as a result of which there was an increase in exports and imports. But the measure seriously affected the indigenous artisans many of whom migrated to towns to serve as factory labourers while others fell back on land creating pressure on agriculture.

In his zeal to establish an empire in India, Dalhousie dethroned several rulers and annexed their territories. But his annexation of Oudh created a great deal of noise in the country. His Policy of Doctrine of Lapse, refusing to recognise adopted sons as heirs hit the right of inheritance of Indian rulers. The States of Nagpur, Satara and Jhansi were annexed to British India in pursuance of this policy. The masses were called upon to resist the measure as a direct interference by foreign rulers on Hindu religion which recognised the rights of the adopted sons. In 1854, the Santhal rebellion in Birbhum, Midnapur and other neighbouring areas in Bengal was ruthlessly put down. But it gave an indication of the extent of discontent among the masses due to loss of their traditional privileges and their being exploited in the new environment. The Santhals demanded that land belonged to them and they must not pay any rent for it. They rose in revolt to "kill all moneylenders and policemen, expel traders and landlords and fight to death all who resisted them." The Hindoo Patriot pointed out that British administrators, having no contact with the masses, could not measure the depth of feelings and discontent of the people".

But Dalhousie did not attach much importance to the comments by the Indian Press though his Government was aware of the influence the newspapers exerted over the people. The European—owned newspapers took delight in parading a sense of racial superiority while Indian—owned newspapers brought out in details stories of crime in England "to show that there are faults with the English too".

Rev. J. Long's report on the Indian Press contradicted many of the charges levelled against many of the Indian newspapers of that period. Some of his remarks were reproduced here as of interest.

"Whether one looks at the stagnation of village life or the need for rousing the native mind from the torpor of local selfishness, the importance of the native newspapers is very great. Let any European look through the files of these papers and he will see there the operations of Darogas and Amlas fully exposed, the want of roads, the fantastic tricks of young European officials, of men in courts, of practices such as swearing on a bundle of rags which for 11 years the people had fancied was the Koran.

If Government wish correct news to circulate in the villages they must use the vernacular Press as organs for diffusing it. The enemies of the English Government are not inactive, already ideas are rapidly spreading in various districts that the English power is on the wane, that the Russians are coming to India and would govern it better than the English do.

The number of newspapers in circulation is small compared with that of other publications. Their influence is great, extending at an average of 10 readers for each paper to 30,000 persons and conveying to numbers in the mofussil their views relating to Government measures. The editors have translated the abuses freely lavished on natives by some English editors and the publication of such matter excites in the reader a spirit antagonistic to Europeans. English newspapers in too many cases cherish the spirit of antagonism of race". (J. Natarajan, History of Indian Journalism, pp 46—47)

However, unlike the Press in Calcutta and Bombay where it was developing fast, the growth of the Press in other parts of the country was very slow. In Bengal newspapers were publishing more of local grievances, official injustice and political affairs. But in Delhi and North-west Provinces the journals made no impact as they were silent on public grievances, political and socio-religious questions. Since they were running at a loss the Government subsidised them by subscribing a few hundred copies of each of the few newspapers for distribution among the officials.

Among the urdu newspapers coming out from Delhi and Agra at that time were *Sayyed-Ul-Akhbar, Oordu Akbar, Mozhur-Ul-Akhbar, Sudder-Ul-Akhbar, Akhbar-Ul-Haquya, Zoobdut-Ul-Akhbar, Siraj-Ul-Akhbar* etc.

In North West Province there were 28 newspapers in 1850 with a circulation of 1497. In 1853 the number of newspapers increased to 35 and their total circulation went to 2216 copies. In 1858 the number of publications came down to 12 only but the circulation increased to

Liberation Of The Press

3223. During the mutiny of 1857 most of the Urdu newspapers stopped publication and of the 12 newspapers that existed only one was edited by a muslim. Official reports deplored the "lack of interest in political matters and the exclusion of public grievances from the Press" during this period.

Commenting on th Press of North—west provinces J. Natarajan observes: "There were other factors peculiar to the Press in NWPS. There were two communities. Persian and Urdu were the current languages. The Hindus were anxious to have the Devnagri script accepted and judicious agitation was carried for its adoption as an alternative script .... The social atmosphere seems to have been such that the mildest controversy on subjects such as comparative superiority of Delhi and Lucknow Urdu and criticism of the practice among the Hindus of not permitting widows to remarry were likely to be misunderstood. The concept of the freedom of the Press as ably propounded by Raja Rammohun Roy in Bengal in 1823 just did not exist in 1853 in North—west Provinces." (History of Indian Journalism, p 55).

In Bombay, Gujrati journalism was started as early as 1822 by the Parsis. Starting with *Mumbaina Samachar* seven papers were established between 1830 and 1858 but a majority of them ceased publication. Other well—known newspapers were : *Mumbaina Chabuk, Doorbin, Rast Gaftar, Chitragnan Durpan, Satya Prakash, Vartaman, Shamsher Bahadsur, Surat Samachar*. Upto the time of the rebellion the main theme of these papers was advocacy of social reforms, such as widow remarriage, education of girls, stoppage of child marriage etc. In Bombay, all the Gujrati newspapers were owned by the Parsis and during the rebellion they blindly supported the British rule, though they vehemently opposed racial antagonism preached by the Anglo-Indian Press. Marathi journalism was inaugurated in 1832 by Bal Shastri Jambhekar, an ex-professor of Elphinstone College. He started *Bombay Darpan*, first as an Anglo-Marathi fortnightly but subsequently converted it into a weekly paper. In 1840 he started *Dig Darshan*, a Marathi monthly magazine and helped to start *Prabhakar*, a weekly in 1841.

An educationist, Jambhekar was free from superstition of all kinds and preached progressive western ideas in the papers. He had trained a band of journalists who carried on the work successfully. The *Prabhakar* earned a reputation for independence and fearlessness under its editor Bhau Mahajan (Govind Vithal Kunte). To defend Hinduism against the attacks of Christian missionaries Pandit Morabhat Dandekar, an ardent disciple of Jambhekar, started in 1844, the *Upadesha Chandrika*, a Marathi monthly journal. Other newspapers which also made considerable impact were *Duyan Prakash* of Poona founded in February 1849, and edited by K.T. Ranade, *Indu Prakash*, the Anglo-Marathi journal established by Mahadev Govind Ranade, the leader of Prarthana Samity (Bombay version of Brahmo Samaj). It was in the columns of this paper that Aurobindo "practised his prentice pen in jornalism". Other papers were *Vartaman Deepika*, *Vichar Lahari*, *Dhoomketu* and *Dhyan Sindhu*.

The first attempt at Tamil journalism was made by the Religious Tract Society in 1831 when it undertook publication of the Tamil magazine. Rev. J. Long in a report submitted in 1859 gives the date of the first newspaper in Tamil and Telegu as 1833. The next newspaper published in Tamil was the *Rajavrithi Bodhini* in 1855. The other weekly paper was the Dinavartaman (1855) edited by Rev. P. Percival. The American Mission Press published the quarterly *Repository*. The Tamil papers were run exclusively by the missionaries and subsidized by the Government. Discussion of social controversies and political matters had, therefore, no place in the columns of these papers. Even English papers were wary of offending the Government.

In the Kannada-speaking area, which was known as

the Southern Maratha country, there were no newspapers before 1857 for a variety of reasons. The first Kannada newspaper was started by Christian missionaries. In Malayalam the printing press was introduced by Christian missionaries towards the end of 15th century. But the first newspaper *Vignyana Nikshepam* (1840) was published from Kottayam and the second one *Paschima Tharaka* (1862) from Cochin.

No newspapers were published in Punjabi, Oriya and Assamese before the rebellion. This was because, as Rev. Long has pointed out, "political awakening and progressive urge for socio-religious reforms did not develop simultaneously all over India and equal degree in all the provinces."

> "Were it left to me to decide whether we should have a government without newspapers of newspapers without a government, I should not hesitate to prefer the latter. But I should mean that every man should receive those papers and capable of reading them."
>
> Thomas Jefferson

6
PRESS AND THE FIRST WAR OF INDEPENDENCE

The growing discontent among the people against foreign rulers exploded in the form of revolts in various parts of the country. The Wahbi rising, the rise of Titumir and Farazis, the Santhal rebellion of 1855 bore testimony to these facts. They were not sudden developments as the Indian Press had forewarned the authority of the looming threat. In his report Rev. Long wrote: "The opinions of the native Press may often be regarded as the safety valve which gives warning of danger; Thus had the native newspapers of January 1857 been consulted by the European functioneries they would have seen in them how the natives were ripe for revolt and were expecting aid from Russia and Persia."

Underscoring the importance of the views of the Press in Indian languages he calculated in his 1859 report that there were six million readers or hearers for the 600,000 copies of hundreds of Bengali books published in 1857, at the rate of 10 per book. Of the newspapers printed for sale, he estimated, 2950 copies with about 30,000 readers at approximately the same rate. In the North-west province the report listed 28 newspapers with a total circulaton of 1497: But in 1853, 39 newspapers and periodicals had a total circulation of 1839 and in 1854 the same newspapers and periodicals had a total circulation of 2216 while in 1858, 12 publishing newspapers and periodicals, account for a total circulation of 3223. It has to be pointed out that the newspapers in the North-west province with large circulation (between 200 and 250 copies) were almost invariably supported by the Government buying about 200 copies of each issue for distribution. The Press in the North- West province was subjected to the most careful scrutiny in the pre-rebellion period and only one case of `objectionable publication' and two cases of "misuse of the editorial chair" in 1852 could be cited. The complaint of 'objectionable publication' related to an attempt to ridicule the notion of British expulsion from India on the ground that "it leaves room for misconception". The 'misuse of editor's chair' related to an editor's complaint against being summoned to court as a witness and publication by another editor of libellous articles against an official for which he was imprisoned for two months. The refrain throughout is that the Press does not adequately reflect public opinion and ventilate public grievances.

However, Long consistently maintained that the Press should be encouraged and restrictions should not be imposed. He wrote: "Much at that period (of the rebellion) was written and spoken on the subject of the native press, and many hasty remarks were made respecting it. While some said it was so radically corrupt that it ought to be abolished .... of late some officials have proposed cutting the knot, and either suppressing the native press, or establishing rigorous censorship. We trust that the perusal of this report will show how suicidal a measure of this kind would be to the interests of good government and sound education. The English newspapers in too many cases cherish the spirit of antagonism of race (Some English editors freely lavished abuse on the natives). Yet during the Punjab War and the rebellion, the native Press, though viewing affairs more from an oriental than an English standpoint, has maintained on the whole a moderate tone --- very different from the Persian and Urdu papers".

But the situation changed once the rebellion started. The first shot was fired in Bengal in March 1857, where, according to Dr Alexander Duff, "Discontent lurks deeply in the hearts of millions". While the rebellion was still in progress affecting large areas in north and central India, the English Press was bringing out news of a highly provocative nature; inflammatory statements to revenge appeared in both the editorial and correspondents columns of the Anglo-Indian newspapers. Writing on the subject six years later Trevelyan said:

"The tone of the press was horrible. Never did the cry for blood swell so loud as among these Christians and Englishmen in the middle of the nineteenth Century. The pages of those brutal and grotesque journals published by Hebart and Marat during the agony of French Revolution, contained nothing that was not matched and surpassed in the files of some Calcutta papers. Because the pampered Bengal sepoys had behaved like double-dyed rascals, therefore every Hindoo and Musalman was a rebel, a traitor, a murderer; therefore, we were to pray that all the population of India were to have one neck, and all the hemp in India might be twisted into one rope. It would be wearisome to quote specimens of the style of that day. Every column teemed wit investives which at the time seemed coarse and tedious, but which we must now pronounce to be wicked and blasphemous. For what could be more audacious than to assert that Providence had granted us a right to destroy a nation in our wrath? -- to slay and burn, and plunder, not in the cause of order and civilisation, but in the name of our insatiable vengeance, and our imperial displeasure? The wise ruler, whose comprehensive and impartial judgement preserved him from the contagion of that fatal frenzy, was assailed with a storm of obliquy for which we should in vain seek a precedent in history. To read the newspapers of that day, you would believe that Lord Canning was at the bottom of the whole mutiny; that upon his head was the guilt of the horrors of Cawnpore and Allahabad; that it was he who had passed round the chaupatties and the lotahs, and spread the report that the Russ was marching down from the north to drive the English into the sea. After all, the crime charged against him was, not that he had hindered the butchery, but that his heart was not in the work. No one had the face to say, or, at any rate, no one had the weakness to believe, that Lord Canning had pardoned any considerable number of condemned rebels. His crying sin was that he took little or no pleasure in the extermination of the people whom he had been commissioned by his Sovereign to govern and protect."

(The Competition Wallah, 1864, pp 299-300 and pp 437-441)

The rebellion was suppressed with ruthless savagery and cruelty. Lord Canning accused the Indian Press of inciting the people to rise in revolt and enacted a hasty legislation, known as the Gagging Act of 1857, to control the Press. While introducing the measure in the Legislative Council, His Lordship said:

"I doubt whether it is fully understood or known to what audacious extent sedition has been poured into the hearts of the native population of India within the last few weeks under the guise of intelligence supplied to them by the native newspapers. It has been done sedulously, cleverly, artfully. Facts have been grossly misrepresented -- so grossly that, with educated and informed minds, the very extravagance of misrepresentation must compel discredit. In addition to perversion of facts, there are constant villifications of the government, false assertions of its purposes and unceasing attempts to sow discontent and hatred between it and its subjects". (M. Donogh, History of the Law of Sedition, pp 183-184)

Lord Elphinstone, the Governor of Bombay, who had least reason to complain against the Press in that area, wrote a strong note supporting the imposition of restrictions, with the avowed object of strengthening the hands of the Governor-General against possible opposition from England or in India to the proposed Act.

The Act to regulate and to restrain in certain cases the circulation of printed books and papers was thus passed, reintroducing the main features of the Adam regulations of 1823. The Act prohibited the keeping or using of printing presses without a licence from Government, which assumed discretionery powers to grant licences and to revoke them at any time. It conferred on the Government the power to prohibit the publication or circulation of any newspaper, book or other printed matter. No distinction was made between publications in English and in the Indian languages. It was applicable to whole of India and its duration was limited to one year. The procedure for obtaining licences was laid down and the conditions imposed on licensed printing presses were as follows:

"That no book, pamphlet, newspaper, or other work, printed at such press or with materials or articles, shall contain any observation or statements impugning the motives or designs of the British Government either in England or in India or in anyway tending to bring the said Government into hatred or contempt, to excite disaffection or unlawful resistance to its orders, or to weaken its lawful authority, or the lawful authority of its civil and military servants.

"That no such book, pamphlet, newspaper or other work shall contain observations or statements having a tendency to create alarm or suspicion among the native population of any intended interference by Government with their religious opinions and observations.

"That no such book, pamphlet, newspaper or other work shall contain observations having a tendency to weaken the friendship towards the British Government or native princes, chiefs, or states in dependence upon or alliance with it".

Under the terms of the Act, the *Bengal Hurkaru* was suspended from September 19 to September 24 and a fresh licence was only granted when the offending editor, Sydney Laman Blanchard, tendered his resignation. A number of Indian editors were persecuted for publishing articles deemed seditious and they were committed for trial. The manuscript press, which was more inflammatory and more widely distributed, was not accessible to the authorities, though the Press Act did have a restrictive effect.

The first warning under Canning's 'Gagging Act' was issued against *Friend of India* for its article on "Centenary of Plassey" which justified the hundred years of British rule by asserting that India's previous rulers had been objectionable on various grounds. The Government warned the Friend of India that its licence would be revoked if it again published so provocative an article. In reply the editor wrote an ironical article entitled "The first warning" which he began with the words: "Lord Canning has done us the honour to select the Friend of India as the subject of his frist experiment under the Gagging Act. Then referring to the Governor-General's erstwhile popularity the editor, Henry Mead, said that today there are not half a dozen Europeans "who would lift up their hands in his favour". These were strong words considering the condition of the country, and the Governor-General was about to revoke the paper's licence when an assurance was received on behalf, of the proprietor that the offence would not be repeated. A few months later, Dr George Buist, the editor of *Bombay Times* acquired similar unenviable notoriety by raising the cry "blood for blood". Here again the proprietors, who were Indians, took the editor to task for his anti-Indian writings. The editor was sacked as he refused to obey the dictates of the management. He was succeeded as editor of the *Bombay Times* by Robert Knight. John Conon, the editor and proprietor of the *Bombay Gazette* expressed his disapproval of the new Press Act in the form of a memorial to the Court of Directors.

But the Governor General maintained a stoic indifference to the vehemence of the newspapers against him personally. After the suppression of the rebellion the Crown took over the Government of India from the East India Company and on November 1, 1858, Queen Victoria's Proclamation announced the transfer. Lord Canning became the first Viceroy of India. The new Act and the Queen's Proclamation restored public confidence to a great extent and the Press which suffered a set-back came to life with renewed vigour. Responsive to the changed circumstances Lord Canning set up an "editor's room' where some State papers were laid on the table for the information of the journalists.

The Queen's Proclamation announced the perpetuation of feudalism and made the Indian Princes the "protected allies of the British Raj". It said, "We shall respect the rights, dignity and honour of the native princes as our own." The real motive behind this new policy was to create a loyal band of aristocracy which will work as a check against any future mass upsurge in the country. Lord Canning suggested this in a speech in which he said "It was long ago said by Sir John Malcolm that if we made all India into Zillas (or British districts) it was not in the nature of things that our empire should last fifty years; but that if we could keep up a number of native States without political power, but as royal instruments, we should exist in India as long as our naval supremacy was maintained. Of the substantial truth of the opinion I have no doubt; and the recent events have made it more deserving of our attention than ever".

The Indian Princes without any political power gradually became servile agents of their imperial masters. Strange enough, the new westernised middle class could not fully realise the real purpose behind this change of policy at that time and they hailed the Queen's Proclamation as a Charter of Rights. This "political hypocrisy" hypnotised, for the time being, the bourgeoisie, aristocracy and barristocracy, but the toiling masses could not be reconciled.

The Gagging Act of 1857 was withdrawn in 1858. "But with a few zigzags, the general policy of the Government was to increasingly curtail the freedom of the Press".

During the period of turmoil caused by the rebellion *Hindoo Patriot* emerged as India's first national newspapers. Under the caption, "The Atrocities and Retribution" *Hindoo Patriot* of May 6, 1858 wrote "History will, we conceive, take a very different view of the facts of the great Indian Revolt of 1857 from what contemporaries have taken of them. What the verdict of the posterity is likely to be may in some measure be anticipated from the judgements of foreign nations and the revulsion already taking place in English feeling. At no distant date it will be found out that while the "atrocities" were in most instances unreal creations of morbid imaginations the retributive excesses were sad realities. "Canning's clemency" will then prove the salvation of the English name as it has proved the salvation of many Indian lives".

At a time when the British sovereignty was being challenged by the Great Revolt and the Press was controlled by the Gagging Act these bold lines came from the pen of Hurish Chandra Mukherjee, editor of *Hindoo Patriot* "who grew with his paper and paper grew with him". He was not a wealthy man. But a keen sense of self-respect and responsibility combined with a desire to fight boldly for the suffering of the humanity made him a great editor. The secret of his success was not his profound learning but his eagerness to become a sincere mouthpiece of the oppressed millions among whom he dwelt. He was recognised as the prophet of nationalism and a leader of men. *The Patriot* editor maintained a balance throughout the mutiny" which was remarkable in an atmosphere of fanatic prejudices".

Hurish Chandra Mukherjee died on June 14, 1861. The paper passed into the hands of Kali Prasanna Sinha who ran it at a loss for a few months before making it over to Pandit Iswar Chandra Vidyasagar who asked Kristo Das Pal to take editorial responsibility of the paper in November 1861. Kristo Das was moderate and restrained in his views, but he was sharp in his criticisms. The relations between him and Sir George Campbell, the Lt. Governor, were strained. When the Gaekwad of Baroda (Mulhar Rao) was deposed in 1874, the *Hindoo Patriot* criticised the Government and exposed the vunerable points in the prosecution. Kristo Das forcefully pleaded for the admission of Indians in increasing to Government appointments and opposed the Verncular Press Act of 1878 though he actively participated in the public agitation. Though financed by the Bengal Zamindars, the *Hindoo Patriot* had a large circulation among the Europeans and Indians and was known for its independence, loyalty and learning.

The rebellion had adversely affected the growth of Urdu newspapers. Many Urdu journals disappeared in May 1857. An interesting aspect of Urdu journalism was that the majority of Urdu organs of the north were edited by Hindus. Before the rebellion their principal topics of discussion were religious and social observances, the various Acts and Notifications of the Government, the niceties of the Urdu language and items of news of general interest from other parts of the country. "The Government officers lived in perpetual fear that the rebellion might at any time break out again. Numerous stories were current of the extraordinary organisation of the May attempt and how the news had been passed from mouth the mouth, through the medium of songs and catch phrases. And the Indian press, as a possible channel of access to the public, was of course, suspected. The Government had established a strict censorship through their district officers and at Peshawar an editor was imprisoned. Presses were also stopped at Sialkot and Multan. One result of the censorship was that the papers concentrated more on general news, mostly culled from journals published in different parts of India" (Barns, The Indian Press, p 260).

It was, however, felt that Calcutta needed a strong Bengali newspaper and when the revolt was over Pandit Iswar Chandra Vidyasagar and Dwarakanath Vidyabhusan of Calcutta Sanskrit College started the *Som Prakash*. Its object was avowdly political. Both Hindoo Patriot and *Som Prakash* were active during indigo disturbances of 1860, to the great advantage of the just case of the Bengali peasants.

A great sensation was caused in newspaper circles in 1861 by which was known as the *Nil Darpan* case. The Indigo Commission which was a subject of protracted controversy in the Indian Press, had submitted its report. Points used to be regularly mentioned in the Press were that the cultivation of indigo was not voluntary on the part of the *raiyats*, that the best lands were forcibly ploughed up and resown with indigo when it had already been sown with other crops, that the *raiyat* became indebted to the factory, lost his personal freedom and was oppressed, kidnapped, imprisoned and outraged by the servants of the factory. The planters had their own case. Action was taken in certain cases on the strength of the Indigo Commission report. At about this time Dinabandhu Mitra's Bengali play *Nil Darpan* created a furore. A translation of this play was made from Bengali to English under the supervision of Rev. J. Long, printed and distributed to a number of officials with the sanction of the Secretary to the Government in Bengal, Mr W.S. Seton-Karr. Enraged, the indigo planters sued Manuel, the printer and Rev. Long for libel in the Supreme Court. The printer was fined and Long was fined as well as sentenced to a month's imprisonment. However, the fine was paid by Kali Prasanna Sinha. Setton-Karr was also in trouble as he had misunderstood or exceeded the instructions of the Lt. Governor. He resigned from the office of the Legislative member for Bengal and Secretary to Government, but the Lt. Governor, Sir J.P. Grant did not accept his resignation. The matter went up to the Governor-General who passed certain strictures on the circumstances in which the mistakes had been perpetrated and ruled on Seton-Karr's resignation.

"His Excellency (Governor-General) in Council cannot consider that the Government is thereby absolved from the duty of making sure that the important ministerial functions of the Secretary to the Government of Bengal shall not be resumed by an officer by whom, from whatever cause, they have been exercised with grievous indiscretion. And in this view it is decidedly the opinion of the Governor-General in Council that, when Mr Seton-Karr shall no longer have to discharge the duties of his present position in the Legislative Council, he should not be allowed to return to the office of the Secretary to the Government of Bengal".

The *Nil Darpan* case figured prominently in the Press, both Indian and Anglo-Indian. Seton-Karr wrote a long letter to the *Statesman* in order to "clear up charges of unfair dealing and of personal hostility to the planters and to make such explanation as was due to persons who felt themselves aggrieved by the publication". Rev. Long received unqualified support of Indian newspapers for his consistent advice against any restrictions on the Press.

In 1861 Manomohan Ghosh, who used to report for the *Hindoo Patriot* on the indigo peasants' unrest started the *Indian Mirror* as an English fortnightly with financial assistance from Devendra Nath Tagore, father of poet Rabindra Nath Tagore. Devendra Nath was the founder of both *Tattvabodhini Sabha* and the *Tattvabodhini Patrika* (1839-1902). Keshab Chandra Sen associated himself with the project and later became its editor. But soon differences grew between them over the basic concept of Hindu religion and social reforms. Devendra nath was opposed to idol worship but he favoured the Hindu form of marriage and disliked widow and inter-caste marriage. Keshab Chandra Sen stood for a complete break with the past. When the two parted company Keshab Chandra Sen retained possession of the *Indian*

Mirror and conducted it until he went to England in 1870 to study the "Christian life as displayed and illustrated in England". On his return to India he started *Sulav Samachar*, a pice newspaper which was a great success. He converted the *Indian Mirror* into a daily and started the weekly *Sunday Mirror*. Credit goes to Keshab Chandra Sen for the passage of the Civil Marriage Act of 1872 which legalised inter-caste marriage, prohibited bigamy and allowed remarriage of widows subject to the condition that the parties declared at the time of registration that they were not Hindus, Mohammedans, Christians, Buddhists, Jains or Parsees. But in 1878 Keshab Chandra Sen himself married his daughter at an early age to the Maharaja of Cooch Behar according to orthodox Hindu rites. The marriage completed his earlier breach with the Brahmo Samaj and he founded the Sadharan Brahmo Samaj on May 15, 1878 as opposed to Tagore's Adi Brahmo Samaj. Later Keshab Chandra Sen broke away once again and established the "New Dispensation Church". Keshab Chandra Sen was a forceful orator and a dynamic personality. He electrified the younger generation and kindled new hopes in them. Largely because of his personal charisma and popularity the *Indian Mirror* and *Sulav Samachar* became a great success. *Sulav Samachar* had 4000 subscribers which was considered very satisfactory during those days.

Girish Chandra Ghosh, who founded the *Hindoo Patriot*, later started the Bengalee in 1868. (1862, according to some). Like the *Patriot* the Bengalee was soon acknowledged to be a fearless exponent of public causes, but it lacked financial stability. The paper was taken over by Becharam Chatterjee and was declining rapidly when Surendra Nath Banerji purchased it through common friends. The *Bengalee* was conducted on independent lines and on occasions strongly differed from its Indian contemporaries. Not only *Som Prakash*, three other papers came out from villages which took up the cause of the oppressed indigo cultivators and helpless *ryots*. They were *Amrita Bazar Patrika*, published in 1868 by Sisir Kumar Ghosh and his brothers from Palua-Magura in the district of Jessore: *Halishahar Patrika*, published in 1870 from Halishahar, a village in the district of 24-parganas and run by young college students; and *Gram Varta Prakashika*, published in 1863, from Kumarkhali, a village in the district of Nadia and conducted by Kangal Harinath Majumdar, a reputed social worker. These papers demanded greater rights for Indians and criticised the administration. Thus a distinct change was noticed in the tone of newspapers which instead of dealing with socio-religious reforms, began now to discuss political matters seriously and regularly.

Of the four newspapers, published from villages, *Amrita Bazar Patrika* deserved special mention. The Ghosh brothers, eight in all, were a remarkable family. It was with the eldest brother, Basanta Kumar Ghosh, that the idea of starting a newspaper first originated. The renamed their village Palua-Magura as Amrita Bazar to perpetuate the memory of their mother, Amrita Moyee Devi. The Ghosh brother's aim was to ventilate the grievances of the rural people, specially the indigo cultivators. They stood by the harassed peasants and fought their case before the Courts as well as Indigo Commission. Sisir Kumar purchased some types and a wooden printing machine with Rs 32 only and picked some skill in composing. On his return Basanta Kumar started a fortnightly journal named *Amrita Prabahini*. This paper died after a few months and with it died Basant Kumar. Soon after Hemanta Kumar and Sisir Kumar gave up their jobs in the Income Tax department and started the Bengali weekly, *Amrita Bazar Patrika*. Soon another brother, Motilal, also joined them. Some leading advocates and friends helped the Ghosh brothers financially. In 1869 it was made a bilingual paper having a few columns in English and in 1871 Sisir Kumar rented a house at Hidaram Banerji Lane and removed the press there with a view to publishing the paper from Calcutta. Here also it was run as a family paper.

Before being shifted to Calcutta *Amrita Bazar Patrika* was involved in a libel case for publishing an article, written by Raj Kumar Mitra, the head clerk of the Joint Magistrate and prosecution was launched against Sisir Kumar, Motilal, their uncle and the printer of their paper Chandra Nath Roy and Rajkrishna Mitra who had injudiciously revealed his identity. Despite most rigorous cross-examination of young Motilal, the identity of the editor could not be established in the court. The result of the eight months' proceedings was that the printer was sentenced to six months and Rajkrishna Mitra to a year's simple imprisonment. Sisir Kumar was persecuted again for withholding material evidence but the prosecution failed.

Ghosh brothers' decision to shift the paper to Calcutta was, doubtless, a wise one because papers published from villages had chiefly local interests to serve and could not, therefore, attract the attention of either the general public of the province or of the government's, provincial as well the imperial. Its removal to Calcutta gave it an opportunity to play a significant role in the forthcoming national struggle and its unearthing of bureaucratic misdeeds and secret documents made it a redoubtable champion of the cause of the people. Dwarka Nath Mitra, a Judge of Calcutta High Court, once told Sisir Kumar, "I have subscribed to your paper. But I am afraid your writings are characterised by a virulence which may afterwards come to influence the masses and spread discontent and disaffection in the country". Sisir Kumar's reply was bold but categorical. He said that "the mission of his paper was to awaken the people and to kindle in them the fire of patriotism. They are now more dead than alive", he said, and "need to be aroused from their slumber. Our language has, therefore, to be loud and penetrating". The patrika held the centre of the stage, so far as Indian Press was concerned, for many years after.

Meanwhile, significant developments took place in other centres of publication. In Bombay the four newspapers -- *Bombay Times*, the *Courier*, the *Standard* and the *Telegraph* were amalgamated in 1861 under the new name *Times of India*. Three other Anglo-Indian newspapers, the *Pioneer* in Allahabad, the *Civil and Military Gazette* of Lahore and the *Statesman* of Calcutta wer established. A fourth paper, the *Madras Mail* was the first evening paper in India. The *Hindu* followed soon after. A number of Urdu journals had ceased publication during the rebellion. Others came up in their places edited by Hindus. Censorship was rigid and an editor was thrown behind the bars in Peshawar and printing presses were confiscated at Sialkot and Multan. Nevertheless, in 1861 there were, besides one missionary publication, 17 newspapers distributed as follows: Urdu 11 and Hindi six. As many as eight were published from Agra, two from Ajmere, two from Etawa and one each from Ludhiana, Meerut, Jaunpur, Shaharanpur, Allahabad and Kanpur. An account is given of these journals in the work quoted as well as a review of the printing presses in the North-western Provinces drawn up by the Director of Public Instruction, Mr Stewart Reid.

Lord Elgin, who succeeded Lord Canning as Viceroy in 1862, did not interfere with the Press. His foreboding that he would never again see his native land proved to be true and he died at Dharmasala about twenty months after assuming the Viceroyalty. Sir Robert Napier then officiated and he was followed by Sir William Denison who retained the office until Sir John Lawrence was able to take over in 1864. Once again the question of a Government newspaper was revived since Sir John Lawrence, grave and conscientious, had deeply resented some attacks by certain newspapers. The same old arguments, both for and against, were once more propounded with the same result; that it was wiser to allow the soundness of the Government's measure to speak for themselves rather than to indulge in special pleadings which could only redound to the discredit of the authority . Moreover, the Government had underestimated the probable cost and when it was realised that this would be prohibitive if the proposed journal were to have any standing, the proposition collapsed.

In 1867, Metcalfe Act for the liberation of the Press was repealed by the Act for the Regulation of Printing Presses and Newspapers, for the preservation of copies printed in British India and for the registration of such books. This Act is still in force. (See Appendix II)

This was a purely regulating Act intended to keep the Government informed of the activities of printing presses and was, in no sense, a restriction on printing presses and newspapers. The Press, more or less, enjoyed complete freedom from 1835 to 1870. But fresh problems arose towards the end of 1875 owing to the prevaling scarcity conditions in Bihar. Leading newspapers, both Indian and European, described it as a famine and urged upon the Government the immediate need for organising relief measures. The *Amrita Bazar Patrika* Correspondent, Hemanta Kumar, toured the affected Bihar villages and reported that there was no famine; it was usual scarcity caused by a fall in the production of crops owing to natural causes. The Bengal Government, however, took a different view and spent some six crores of rupees on relief. At the time the Lieutenant Governor of Bengal, Sir George Campbell, favoured prohibition of export of grain and Robert Knight supported him. The Governor General Lord Northbrook and his Finance Member, Sir Richard Temple, disagreed with this view and Robert Knight attacked both of them. He was an official, editing an official news journal, *Agricultural Gazette of India*. Even the *India Economist* he had started in Calcutta in 1872 was being subsidised. The subsidy was reduced and later withdrawn altogether and the two questions of freedom of the Press and the association of Government servants with newspapers were reopened.

On freedom of the Press, Sir George Campbell expressed himself in no uncertain terms, possibly because of frequent attacks on him by the Indian Press generally and by *Amrita Bazar Patrika* in particular. He repeated the earlier argument that a free Press and a despotic Government were incompatible, that newspapers were almost against the Government and there was no Press to answer them. He even went so far as to say that the law of libel was no remedy because a protracted trial gave the editor "all the notoriety that the most ambitious libeller could desire."

On the other point a notification was issued by the Home Department on July 8, 1875. It reserved to the Government the right to decide whether the association of officers with the Press was consistent with the discharge of their duty.

The trouble was brewing for sometime and Robert Knight, in anticipation of the shape of things to come, resigned in 1874 and founded the *Statesman* on January 1875 with the financial support of 24 merchants who took share in the venture. Knight tried to acquire the *Friend of India*, which was a source of inspiration for him, but the negotiations were protracted and were not put through till April 1875 when he bought the journal for Rs 30,000 and moved the paper to Calcutta. The two papers were published separately till 1877. T*the Statesman* as a daily and the Friend of India as a weekly. The *Friend of India* was incorporated with the weekly overseas edition of the *Statesman* and for many years the daily paper was headed "The Statesman and Friend of India". In deference to the wishes of the founder *The Statesman* to this day bears the legend "incorporating and directly descended from the *Friend of India* — founded in 1818."

The Government, meanwhile, was getting increasingly worried about the attitude of the Press. It was particularly concerned about the Indian Press on whom it had to depend for information relating to goings-on in the

Indian society. Rev. Long, it will be recalled, made the categorical assertion that if the North-western provinces' newspapers had been carefully studied in 1856-57, the rebellion could have been anticipated and prevented. It was repeatedly impressed on the local officials that a most careful watch should be kept on the Indian language Press and the complaint was frequently recorded that the annual reports submitted were inadequate and left much to be desired. The effect of all this was that a formidable document had been compiled of all the trangressions of Indian language Press and it hung like Damocle's Sword over the head of the officials.

"If language is not correct, then what is said is not what is meant; if what is said is not what is meant, then what ought to be done remains undone".

Confucius

7
REPRESSIVE MEASURES

When Lord Lytton became the viceroy of India in 1876 he had before him the findings of Sir George Campbell who had instituted an inquiry into the state of Indian-owned Press of Bengal three years earlier. Forthwith he decided to seek opinions on improving relations between the Press and the Government. Robert Knight was of the opinion that the attitude of the Press towards the Government derived directly from the attitude of the Government towards the Press. Knight said, "If the Government shows no sympathy, is jealous of all appearance of consulting it, excludes from all information upon subjects of current interest, shows no deference to public wishes, however reasonable, looks upon the Press as factious and inspired by no real desire for the public good and gives neither the support nor the encouragement it might reasonably expect then the want of representative institutions become unendurable and the whole Press glides insensibly into the attitude of hostility to the Government......"

"At present there is not the slightest sympathy with the Press, nor the least disposition to asist it. Instead of any desire being evinced to conciliate its sympathies, it is made to feel that it is a matter indifference to the Government whether it sinks or swims .... The Goverment practically treats the Press as though it were Bohemian, and in all passive ways, ignores and discourages it. The attitude is felt sensibly and calls forth a corresponding one on the other side .... It seems to me most desirable that the Government must possess some means by which it might communicate to the Press as far as may be prudent and possibly to do so, the course of its proceedings, the information it is receiving, the views with which it is regarded, the purposes and desires of the Government and the special difficulties that embarrass its course." (S.C. Sanial in The Calcutta Review Oct., 1908).

Knight suggested that there should be a special Press Bureau in the Government, the duty of whose Director should be to acquaint himself with the writings of every journal in the country. Moreover, the Press should be invited to communicate freely with such an oficer on all questions concerning which they might desire information. Knight believed that by a wise attitude towards the Press the Government might improve its character infinitely and settle its loyalty. "The Government should abandon its attitude of total indifference to the Press and should frankly recognise in it an opposition with which courteous and friendly relations were to be maintained; and in all reasonable and proper ways it should be recognised, honoured and assisted." The only other person to support this point of view was Arthur Hobhouse (Later Lord Hobhouse).

"Neither knowledge nor freedom of speech be acquired without unpleasant excesses. We have chosen the generous, I think the wise, policy of encouraging both, and we ought not to be frightened because some of the symptoms appear. People who increase their knowledge are sure to be discontented, unless their power increases too, and will probably be impatient to acquire that power; and people who have newly pacquired freedom of speech are likely at times to use their tongue with discretion. All that we must take as the drawback necessarily attendent on the benefit of having a more intelligent and less reticent people in India."

The Press in Indian language was growing rapidly. At that time there were about sixty-two such papers in the Bombay Presidency; about sixty in the North-west Provinces; some 28 in Bengali; about nineteen in Madras. Their circulations were, of a necessity, restricted but they were nevertheless expanding. It was computed about this time that there were probably 1,00,000 readers of such papers and that the highest circulation of any one paper was in the neighbourhood of 3000.

During Lord Lytton's opening year of office, 1876, *The Civil and Military Gazette* was first published from Lahore. Originally, the paper was intended to cater for the Services. But on February 1, 1873 when the paper changed hands the management decided that the paper would not descend to be the organ of any clique. "Its columns will be open to all representations and claims which seek only a full and impartial consideration and its aims will be to represent in the best sense that honourable spirit which has made our English Fourth Estate the power it is."

On February 28, 1877 The Civil and Military Gazette purchased the *Lahore Indian Public Opinion* and the two papers were amalgamatedo Reuters telegrams only occupied half a column of the first page in those days while Indian telegrams took only about one eighth of a column. The rest of the Indian news were taken from the newspapers of Calcutta, Bombay and Madras.

In 1882 Rudyard Kipling, who was then seventeen, was taken on the staff of The Civil and Military Gazette as an apprentice. Kipling left *the Gazette* in 1887 to become Assistant Editor of *the Pioneer*, then at Allahabad . He remained in this post for two years when the paper sent him round the world and the vivid impression of his travel in the United States and Japan were published in *the Pioneer*.

Another important Lahore newspaper, *Tribune*, had been established by this time. Sir Surendra Nath

Banerjea relates how in 1877, he met Sirdar Dayal Singh Majeetia and recalls:

"I persuaded him to start a newspaper at Lahore. I purchased for him at Calcutta the first press for the *Tribune* newspaper and to me he entrusted the duty of selecting the first editor. I recommended the late Sitala Kanta Chakravarty of Dacca for the post, and his successful career as the first editor amply justified my choice. His fearless courage, his penetrating insight into the heart of things, and above all his supreme honesty of purpose, the first and last qualification of an Indian journalist, soon placed him in the front rank of those who weilded their pen in the defence of their country's interest." (A Nation in making, p 47).

The *Tribune* rapidly became a powerful organ of public opinion; it is now (1926) perhaps the most influential Indian journal in the Punjab, and is edited by a gentleman who in his early career was associated with me as a member of the staff of the Bengalee.

On January 1, 1877 Queen Victoria was proclaimed Empress of India. In her message, she declared:

"We trust that the present occasion may tend to unite in bonds of yet closer affection ourselves and our subjects; that from the highest to the humblest all may feel that under our rule the great principles of liberty, equity and justice are secured to them; and to promote their happiness, to add to their prosperity and advance their welfare, are the present aims and objects of our empire."

The object involved--- in the words of then Viceroy, Lord Lytton--- "administrative problems unsolved by Caeser, unsolved by Charlemagne and unsolved by Akbar."

It was the view of many Indians that these problems could be more adequately solved if they had a greater share in their examination and there began a forward movement which has never since lost momentum.

"The history of progressive ideas in Britain was not unknown to Indian youths who, since 1836, had been taught about the British struggle for emancipation and they drew their inspiration from the stories and also from those of an ancient Hindu culture with which the Hindu reformers were endeavouring to revitablise the community" (Barns, The Indian Press, p 279).

The new spirit was briefly reflected in the Indian-owned Press. Two years before Queen Victoria was proclaimed the Empress of India the then Secretary of State Lord Salisbury had drawn the attention of the Government of India to "various articles in the native Press which are not calculated to bring the Government into contempt, but which palliate, if they do not absolutely justify as a duty, the assassination of British officers." Lord Northbrooke's Government had replied that it was not desirable in the then state of law for the Government to prosecute except in the case of systematic attempts to excite hostility against the Government."

Faced with growing criticism of the Press, Lord Lytton studied various methods of meeting the situation. In the autumn of 1877 he prepared a Minute which was circulated to the members of his Council and to each local Government and Chief Commissioner. All, with the exception of Madras (where the Press in Indian languages was not yet strong), concurred in the principles of taking legislative action. Consequently, a Bill was prepared and its substance was telegraphed to the Secretary of State whose permission was sought for its introduction.

For sometime the India Press had been aware that repressive measures were under contemplation. Sir Surendra Nath Banerjea records how in 1877 the Press was invited to the Delhi meeting and how he attended it as the correspondent of The *Hindoo Patriot*, then the leading paper in Bengal, under the editorship of that prince of Indian journalists, Kristo Das Pal. Sir Surendra Nath describes the presentation of an address to the Viceroy by the newspaper and adds:

"In the address we made a pointed reference to the report about the coming restrictions on the Press, and we expressed the hope that the liberties so long enjoyed might be continued. The Viceroy, as might have been expected, was reticent and said nothing in reply to this part of the address. We felt that we had done our duty in communicating our hopes and fears, and for the time the matter ended there. Within less than fifteen months, the vernacular Press all over India, save that of Madras, was muzzled."

He further writes, "In the Council chamber not a single dissentient voice was raised. Maharaja Jatindra Mohan Tagore, who was then a member of the Council, sent for and spoken to by the viceroy and he voted with the Government. The *Hindoo Patriot* wrote against the measure, but not with the warmth that usually characterised its patriotic utterances. "(A Nation in Making, p 59)

The Vernacular Press Bill was introduced in the Governor General's Council and passed as Act IX of 1878. Its objects, briefly, were to place newspapers published in the Indian languages under" better control" and to furnish the Government with more effective means than the existing law provided, of punishing and repressing seditious writing calculated to produce disaffection towards the Government in the minds of ignorant population. It was also claimed to be intended to prevent unscrupulous writers from using their papers as a means of intimidation and extortion. Although the bill was introduced by Sir Arbuthnot, Sir Ashley Eden, the Lt. Governor of Bengal, was the figure round whom there was a storm of controversy. It will be remembered that the chief grievance of the European community in India against Lord Canning was that he refused to discriminate between the "disloyal native" and the "loyal British" in the Press Act and the Arms Act of 1857. The grievance figured prominently in the memorial presented to the Queen for his recall.

Motilal Ghosh's version of the circumstances in which the Act was passed, is also relevant.

Repressive Measures

"An autocrat of autocrats, Sir Ashley sought to rule Bengal with an iron hand. The *Amrita Bazar Patrika* was, however, a thorn in his side. He, therefore, conceived the idea of winning over Babu Sishir Kumar partly by kindness and partly by threats. He had managed to make Babu Kristo Das Pal, Editor of the *Hindoo Patriot* his ardent admirer, and his next move was to entrap and muzzle Sisir Kumar Ghose. So, Sir Ashley sent for him one day, gave him a cordial reception when he came, and offered him a "share of the Government" if he would follow his advice. Here is the purport of what His Honour proposed :-

"Let us three -- I, you and Kristo Das -- govern the province. Kristo Das has agreed to conduct his paper according to my direction. You will have to do the same thing. I shall contribute to your paper as I do to The *Hindoo Patriot*. And when you write an article criticising the government, you will have to submit the manuscript to be before publication. In return, the Government will subscribe to a considerable number of your paper, and I shall consult you as I consult Kristo Das in carrying on the administration of the province.

Babu Sisir Kumar was at the time a poor man. His position in Calcutta society was not high. The tempting offer came from the ruler of the province.... any other men in his circumstances would have succumbed to his temptation. But he was made of a different stuff. He resisted and did something more. He thanked His Honour for his generous offer, but also quitely remarked, 'Your Honour, there ought to be at least one honest journalist in the land'. The expected result followed. Sir Ashley flew into an unconquerable rage. With seething sarcasm, he told Babu Sishir Kumar that he had forgotten to whom he was speaking, that as the supreme authority in the province he could put him in jail any day he liked for seditious writings in his paper, and that he would drive him back to Jessore bag and baggage from where he came in six months. It was not a vain threat. The Vernacular Press Act owed its origin to this incident. It was to take his revenge on Babu Sishir Kumar that Sir Ashley Eden persuaded Lord Lytton to pass this monstrous measure at one sitting. The blow was aimed mainly at the *Amrita Bazar Patrika* which was then an Anglo-vernacular paper and fell within the scope of the Act. But Babu Sishir Kumar and his brothers were too clever for Sir Ashley. Before the Act was put in force they brought out their paper in wholly English garb and thus circumvented the Act and snapped their fingers at the Lieutenant Governor; for, a journal conducted in the English language was beyond the jurisdiction of Lord Lytton's Vernacular Press Act. Sir Asheley was a very outspoken man and he did not conceal his chagrin and bitter disappointment at the escape of the *Patrika* from several of his Bengali friends. He told them that if there had been only one week's delay on the part of the proprietors ,to convert the *Patrika* into English, he would have dealt a deadly blow at it by demanding a heavy bail-bond from them." (Natarajan, History of Indian journalism, p 83).

Motilal Ghose's reading of Sir Ashley Eden's intention was substantially correct and that the bill was aimed at *Amrita Bazar Patrika* as one of the papers which indulged in sedition. *Patrika* was then a bi-lingual weekly. On March 21, 1878, it came out, almost "overnight", as an English weekly to defeat the rigours of the vernacular press Act. In the English editon of the paper no mention was there of the Act. Only the editorial informed the readers with "deep regret" the decision to drop the Bengali section. Such a changeover with borrowed types to avoid the Act was a feat. Mr W.S. Caine did not exggerate when he said, "The change effected in a single day, with the help of borrowed type- - a remarkable feat of journalism."

Though *Amrita Bazar Patrika* came out unscathed, *Som Prakash* could not. Proceedings were instiued against the paper for publishing seditious matters and a bond was demanded from the printer. The printer executed the bond, but the paper ceased publication soon after and in its place was published *Navabi Bhakar*. Permission to revive *Som Prakash* was sought and granted in 1879 and the editor gave an undertaking for its future good conduct.

The V.P. Act was comprehensive and rigorous. It empowered any magistrate of a district, or a Commissioner of Police in a presidency town to call upon the printer and publisher of a newspaper to enter into a bond undertaking not to publish certain kind of materials, to demand security and to forfeit if it was thought fit, such presses and confiscate any printed matter as it deemed objectionable. No printer or publisher against whom such action had been taken could have recourse to a Court of Law.

A Press Commissioner was appointed; his function was two-fold. (One) to supply the press with early and accurate information inregard to public measures and (two) to act as a channel of communication between the Government and the press published in Indian languages. Mr Roper Lethbridge was appointed the Commissioner.

The Anglo-Indian journals resented the Press Commissionership as they had previously established their own sources of information. *The Statesman* went so far as to ridicule some of the communications from the officer as "Fatuous flap-doodle". In reply, the Government immediately stopped all communications from being sent to the paper. Good relations were eventually restored, but not before Lord Lytton had begun to doubt the utility of the Press Commissioner's office. It was, however, left to the new Viceroy Lord Ripon to order its abolition in March 1881. High establishment cost was shown as the main reson for abolition.

But the decision was not to the liking of the European papers. About 124 newspaper editors and proprietors (representing the bulk) of the Press (with the exception of *Pioneer, The Civil and Military Gazette* and *The Satesman*) presented a Memorial to the Viceroy urging the retention of the office. The signatories concluded by saying:

"We do not wish to occupy your Lordship's time by pointing out in this Memorial the evils likely to arise from any competition to obtain Government secrets for publication by underhand means, whether by payment or by flattery. An official who can be bribed by either method is unworthy of Government confidence. Every Government in England supplies important information to the Press either generally or to its own special organs which are well-known. It remained, however, for the Government of India to establish the precedent of supplying information to all papers whether supporters or opponents alike.

We would, however, specially call your Lordship's attention to the marked improvement in the Vernacular Press since the institution of the office of the Press Commissioner, a fact prominently noticed in several of the letters from the proprietors and editors of Vernacular newspapers attached to the Memorial. No longer dependent chiefly on bazar rumours for their information, the writers in the vernacular Press are now able to discuss actual facts, and the Government is thus provided with an opportunity of knowing the real sentiments of the people on all subjects of importance, a fact which is of itself sufficient to justify the retention of the appointment. The same argument applies, though, of course, in a less degree, to the English papers and the native papers published in English.

We have as yet failed to see any valid argument brought forward for the abolition of the appointment. It has been said that the procuring of news should be left for private enterprise, and though this may be true so far as ordinary news is concerned, in the case of special Government news, it simply means bribery and corruption in some form or other which every Government must wish to prevent. The expense of the maintenance is but trifling, regard being had to the benefits mutually conferred and received by the Government and the public .... We would therefore, humbly request your Lordship that the appointment of the Press Commissioner may be maintained and that all the heads of offices may be directed to supply the Press Commissioner without delay with all important information, which may be advantageous or useful to the public to know, without revealing confidential communications." (The Indian Press, pp 292-293)

This request notwithstanding, Lord Ripon abolished the Press Commissionership in March 1881. In his reply he said that the system "seemed to be working satisfactorily so far as it went, but that the duties of the Press Commissioner were practically limited to the daily distribution to the Press of such items of official news as the Government thought expedient to publish, and that the scale of his salary, and the cost of his establishment were out of all proportion to the duties thus discharged". The highly paid post of the Press Commissioner was to be abolished but other methods were to be devised for affording direct information to the Press.

Meanwhile, opposition to V.P. Act grew throughout the country . One result was the foundation of what is today one of the leading Indian-owned newspapers, *The Hindu* of Madras. The paper first came out on September 20, 1878, the year following Queen Victoria's Proclamation as Empress of India.

Sir Surendra Nath Banerjea, who became editor and proprietor of *The Bengalee* in 1879, gave a vivid description of journalism in Bengal of this period.

"With the exception of *The Indian Mirror*, all our newspapers in Bengal, including the most influential, were weekly. The craving for fresh news was then most general; and Indian readers for the most part were content to have a weekly supply of news and comments thereon. I remember speaking at the time to the headmaster of a Government high school, a man of education and culture, who said to me that it took him a week's time to go through the Bengalee (then a weekly paper) and that if it were a daily paper he would not know what to do with it" (A Nation in Making, p 50)

Less than two years after the inception of *The Hindu*, Lord Lytton was succeeded by Lord Ripon" who will always be remembered in India and elsewhere for the practical interpretation he gave to his liberal ideas. Notwithstanding the conservative attitude of his Council, he was quick to perceive the general discontent throughout the country and considered a despotic policy not only insulting to India's own civilisation but one which could not but assist the deterioration and possibly the disintegration of political relationships" (The Indian Press, p 295)

The wave of protests against the V.P. Act also reached the shores of Great Britain. Gladstone himself objected to the Act in British Parliament. At last on December 7, 1881 a bill was introduced for the repeal of the V.P. Act on the grounds that in the opinion of the Government, circumstances no longer justified existence of the Act.

Lord Ripon further stimluated political enthusiasm by inviting the cooperation of qualified Indians for the work of local and municipal administration, and by giving his support to a more vigorous educational policy. So far as Madras was concerned, one result of this increasing political consciousness was the conversion of Hindu from a weekly to a tri-weekly paper and as such it was printed from October 1883.

Mention has to be made at this stage of the famous case in which Surendra Nath Banerjea was involved since he claimed "the honour of being the first Indian of my generation who suffered imprisonment in the discharge of public duty." A news item appeared in *Brahmo Public Opinion* in March 1883 to the effect that Justice Noris of Calcutta High Court had insulted Hinduism by compelling the Hindu idol (Shalgramshila) to be produced before the Court during hearing of a particular case. Surendra Nath wrote a strong editorial in *The Bengalee* on April 2, 1883 in which he said, "The judges of the High Court have hitherto commanded universal respect of the community: Of course, they have often erred and grievously failed in the performance of their duties. But their errors have hardly ever been due to impulsiveness or to the neglect of the commonest consideration of prudence and decency. We have now, however, amongst us a judge who, if he does not actually recall to mind the days of Jeffryes and Scroggs, has certainly done enough within the short time that he has filled the High Court bench, to show how unworthy he is of his high office and how by nature he is unfitted to maintain those tradition of dignity which are inseparable from the office of the judge of the highest court in the land." Surendra Nath was charged with contempt of court and jailed for two months. It was a blessing in disguise. According to Surendra Nath, effect of the case was to give a stimulus to the Press.

"It gave an impetus to journalism. *Sulav Samachar* had been started as a pice paper by the late Keshub Chandra sen, but the movement for cheap journalism had languished. Now however, it received an awakened implulse in the passionate desire for news. Babu Jogendranath Bose started *Bangabasi* as a pice paper. *Bangabashi* and *Sanjivani* still continue to hold an important place in the journalistic world of Bengal. " (A Nation in Making, pp 74-84). While appreciating Lord Ripon's efforts educated Indians thought that a mere advisory place in the country's administration was quite inadequate. But they still lacked a national forum for voicing their views, though a number of provincial organisations were in existence, such as the Indian League in Bengal. In 1885, a year after Lord Ripon retired from Viceroyalty an organisation was born which has since answered this demand. It was Indian National Congress.

Much of the credit for the foundation of the Congress

goes to Allan Octavian Hume, the son of Joseph Hume, the Liberal. The younger Hume had served in the Indian Civil Service from 1849 till 1882 and had been decorated for his work in the Mutiny. On his retirement he spent most of his time in introducing the tenets of English Liberalism to educated Indians. Perceiving the rising discontent among the Indians at being shut out from the control over their country, he wrote that he considered it "of paramount importance to find an overt and constitutional channel for the discharge of the increasing ferment which had resulted from western ideas and education." He was assisted in his move to establish Indian National Congress by Robert Knight of the *Statesman*, Sir William Wedderburn, Wilfred Blunt and a number of leading Indians. Incidentally, when Robert Knight died in 1890 the Indian Press called him "the Bayard of India" and paid moving tributes to the part he had played in building up public opinion.

In March 1883, Hume had addressed an open letter to the graduates of Calcutta University as representatives of the intelligentsia urging them to support the organisation. The following is the concluding part of the long letter which speaks of the burning zeal which animated this remarkable man to undertake this venture:

"And if even the leaders of thought are all either such poor creatures, or so selfishly wedded to personal concerns that they dare not strike a blow for their country's sake, then justly and rightly are they kept down and trampled on, for they deserve nothing better. Every nation secures precisely as good a government as it merits. If you, the picked men, the most highly educated of the nation, cannot, scorning personal ease and selfish objects, make a resolute struggle to secure greater freedom for yourselves and your country, a more impartial administration, a larger share in the management of your own affairs, then we, your friends, are wrong and our adversaries right, then are Lord Ripon's noble aspirations for your good fruitless and visionary, then, at present at any rate all hopes of progress are at an end, and India truly neither lacks nor deserves any better Government than she enjoys. Only, if this be so, let us hear no more factious, peevish complaints that you are kept in leading strings and treated like children, for you will have proved yourself such. Men know how to act. Let there be no more complaints of Englishmen being preferred to you in all important offices, for if you lack that public spirit, that highest form of altruistic devotion that leads men to subordinate private ease to the public weal, that patriotism that has made Englishmen what they are -- then rightly are these preferred to you, rightly and inevitably have they become your rulers. And rulers and task-masters they must continue, let the yoke gall your shoulders never so sorely, until you realise and stand prepared to act upon the eternal truth that self-sacrifice and unselfishness are the only unfailing guides to freedom and happiness."

The response was overwhelming. The result was the first session of the Indian National Congress in Bombay in December 1885. The declared objects of the Congress were, first, to enable the most earnest labourers in the cause of national progress to become personally known to each other, and, secondly, to discuss and decide upon the political operations to be undertaken during the ensuing year. It was declared: "Indirectly, the conference will form the germ of a native parliament, and if properly conducted, will constitute in a few years an unanswerable reply to assertion that India is still wholly unfit for any form of representative institution". Lord Ripon was succeeded by Lord Dufferin in 1884 whose attitude towards the Press was one of friendliness and confidence and who allowed the Government servants to contribute to newspapers.

During Lord Dufferin's term of office the *Amrita Bazar Patrika* published certain facts about the administration of Bhopal and commented adversely on the conduct of Sir Lepal Griffin, the Agent of the Governor General for Central India. Sir Lepal appealed to the Viceroy for legal proceedings to be instituted against the paper and, on the latter refusing to do so, he tendered his resignation and retired from service.

Again in 1889, during the Vice-royalty of Lord Lansdowne, who succeeded Dufferin, *Amrita Bazar Patrika* made yet another history by publishing a confidential foreign office document. The idea of annexing either the entire State of Kashmir or at least its part, the Gilgit region, was entertained by the Political Agents of the British Indian Government for a long time and the *Amrita Bazar Patrika* was noticing the development in the editorial columns. It was in its issue of October 2, 1889 while going on leave for the Puja holidays the Patrika editor wrote dramatically: "Today we shall publish a document which will startle India-- probably Lord Lansdowne himself".

The document was the memorandum, the opinion of the Foreign Secretary Sir H.M. Durand, on the question of occupation of Gilgit as suggested by the ex-Resident Plowden .. " If we annex Gilgit or put an end to the suzerainty of Kashmir over the petty principalities of the neighbourhood," wrote the Foreign Secretary, "and above all, if we put British troops into Kashmir just now, we shall run a risk of turning the Durbar against us and thereby increase the difficulty of the position. I do not think this is necessary. No doubt we must have practically the control of Kashmir relations with those principalities, but this we already have. Indeed the Durbar has now, since the dismissal of Lachman Dass, asked Plowden to advise the Gilgit authorities direct without reference to them. If we have a quiet and judicious officer at Gilgit, who will get the Kashmir force into through order and abstain from unnecessary exercise of his influence, we shall, I hope, in short time, have the whole thing in one hand, without hurting any one's feelings". Dufferin to whom the Durand memorandum went, disposed it with the comment— "very well".

The disclosure expectedly caused utmost sensation.

Whatever doubt was there about the authenticity of the document was soon dispelled. The Government was already considering at the time to introduce a Bill to make penal the publication of official secrets. During the discussions in the Legislative Council, Lord Lansdowne confirmed the first two paragraphs as substantially accurate and added that there could be no doubt whatever that it must have been communicated to the Press by a person who had had the opportunity of copying or committing to memory at least a part of Sir Mortimer Durand's minute. The rest of the document as published in the *Amrita Bazar Patrika*, Lord Lansdowne characterised as : "sheer and impudent fabrication".

Lord Lansdowne added :

"The responsibility which rests upon those who are ready not only to give to the public documents which they are well aware could not have been obtained except by a distinct and a criminal breach of trust, but who are not even at the pains to satisfy themselves that these documents are genuine, is a very serious one.

Not content with persistently misrepresenting the Government of India, the publishers of the article have not scrupuled to present to the public a garbled version of a confidential note, written more than a year ago, in order to give an entirely distorted account of the then views and actions of the Government ... and I believe that an exposure of the practices to which our critics have not scrupuled to resort in the present instance may have the effect of, in some degree, opening the eyes of the public as to the methods which have been adopted for the purpose of prejudicing its judgement in regard to this important case.

Alluding to the speech, the Statesman commented:

"Since the receipt of the full text of the Viceroy's speech on the official Secrets bill, which we publish in another column, we have been at some pains to compare carefully what is therein stated with the suggestions contained in Sir M. Durand's alleged minute as published by the *Amrita Bazar Patrika* three weeks ago. As a result of this comparison we feel bound to say that the Viceroy's repudiation of the authenticity of all but first two paragraphs of that document, as it appeared in the columns of the *Patrika*, is scarcely borne out by the admissions in His Excellency's own speech ...... The main allegations of the *Patrika* are practically admitted, and it seems to us only fair to say that the inaccuracies which have been found in the published version of Sir M. Durand's minute must be due rather to the circumstances under which, apparently, the copy was made, than to any wilful garbling or manipulation of the documents on the part of the Patrika, for the purposes of misrepresenting the motives and intentions of the Government, as the Viceroy's speech would seem to imply".

The subsequent history of the restoration of the Maharaja to full power following the *Patrika* exposure of the conspiracy was simple. The issue was debated in Parliament, the lead being taken by Charles Bradlaugh, M.P, then known as a friend of India and hammered outside by another friend, William Digby. Placed in a predicament the Government of India, without allowing grass to grow under its feet, hit upon the official Secrets Act on October 9, 1889 to prevent disclosure of official documents and information. In England the Official Secrets Act had been placed on the Statute Book by that time. The Indian Act which was modelled on the The British Act provided a penalty of imprisonment for a year to two years and/ or a fine. This Act was amended by Act V of 1904 and later replaced by Official Secrets Act of 1923.

"Time was marching on. While the 19th century had begun in England with very marked developments in social ideas, it closed at a period when science was rendering many old forms obsolete. Universal education, the railway, a cheap press, the electric telegraph, indeed mechanical inventions of various kinds were all tending to democratise national life. Inevitably, the influence of these changes was felt in India and succeeding

Repressive Measures

sessions of Congress provided evidence that Indian political opinion was far in advance of what the Government in England and India deemed advisable". (The Indian Press).

There were, moreover, internal reasons for the progress of public opinion. The chief of these were the Ilbert Bill of 1883, the Age of Consent Bill of 1891, the Indian Councils Act of 1892 and the Government's measure to cope with plague in Bombay in 1896.

The Ilbert Bill controversy had its origin in racial discrimination. Under the existing law the Indian judges were held not capable of hearing charges against Europeans within their jurisdiction. This created an anomalous situation. Therefore, Sir Courtney Ilbert, the Law Member, introduced a bill to confer on Indian District Judges the same powers as were enjoyed by their British colleagues. The measure was opposed by the European community, the indigo and tea planters in particular, as they feared that they would liable to be exposed to unfounded charges. The Government bowed to the strong protests and amended the bill so as to give Europeans, accused of criminal offences in the mofussil, the right of demanding trial by jury, of which at least half the members were Europeans or Americans. Naturally, the Indian sentiment was shocked by the discrimination and by the underlying implication that India judges could not be relied upon to maintain judicial standards.

The Age of Consent Bill was in a different category. Following the death of a Hindu child-wife in Calcutta, Lord Lansdowne's Government passed the Bill prohibiting consumation of marriage until the wife was at least twelve years old. Orthodox Hindu opinion throughout the country objected to the measure on the ground that it was in the nature of unwarranted interference with religious custom. The editor, manager and printer of *Bangabashi* of Calcutta, which expressed this view, were prosecuted for sedition. Tilak, in his Marathi journal, Kesari, denounced the measure and declared that every Hindu supporter of it was a traitor to his faith. He wanted to harness the criticism of the bill to the existing political discontent. The bill also affected the destiny of the *Amrita Bazar Patrika*. It was still being published as a weekly and Hindu opinion required a daily organ of expression. Therefore, on February 19, 1891, the Patrika began its career as a daily newspaper.

Another journal founded during this period of national awakening was the *Indian Social Reformer*. The *Reformer* was started in 1890 with the principal objects of advocating social reforms, women's education, the abolition of caste, the removal of the ban on remarriage of widows and the raising of the marriage age of girls. "Believing in evolution, as opposed to revolution, the *Reformer* advocated ordered progress, in conformity with the genius of the Indian people" (The Indian Press).

The Indian Councils Act, 1892, provided for the enlargement of the legislative councils to which local boards and corporations were permitted to return members subject to the approval of the Government. The scope of debate and the power to ask questions were restricted and the Government was rendered secure by its majority representations. Newspapers expressed disappointment with the inadequacy of the measure and at the end of the year the Congress too recorded its disappointment that it should have fallen so very short of Indian aspirations.

Lord Elgin succeeded Lord Lansdowne in 1894. His regime, so far as the Press was concerned, was noteworthy on account of the amendment which was made to the Sedition section of the Indian Penal Code. In 1896 a famine broke out in Bombay which was followed by an outbreak of bubonic plague. In dealing with the situation the Government decided to segregate the victims. British troops were used in Poona to search the houses of suspected cases as many families would like to keep their stricken members on their homes. Though the administration acted in the best interest of the community

Repressive Measures

the measure was construed as encroachment on liberty and privacy. Tilak, in the columns of *Kesari*, accused the military of having offended the religious susceptibilities of the people and conjured up visions of Shivaji, the great Maratha hero, ever "tolerating such persecution." The material on which he worked was highly inflamable and two Chitpaban Brahmins (Tilak's own community) were tried for the murder of a military officer and the Indian civilian in charge of plague precautionery measure at Poona. The accused were convicted and executed and Tilak himself was tried for sedition and imprisoned for eighteen months.

Seriously alarmed at the outbreak of violence and similar outrages which had taken place elsewhere and also suggestive propaganda appearing in the Press the Government proposed to add sections to the Indian Penal Code to enable them to deal legally with the situation. However, the new amendment did not alter the law of sedition but merely reinstated it in plainer language.

The new factors influencing the Press during the era were the establishment of the Indian National Congress in 1885, the Indian Councils Act of 1892 and the interest in technical matters which had spread from the West. Recognising the fact that the Indians had the right to choose their own representatives throgh approved public bodies and constituencies, the Council Act gave a notable impetus to journalism. Indeed it influenced its development to the extent that the debates in the legislature became a leading feature of the news. Speeches of public men were the subjects of discussions and criticisms. This set a trend that eventually gave Indian daily journalism its present bias in favour of news of a wholly political character.

Hitherto, English politics had been the main interest of newspapers in India. The Irish question and the possibility of invasion of North-western frontier were favourite topics. Towards the end of 19th century, weekly and technical journalism become a feature of Indian newspaper world. On January 3, 1880 *The Times of India* published a weekly summary of the news incorporating the leading and special articles of the daily papers. This was before the era of news photos. But during the great Famine a few illustrations were published to supplement the letters of the special correspondents in the affected areas. The general appreciation of this innovation inspired the proprietors to bring out, twenty years later, *The Times of India Illustrated Weekly*.

In 1888, Shirley Tremearne, who was both a lawyer and a journalist, founded *Capital* in Calcutta. The journal, as its name implies, dealt with the news and views of a commercial and financial character. About the same time *Indian Engineering* was founded by a civil engineer, Pat Doyle. This journal was followed by *The Eastern Engineer*.

Sports journalism was represented by The *Asian and Indian Planters' Gazette*. The circulation of these papers was practically restricted to the non-Indian section of the reading public although in course of time news of sporting events was to occupy a prominent place in Indian newspapers.

In 1899 Sachchidananda Sinha, a well-known politician of Bihar, founded and edited "*The Hindustan Review*", a monthly periodical devoted to articles and reviews of topics of political, historical and literary interest.

"The close of the century saw a critical state of affairs. The intelligentsia was clamouring for rapid political advance. And in the absence of what was considered an adequate response from the authorities, much of the agitation had been driven underground and the terrorist movement grew in force. Briefly, the problem before the Government was to devise a policy which would meet what were in their view reasonable demands and yet would yield nothing to forces of extremism. The story of how the administration has attempted to solve the dilemma is the story of the present century." (The Indian Press, p 308)

8
NEW ERA OF SWADESHI

The dawn of the twentieth century marked a new era in Indian politics and in the development of the Press as well. For Indian journalism 1900 was a memorable date when G.A. Natesan first published his *Indian Review* devoted to the cause of the country's welfare. The *Review* was remarkable for the list of distinguished number of contributors who used to write in the paper. C.Y. Chintamoni (later Sir) was another promising youngman at this time who grew up as an eminent journalist and writer and was widely known for his photographic memory on all matters concerning literature and politics. N.C. Kelkar and K.P. Khadilkar were two other powerful journalists and publicist. As the trusted lieutenants of Tilak, they ably edited *Kesari* and *Mahratta* in the absence of Tilak who was in prison serving a term for sedition. Closely associated with Kelkar and Khadilkar was J.S. Karandikar who succeeded Kelkar as the editor of *Kesari*. Karandikar was near to Khadilkar in style while he resembled Kelkar in informed criticism. *Kesari* had a large circulation all over Maharastra. Even in remote districts *Kesari* was almost a synonym for newspaper.

Mahadev Govind Ranade's death in 1901 brought

into the open the ideological conflict between his two proteges— Gokhale and Tilak --- which had remained dormant when Ranade was editing the Anglo-Marathi weekly, *Indu Prakash*. Ranade was a source of inspiration for every movement of this time in Maharashtra and was the brain behind the Deccan Education Society. Because of his patience and deep study Gokhale was nearer to Ranade than Tilak. Ranade himself had invited Gokhale to accept the editorship of the quarterly journal *Sarvajanik Sabha*, a journal devoted to the careful and thorough study and discussion of current problems of the day .. Later Ranade made Narayan Ganesh Chandavarkar the editor of *Indu Prakash*. Gokhale also edited *Sudharak*, or *Reformer*, an Anglo-Marathi weekly of Poona. In this task he was assisted by Agarkar who had earlier left *Kesari* and *Mahratta* owing to differences with Tilak on the questions of politics and social reform.

While Ranade's death in 1901 brought in sharp focus the ideological conflict between Gokhale and Tilak which had far-reaching consequences for Indian politics the death of Queen Victoria in the same year, during the Viceroyalty of Lord Curzon, brought to an end the period of sporadic agitation and the following years were to see the organisation of public opinion in a manner hitherto not contemplated.

The country was in a ferment over the question of partion of Bengal which was presented to the people by Lord Curzon in December 1903. It gave rise to an wave of indignation in the country, particularly in the eastern part of Bengal. The province, which was in the vanguard of intellectual reawakening, became scene of revolutionery upsurge and militant nationalism. The Swadeshi Movement that began in 1905 marked, in the true sense of the term, the first phase of India's stuggle for independence. In the eyes of the new generation, whose outlook was moulded by Bepin Chandra Pal, Brambndhav Upadhya, Bhabani Charan Bandopadhyay and Aurobindo Ghosh, the English rulers forfeited their claims to Indian

New Era Of Swadeshi

loyalty and cooperation because of their century of misgovernment.

As the Swadeshi movement, triggered by partition, progressed, political extremism growing in the country found its convenient vehicle in journals like *Jugantar* and *Bande Mataram*. Incidentally, the *Bande Mataram* song was first sung on the Congress platform in 1896 by Rabindra Nath Tagore. The daily *Bande Mataram* was unique in many respects. It told the people that it is not by prayer and petition to alien Government that a nation's liberty was bought but by a grim battle with the rulers and shedding the martyr's blood". Lord Curzon, however, did not remain in India to see the effects of partition. A difference of opinion with the Commander-in-Chief, Lord Kitchener, regarding the status of the military member of the Viceroy's Executive Council led to a controversy in which Curzon was not supported by the Secretary of State for India. Curzon, in consequence, resigned.

Lord Minto, who succeeded Curzon, inherited a turbulent situation and tried to deal with it by widening the scope of the Official Secrets Act, the Public Meetings Act, The Press Act, the Sedition Law, the Explosives Act and many other ordinances and circulars abridging the right of free speech and free critisism. The principal object of amending the Indian Official Secrets Act of 1889 was to place civil matters on a level with naval and military matters and to extend to whoever "without lawful authority or permission (the proof whereof shall be upon him) goes to a Government officer, and commits and offence under the Act". All offences under the Act were cognisable and non-bailable. Such a piece of legislation gave the Government undefined and complete authority to prosecute.

The Englishman of Calcutta sharply criticised the proposal as "Russianising" the administration. Appreciating the comment Gokhale said, "The Bill even if it became law, would not in practice affect writer or the other editors of the Anglo-Indian papers. "I would", he said, "like to see the official who would venture to arrest and march to the police thana the editor of an Anglo-Indian paper. But so far as Indian editors are concerned, there are, I fear, officers in this country, who would not be sorry for an opportunity to match whole battalion of them to the police thana. It is dreadful to think of the abuse of authority which is almost certain to result from the placing of Indian editors, especially the smaller ones among them, so completely at the mercy of those whom they constantly irritate or displease by their criticism. Earlier, the English journalists who had the temerity to criticise the administration used to be deported and otherwise punished. But now with the rise of the Indian journalism, the Anglo-Indian papers changed their role and became supporters of the Government and, as Gokhale pointed out, the prospect of an editor of an Anglo-Indian paper being arrested had become unthinkable. Gokhale rightly said:

"The proper and only remedy worthy of British Government, for whatever is really deplorable in the present state of things, is not to gag newspapers as proposed in this bill, but to discourage the issue of confidential circulars which seek to take away in the dark what has been promised again and again in Acts of Parliament, the Proclamations of Sovereigns, and the responsible utterences of successive Viceroys. From the standpoint of rulers, no less than that of the ruled, it will be most unfortunate if the Indian papers were thus debarred from writing about matters which agitate the Indian community most." (Speeches of Gopal Krishna Gokhale, pp 214-215)

Although the bill was amended in several details by the Select Committee its potentiality to curtail the freedom of the Press led Gokhale to condemn such restrictions.

He declared with great eloquence:

"Nowhere throughout the British Empire is the

Government so powerful relatively to the governed as in India. Nowhere, on the other hand, is the Press so weak in influence, as it is with us. The vigilance of the Press is the only check that operates from outside, feebly, it is true, but continuously, upon the conduct of the Government, which is subject to no popular control. It is here, therefore, of anywhere, that the legislature should show special consideration to the Press, and yet here alone it is proposed to arm Government with a greater power to control the freedom of the Press than in any other part of the Empire. My Lord, we often hear Government complaining of the distrust shown by the people in this country, and the people complaining of the Government not trusting them enough. In such a situation, where again the question is further complicated by a tendency on the part of the Government to attach undue importance to race or class consideration, the wisest and safest and most statemanlike course for it is to conduct its civil administration as far as possible in the light of the day. The Press is, in one sense, like the Government, a custodian of public interests, and any attempt to hamper its freedom by repressive legislation is bound to affect these interests prejudicially, and cannot fail in the end to react upon the position of the Government itself .... In England the Government dare not touch the liberty of the Press, no matter how annoying its disclosures may be, and has to reconcile itself to the latter, regarding them as only so much journalistic enterprise. In India the unlimited power which the Government possesses inclines it constantly to represive legislation. This single measure suffices to illustrate the enormous difference between the spirit in which the administration is carried on in England." (Ibid, pp 215-216)

Meanwhile, as the anti-partition agitation spread all over the country cementing the ties among the nationalist leaders in different provinces, the steam-roller of repression moved mercilessly to crush all protests. Tilak's arrest had electrified the youths of Bengal more than any other province. As the Cambridge History of India noted," Nowhere did Tilak's methods and organisations attract more attention than in Bengal. His influence is plainly to be seen in the accompaniment of subsequent revolutionary movement in that province. His example in brigading school boys and students in gymnastic societies for the purpose of political education was followed there. Effort was even made to introduce in Bengal, the very province which in pre-British days had been scourged by Maratha raids, the singularly appropriate cult of Shivaji."

The stage was set for trouble. And trouble was in plenty. A train in which the Lt. Governor, Sir Andrew Fraser, was travelling was derailed by a bomb explosion at Midnapore in 1907. The District Magistrate of Dacca was shot in the back at a railway station. However, he was not fatally injured. In Muzaffarpur in Bihar, a bomb was thrown into the carriage in which Kennedys -- mother and daughter -- were killed in April 1908. The target was Kingsford, the Chief Presidency Magistrate of Calcutta. Khudiram Bose, then a student and Prafulla Chaki were arrested. Khudiram was executed and his accomplice Prafulla shot himself dead.

There was trouble in Punjab. Riots broke out at Lahore and Rawalpindi. Serious disturbances which followed a series of public lectures by Bepin Chandra Pal, were reported from Madras. Also from the United and Central provinces reports came about seditious writings and secret organisations.

In London India House was set up by one Shyamaji Krishnavarma, son of a Kathiwad merchant, who was publishing a paper, The *Indian Sociology*. And in July 1909, Sir William Curzon Wylie and Dr Lalkaka, who attempted to save him, were shot dead by a young student named Madanlal Dingra. Tilak persued his campaign through the columns of *Kesari* and *Desha Sewak* of Nagpur. Indian opinion found expression in the columns of *Bengalee* edited by Surendra Nath Banerjea who is remembered for, amongst other things, his vigorous campaign against the Partition of Bengal. In Madras The *Hindu* mirrored the Indian point of view while The *Madras Mail* was backed by the European community. In Bombay, though The *Times of India*, *Bombay Gazette* and The *Advocate of India* were the leading dailies there was no daily newspaper expressing Indian opinion. However, The *Indian Spectator*, edited by Byramji Malabari, gave a weekly survey of Indian affairs.

In June 1908 the Government passed the Newspaper (Incitement to Offence) Act which empowered the authorities to take judicial action against the editor of any newspaper which published matters" which, in the view of the Government, amounted to incitement to rebellion". At the same time the Bombay Governor declared in the Legislative Council at Poona that the Government was determined to put down seditious agitation in the province. In Bombay S.M. Paranjpe, the editor of the *Kal*, was under trial for seditious writings. His writings were acclaimed as incomparable and unequalled in Marathi literature and journalism even to this day. Tilak went to Bombay to assist Paranjpe but his help was not available as Tilak himself was arrested and tried in respect of two articles on three charges. A jury of seven Europeans and two Parsis found him guilty by a majority of 7 to 2. Tilak was sentenced to six years' transportation, detained in Ahmedabad for a while and then sent to Mandalay.

Lajpat Rai and Ajit Singh had already been deported in 1907 and in Bengal as many as nine were singled out for deportation. They were: Krishna Kumar Mitra, Aswini Kumar Datta, Shyam Shundar Chakravarty, Subodh Chandra Mallick, Sachindra Prasad Bose, Satish Chandra Chatterji, Pulin Behari Das, Manoranjan Guha and Bhupesh Chandra Nag. Prominent among editors prosecuted in Bengal were Aurobindo Ghose of *Bande Mataram*, Brahma Bandhabh Upadhyay, editor of *Sandhya* and Bhupendra Nath Datta, the editor of *Jugantar* and brother of Swami Vivekananda with whom was associated Barindra Kumar Ghosh, brother of Aurobindo Ghosh. Barrister Chitta Ranjan Das appeared for the editors of *Sandhya* and *Jugantar*. The former, however, refused to defend himself as he did not hold himself accountable to an alien Government. He died in Campbell Hospital in Calcutta, when the case was still in its initial stage. The editor of *Jugantar* was sentenced to a year's rigorous imprisonment. C.R. Das also defended Aurobindo Ghose and Barindra Kumar Ghose in the famous Alipore Bomb case of 1908. About 36 persons involved in the conduct of an organisation which had a bomb factory at Manicktolla. Some of the persons arrested made startling confessions. Aurobindo Ghose was acquitted because of C.R. Das' able advocacy but Barindra Kumar Ghosh and Ullaskar Dutt were sentenced to be hanged and Hemchandra Das and Upendra Nath Bandopadhya and others were transported for life. Later Barindra and Ullaskar were also given life transportation.

Bande Mataram editorially referred to the reforms proposed by Lord Morley in the middle of 1907 as "Comic opera-- the right place for this truely comic Council of Notables with its yet more comic functions is an opera by Gilbert and Sullivan and not an India seething with discontent and convulsed by the throes of an incipient revolution".

In a series of seven articles published between April 9 and April 23, 1907, Aurobindo propounded the doctrine of passive resistance as an instrument of political action. "We have not only to take up all branches of our national life into our hands, but in order to meet bureaucratic opposition and to compel alien control to remove its hold on us, if not at once, then tentacle by tentacle, we must organise defensive resistance .... our immediate problem as a nation is not how to become intellectual or well-informed or how to be rich and industrious, but how to stave off imminent national death, how to put an end to the white peril, how to assert ourselves and live ..... In a peaceful way we act against the law or the executive but we passively accept the legal consequences". Gandhi's philosophy of passive resistance was thus anticipated by twenty years. However, there was a difference. Aurobindo made the reservation that resistance should be peaceful and passive only so long as official action was "peaceful and within the rules of the fight". These articles were the cause of prosecution already referred to. Bepin Chandra Pal who was called to give evidence of Aurobindo's editorship (because few outside Bengal have heard of Aurobindo Ghose) refused to do so and for this offence he was sentenced to six months' imprisonment. In delivering his judgment, the Chief Presidency Magistrate Kingsford acknowledged that "the general tone of the Bande Mataram is not seditious". He nevertheless, sentenced the printer to imprisonment for a few months.

In May 1907 Aurobindo was arrested in connection with the Alipore Bomb case and during the trial which lasted for a year, he was held in detention, for a period in solitary confinement. He gave himself up to religious meditation and self discipline. When he was released, Aurobindo found that all his political friends and associates had been put out of action. He refused the editorship of *Bengalee* and also to restart *Bande Mataram* which had closed down during his trial, but started two weekly papers, the *Karmayogin* in English and *Dharma* in Bengali, both devoted to the dissemination of the principle of the Sanatan Dharma.

Meanwhile, the Indian national Congress met in Surat in December 1907. There were clashes between the Moderates and the Extremists as the latter were becoming impatient of Moderates' attachment to constitutional forms of agitation. Uproarious and violent scenes were witnessed and the session had to be suspended sine die. Eventually, the police restored order. Moderates and the Extremists parted company— Gokhale leading the former and Tilak taking charge of the latter. It almost appeared as if the future of the national movement were threatened and the Indian Press had now to take its stand for one party or the other.

Tilak pursued his campaign in the columns of *Kesari* and *Desha Sevak* of Nagpur and on the platform. (briefly mentioned earlier) under the newspaper (Incitement to offences) Act, nine prosecutions in all, were instituted. Seven resulted in the confiscation of presses— four in Bengal, two in Punjab and one in Bombay. In one instance, the Government of Bengal ordered the restoration of the presses on the owner's tendering an apology and giving an undertaking that the liberties accorded would not be misused in future. In another instance the Government order was aside on an appeal to the High Court. All these prosecutions took place in one year. But for the next eleven years (until the Act was replaced) it remained a dead letter. Moreover, the provisions of the Statute were somtimes evaded as the result of mere nominees declaring themselves as printers and publishers while those who were really responsible maintained anonymity. Sometimes, as in the case of prosecutions against *Jugantar* and *Sandhya*, the proceedings were protracted and in the meantime the papers vastly increased their circulation. On one occasion five editors of the same paper were convicted one after another and fresh dummy editors took their places.

In 1905 a decision had already been formulated that a half of the elected members in all the Councils should be Indians and for the appointment of three Indians to the Council of the Secretary of State. At the Calcutta session of the Congress which met under the Presidentship of Dadabhai Naoroji, a demand was made that the system of Government obtaining in the self-governing British colonies should be adopted in India. Difference of opinion among the Indian leaders on the country's constitutional goal led to the emergence of two schools of thought— Moderates and the Extremists.

Well aware of the trend of public opinion, Lord

Minto fully realised the desirability and necessity of trying to appease the Moderates. In February 1907, in a despatch to Lord Morley, the Secretay of State, he advocated the inclusion of an Indian in the Viceroy's Council . He wrote:

"The reasons against it as stated in the Notes of Members of Council (Minto had only one supporter among his colleagues) are generally very narrow, based almost entirely on the assumption that it is impossible to trust a native in a position of great responsibility, and that the appointment of a native member is merely a concession to Congress agitation. The truth is, that by far the most important factor we have to deal with in the political life of India is not impossible Congress ambitions, but the growing strength of an educated class, which is perfectly loyal and moderate in his views, but which, I think, quite justly considers itself entitled to a greater share in the government of India, I believe that we shall derive the greatest assistance from this class if we recognise its existence, and that, if we do not, we shall drive it into the arms of the Congress leaders." (John Buchan, Lord Minto, p 253)

But Minto's proposal was opposed not only by the majority of his own Council but also of King Edward VII to whom he had written a long personal letter explaining the reasons of his proposal. In his reply the King wrote:

"My dear Minto, many thanks for your long and interesting letter of 4th instant in which you gave me your reasons why you consider it desirable that a Native of India should form part of the Viceroy's Executive Council. As you hold such strong views on the subject and have given me many cogent reasons for such a new departure, I am very unwilling to differ from you as well as the Secretary of State on the subject. At the same time I hold very strong and possibly old-fashioned views on the subject, which my son, who has so recently been in India, entirely shares.

During the unrest in India at the present time and the intrigues of the natives it would, I think, be fraught with the greatest danger to the Indian Empire if a Native were to take part in the Councils of the Viceroy, as so many subjects would be likely to be discussed in which it would not be desirable that a Native could take part. Besides, if you have a Hindu, why not a Mohammedan also? The latter would strongly claim it. If the present view which you so strongly advocate is carried into effect, and you find it does not answer, you will never be able to get rid of the Native again. The Indian Princes, who are ready to be governed by the Viceroy and his Council, would greatly object to a Native, who would be very inferior in caste to themselves, taking part in the government of the country. However clever the Native might be, and however loyal you and your Council might consider him to be, you never could be certain that he might not prove to be a very dangerous element in your Councils and impart information to his countrymen which it would be very undesirable should go further than your Council Chamber.

I have, however, informed the Secretary of State that owing to the great pressure which has been put upon me by my Government, I unwillingly assent but wish that my protest should remain on record, as I cannot bring myself to change my views on this subject.

That you never repent the important step now made is the ardent wish yours very sincerely,

Edward, R. & I."

Lord Minto, eventually, had his way. In March 1907 he sent another despatch to London proposing liberal administrative reforms. The following year was the fiftieth anniversary of Queen Victoria's Proclamation as Empress of India, and it was decided to mark the occasion by a message from the King to the people of India foreshadowing the forthcoming reforms which were the subject of close and constant discussion between the Viceroy and the Secretary of State, Lord

Morley. The time had come, the message ran, when the principal representative institutions must be prudently extended and when valour and fidelity of the Indian troops should receive recognition. The latter promise was due to a strong feeling on the part of Lord Minto that army careers should be opened to Indians.

A short while later Morley-Minto reforms became law. In 1909 the new Act enlarged the Legislative Council and the number of elected members who were given the powers to move resolution on matters of general public interest, to discuss annual budgets and to put supplementary questions. In addition, an Indian was to be appointed to the Viceroy's Council and separate electorates were instituted.

All parties were disappointed by the reforms; but the Moderates were of the opinion that they should be worked for what they were worth. Minto himself made it known that he had no intention of introducing a parliamentary system of Government in India.

The Morley-Minto scheme was supported by the Anglo-Indian Press. But the Indian Press was in a dilemma. In publishing views of both the Moderates and the Extremists they had to adopt a policy which would antagonise neither section. Yet they could not but condemn the repressive aspects of Minto's administration while commenting on the reforms, especially after the arrests of Tilak, Bepin Chandra Pal, Upadhyay, Aurobindo Ghosh, Lala Lajpat Rai and others.

Moderates, such as Sir Phiroz Shah Mehta, Sir Dinsha Wacha and Gokhale were deeply conscious of the need of an organ to propagate their views. The *Leader*, established at Allahabad in October 1909 by Pandit Madan Mohan Malaviya met the need to some extent.

An avowed extremist, Tilak was not very concerned with the language he used in advocating his political programme. In Bengal, a section of the Press adopted an unrestrained style of writing. Anarchical ideas were, doubtless, gaining ground, largely as a result of discontent over the partition of Bengal. After a review of writings in several newspapers which, in the opinion of the authorities, "exceeded the bounds of responsible criticism and which could not be tackled by ordinary law of the land the Government introduced a legislation which was embodied in Act No. 1 of 1910 (an Act to provide for the better control of the Press). As Objects and Reasons of the Act it was stated:

"The continued recurrence of murders and outrages has shown that the measures which have hitherto been taken to deal with anarchy and sedition require strengthening and that the real source of the evil has not yet been touched. Prosecutions have invariably proved successful, but have produced no permanent improvement in the tone of the Press".

At first the Indian members of the reformed legislative Council were hesitant to support the Act which, in the opinion of the Law Member, Mr S.P. Sinha (aftewards Lord Sinha) was "incompatible" with the spirit of the reforms. Gokhale saw in it a "cruel irony of fate that the first important measure to come before the reformed Council was a measure to curtail a great and deeply cherished privilege which the country had enjoyed, with two brief interruptions, for three quarters of a century". But they had changed their mind and supported the measure after an incident on January 24, 1910 when a police officer was shot dead by an anarchist within the precincts of Calcutta High Court in broad daylight. Addressing the Council the following day Lord Minto declared:" We can no longer tolerate the preachings of a revolutionery Press. We are determined to briddle the literary licence".

The new Press Act empowered the Government to instruct the Government Solicitor to go before the Presidency Magistrate to demand security from any newspaper publishing matter considered offensive. In other words, punitive action could be taken at the discretion of the executive. Lord Morley approved of the measure but he has left it on record that he was very unwilling to allow the Act to be introduced, but that his hands were forced.

The measure had a number of obnoxious features. First it substituted the discretion of the executive for the rights of publicity, audience and appeal. Secondly, it specifically violated the principle of jurisprudence by directing the accused to prove that he was innocent; thirdly, though an appeal was provided for, it had been pointed out both in the Calcutta and Madras High Courts that the High Court had no power to question the discretion of the executive. Fourthly, the Act had the effect of humiliating the intelligentsia since journalists were asked to furnish security, at the discretion of the executive, before they could publish a newspaper.

Naturally, the Act caused considerable disaffection in the country. It was strictly enforced and by 1919 over 350 presses were penalised; 300 newspapers subjected to security amounting to 40,000 pounds and 500 publications proscribed. Owing to the demand for security 200 presses and 130 newspapers could not be started.

Meanwhile, administrative changes of far-reaching consequences were taking place. In August 1911 Lord Hardinge, who succeeded Lord Minto, sent a secret dispatch to the British Government recommending the formation of a Presidency Government for a re-united Bengal, a separate Lieutenant Governorship for Bihar and Orissa and the transfer of the imperial capital from Calcutta to Delhi.

These measures were announced as a "boon" to the people of India by King George V at his Coronation Durbar at Delhi on December 12, 1911. "It is our earnest desire", he said, "that these changes may conduce to the better administration of India and the greater prosperity and happiness of our beloved people".

Opinions however differed whether the hopes wer fulfilled or not.

The interesting feature of the time that could not escape notice was that although Bombay succeeded Calcutta as the centre of nationalist agitation the province had no daily paper which could be used for the expression of the Indian viewpoint. At this time three English-owned newspapers existed in Bombay— *Times of India*, *The Bombay Gazette* and *The Advocate of India*. The expression of Indian opinion was restricted to the columns of Kaisari-i-Hind, a weekly Anglo-Gujrati paper and *The Oriental Review* which supported the political activities of Sir Pherozshah Mehta and *Indu Prakash*, an Anglo-Marathi daily. The need for Indian-owned English daily newspaper was badly felt by the nationalists. In Madras there was *The Hindu*, in Calcutta *Amrita Bazar Patrika* and *The Bengalee*, in Allahabad *The Leader* and in Lahore *The Tribune*. Sir Pherozshah had already founded an Indian bank and had laid the foundation of a national medical college. The establishment of an english daily newspaper was a further object which he greatly desired to see achieved. The object was at last achieved. On March 3, 1913 the first copy of The *Bombay Chronicle* was on sale on the streets of the city. Ably guided by Sir Pherozshah Mehta as Chairman and brilliantly edited by Benjamin Guy Horniman it rapidly gained popularity amongst Indian readers. Horniman who had served on *The Manchester Guardian* and later on *The Statesman* of Calcutta was known for his powerful and impartial pen. During the protest in Calcutta over the partition of Bengal, he had walked in the procession barefooted through the streets wearing Indian dress.

Sir C.Y. Chintamani, the distinguished editor of *The Leader* of Allahabad, has recorded the great service rendered by Horniman to the oppressed Indians of South Africa during their passive resistance campaign of 1913 and the fact that Gokhale specially mentioned The *Bombay Chronicle* and The *Leader* as the two papers which most helped him and Gandhi in the struggle. The then Secretary of State Montague described The *Bombay Chronicle* as the most brilliantly written paper in India. In the words of Chintamoni, this tribute was all the more valuable because Horniman was amongst the severe critics of Montague's reform scheme.

"Indian political thought was at this time largely concentrated on the position of Indians in South Africa. Many had settled down in that country after their term of service as indentured labourers had expired. In course of time they were joined by Indian professional men and a self-contained community grew up. Outside their own circles, however, Indians were subjected to severe discrimination by other south African colonists, both British and Dutch.

The formation of Union of South Africa in 1909 vested authority in the Union Government and the British Government declared that they could not interfere with the rights of a self-governing colony. The history of Gandhi's passive resistance movement is well-known. Naturally, the welfare of their brethren overseas was a constant preoccupation of the Indian Press and it was to this question that its columns were largely devoted when war was declared in Europe", writes Margarita Barns in her "Indian Press".

9
PRESS AND WORLD WAR I

The outbreak of World War I in 1914 was not without its impact on the Press as it mirrored the turns and twists in the country's political life. India was being asked to give her support to a war to defend the principle of self-determination; the very principle which she herself was seeking to establish. Simultaneously, attempts were also being made to enlist foreign support in our fight for freedom. Muslims and Hindus took part in them, the former being particularly "out of humour" with the British on account of their attitude towards Turkey, whose Sultan was Khalifa to the Islamic world. The Congress and the Muslim League (the latter set up in 1906 with the Government having a hand in it rather like in the case of the Congress) supported the war in resolutions of loyalty, but the country's temper was different.

The Press differed on the question of India's support to war efforts. The Anglo-Indian Press viewed that the nationalist should have given way to the necessity created by the emergency of war. The Indian Press, however, felt that the spontaneous response of the princes and people of India for help and cooperation should be acknowledged by the British Government by according to India the same rights and liberties for which the allies were fighting in Europe.

While some leaders trusted in the British Government there were others who felt that Indian claims should be pressed without delay. So the Home Rule Movement was born. Inspired by Annie Besant and supported by Tilak, a number of Home Rule Leagues were established and at the 1916 session of the Congress held at Lucknow in December the Congress and the Muslim League came to an accord over a draft constitution designed to secure self-government. Mrs Besant acquired the control over *The Madras Standard* which she renamed New India and through the columns of which she and her followers persistently advocated a dominion constitution for India. *New India* was a fiery champion of Home Rule for India and Mrs Besant's forthright attacks on the Government of the day enhanced the popularity of the paper. When proceedings were instituted against the paper during the Governorship of Lord Pentland, she appeared before the High Court herself and argued the first case for her paper. Dr. C.P. Rama swamy Aiyar argued the other cases on behalf of New India. The paper was asked to furnish a security of Rs 2000 in the first instance which was forfeited and a second security of Rs 10,000 was demanded of the paper.

Before and during the internment of Annie Besant arrangements were made for the conduct *of New India* and the allied publications. P.K. Telang was chosen to be the editor and he ran the paper with the assistance of Arundale, B.P. Wadia, Dr C.P. Ramaswamy Aiyar, all of whom were intended to step into the breach successfully in case of arrest or internment. *New India* attained a phenomenal circulation which was maintained until Mrs Besant, both personally and in the editorial columns of the paper, spoke against Gandhi's Non-Cooperation and Satyagraha Campaign. After her well-known saying that brickbats cannot be met with bullets the circulation of *New India* fell considerably.

Annie Besant favoured the total repeal of Newspapers (incitement to offences) Act of 1908 as well as of the Indian Press Act of 1910. She was of the view that the Press and Registration of Books Act should be amended to require a declaration by the editor. She maintained that newspapers guilty of incitement to violence and sedition should be dealt with under the ordinary law after a judicial trial. She was a strong critic of direct action and of Gandhi's writings in *Young India*. In a written statement to the Press Law Committee she said:

"Mr Gandhi in *Young India* is allowed every week to incite hatred and contempt against the Government in language compared with which criticism of Government that have ruined many papers are harmless; he is even allowed to approach perilously near high treason by saying that he would' in a sense' assist an Afghan invasion of India, while papers that one has never heard of, weilding little influence, have their security forfeited or heavily enhanced. And administration which with flagrant injustice allows the main offender and inspirer of hatred, who proclaims "war against Government" speaks of paralysing or "pullling it down" to go scot free while crushing small offenders encouraged by the example undermines in the community all respect for law and for the Government and the law thus abused should immediately be repealed. I rejoice that the Government is strong enough to treat Mr Gandhi's vapourings with contempt instead of bestowing on him the martyrdom Le courts. But I urge that a law not enforced against the influential should not be allowed to crush the weak and the poor."

Annie Besant strongly criticised Gandhi's non-cooperation policies. In February 1919 when Gandhi announced his intention to resort to passive resistance against the Rowlatt Act, Annie Besant warned him that any such movement would result in the release of forces whose potentialities for evil were incalculable. She supported the Rowlatt Bills on the ground that they contained nothing to which an honest citizen could take exception and wrote in *New India* that "when the mob begins to pelt them, solidiers, with brickbats, it is more merciful to order the soldiers to fire a few volleys of buckshot". There was country-wide indignation at this comment and Annie Besant's popularity waned fast, but undettered , she persisted in her unsparing criticism of the Government as well as her condemnation of passive resistance and direct action. In 1930 she described Gandhi's Salt March as "the clash with authority with mock fight".

Sometime after *New India* was started in 1915, the Justice (non-Brahmin) Party came into existence with a newspaper called *Justice*. Annie Besant's *New India* had made serious dent into the circulation of *Indian patriot*, edited by Karunakara Menon. The non-Brahmin Party organised by P. Theagaraya Chetty, T.N. Nair, the Raja of Panagal and others was looking out for a paper of their own. In the decline of *The Indian Patriot* they saw an opportunity to control the paper. Another reason was that *The Indian Patriot* press had issued a number of bulletins entitled "non-Brahmin letters" which set forth the grievances of the community in the matter of their exclusion from the public service. Karunakara Menon, however, declined to sell the paper or to change its policy to suit justice Party. T.M. Nair himself became the editor of *Justice* which was started from scratch in 1917. He was succeeded by Sir A. Ramaswamy Mudaliar under whose able control the paper flourished from some years. The Justice Party favoured acceptance of office and the assumption of power by it contributed to its strength. Sir A. Ramaswamy Mudaliar had to give up the editorship of the paper after he joined the Government of India. When the Justice Party went out of power in the State the paper languished and ultimately folded up. Its successor, The *Liberty*, edited by Dr K. Mudaliar also ceased publication in 1953. One reason for the weakness of the Justice Party and the paper was that it could never live down the reputation of having been sponsored by the British. *The Indian Patriot* ceased publication in the early twenties.

In 1920 when Gandhi launched his first non-cooperation movement, the Congress felt the need for a paper of its own in the Madras Presidency. This need was met by *Swarajya* started by T.Prakasam in 1922. Among his colleagues were G.V. Krupanidhi, Khasa Subha Rau, K. Ramakotiswara Rao, K. Srinivasan and N.S. Varadachari. The paper gained in popularity in no time. But it did not last long.

In Bengal also the war years saw rapid development in the newspaper world. The process of modernisation started in 1914 when the Bengali daily *Basumati* appeared. *Basumati* was the first Bengali newspaper to roll out of a power-operated rotary press and which used Reuter's news.

It was also the first newspaper sold by hawkers. *Basumati* apart, *Nayak* was another newspaper which had earned popularity. C.R. Das who had, with Gandhi's consent, formed the Swaraj Party to wreck the Constitution from within the legislature, also felt the need for a newspaper. In 1923 he started *Forward* as the daily organ of the Swaraj Party. Like the *Swarajya* of Madras, *Forward* captured public imagination in Bengal. The *Forward*, however, declined precipitately after the death of Das in June 1925 and finally closed down in 1929 when it was fined a lakh of rupees. It was restarted under the name of *Liberty* and few years later reappeared as *Forward*. But its promoter failed to establish the paper because of successive prosecutions. In the same year *Advance* was founded by J.M. Sen Gupta which continued for several years even after independence. But later the paper ceased publication. Other newspapers that made a mark in Bengal's journalism were *Ananda Bazar Patrika* which began its journey in 1922 and is still going strong, the daily *Servant* brought out by Shyamsunder Chakravarty. Other papers were *Atma Shakti*, the Bengali edition of *Forward*, daily *Banglar*

Katha, Bangabani and *Nabashakti*. All these papers provided impetus to the political movement in Bengal.

At the turn of the century and during the first two decades, a number of important newspapers and periodicals came into existence. In 1899, Rabindranath Tagore started *Sadhana* under the editorship of his nephew, Surendra Nath Tagore. Ramananda Chatterjee embarked on his long and distinguished journalistic career as editor of *Kayestha Samachar*, an English weekly started from Allahabad by Sachidanand Sinha. It was converted into *Hindustan Review* the following year and published from Allahabad till 1921. It was shifted to Calcutta in 1925 under the editorship of K.C. Mahindra and later removed to Patna when Dr Sachidanand resumed its editorship.

The Indian Review was started in Madras by G. Natesan in 1900 and Ramananda Chatterjee who was editing Dr Sinha's weekly, founded the *Prabasi* to be followed seven years later by *The Modern Review* which heralded a new era in journalism. In 1908 Chatterjee shifted the Prabasi and *The Modern Review* from Allahabad to Calcutta. *The Modern Review* was produced with great care by Ramananda Chatterjee. It fully lived up to the claim of being a complete record of important events and comments with deft touches from the editor's analytical pen. Its columns were open to established and young writers. The paper's prestige was so high that it was considered to be a privilege to get one's article published in *The Modern Review*. Old volumes of the monthly are still prized as valuable works of reference.

In 1909, Bepin Chandra Pal founded the monthly *Swarajya* in London and in 1918 Aurobindo Ghosh started the *Arya*, an English monthly from Pondicherry. Other important weeklies published during this period were Mohammed Ali's *Comrade* established in Calcutta in 1911 and transferred to Delhi in the following year, the Servant of India founded at Poona in 1918 by the

Servants of India Society and *Young India* founded by the Home Rule Leaguers of Bombay with Jamnadas Dwarakadas as the editor, shortly after the departure of B.G. Horniman, editor of *Bombay Chronicle*. In 1919 Gandhi took over the editorship of *Young India* and of *Navjivan*, a Gujrati monthly converted into weekly. The two papers were edited by C. Rajagopalachari, Jairamdas Daulatram and George Joseph when Gandhi was in Jail from 1922 to 1924. *Young India* ceased publication for a time when the Swaraj Party was in power but Gandhi started the *Harijan* soon after under the editorship of Mahadev Desai.

Gandhi's papers carried no advertisements. They enjoyed a wide circulation and his articles were often circulated by the news agencies to the daily Press for publication simultaneously on the day after. His clear and simple style, direct and free from all flourishes, gave Gujrati a strength and vividness of expression which was a valuable contribution to the development of the language. In his autobiography, Gandhi defined the objects of journalism as follows: "One of the objects of a newspaper is to understand the popular feeling and give expression to it; another is to arouse among the people certain desirable sentiments; and the third is fearlessly to expose popular defects." In his endeavour to achieve this in his own journals, he imposed the most rigid discipline on himself which he did not necessarily recommend to other editors. Writing in Young India of July 2, 1925 he explained:

"Reference to abuse in the State is undoubtedly a necessary part of journalism and it is a means of creating public opinion. Only my scope is strictly limited; I have taken up journalism not for its sake but merely as an aid to what I have conceived to be my mission in life. My mission is to teach by example and present under severe restraint the use of matchless weapon of satyagraha which is a direct corollary of non-violence. It is a solvent strong enough to melt the stoniest heart. To be true to my faith, therefore, I may not write in anger or malice. I may not write idly. I may not write merely to excite passion. They can have no idea of the restraint I have to exercise from week to week in the choice of topics and vocabulary. It is a training for me. It enables me to peep into myself and to make discoveries of my weaknesses. Often my vanity dictates a smart expression or my anger a harsh objective. It is a terrible ordeal but a fine exercise to remove the weeds. The reader sees the pages of the *Young India* fairly well dressed-up and sometimes with Roman Rolland. He is inclined to say" what a fine old man this must be". Well, let the world understand that fineness is carefully and prayerfully cultivated. And if it has proved acceptable to some whose opinion I cherish let the reader understand that when that fineness has been perfectly natural i.e. when I have become incapable of evil and when nothing harsh or haughty occupies, be it momentarily, my thought world, then till then my non-violence will move all the hearts of the world. I have placed before me and the reader no impossible idea or ordeal."

During the period a number of important and politically-oriented language newspapers came out. The Hindi papers were *Abhyudaya*, a weekly founded and edited by Pandit Madan Mohan Malaviya in 1900 and later edited by his son, Pandit K. Malaviya; the daily *Pratap* of Cawnpore (1913) founded and edited by Ganesh Shankar Vidyarthi; the daily *Biswamitra*, founded and edited by Mahendra Chandra Agarwal in Calcutta in 1916 and the daily *Aj* (1920) of Banaras founded by Shivaprasad Gupta.

The Urdu papers included Maulana Abul Kalam Azad's daily *Al Hilal* (1912) from Calcutta, the *Hamdam* started from Lucknow by Abdul Bari Saheb with the help of Raja of Mahnudabad and weekly *Haquiqat* (1919) owned and edited by Anis Ahmed Abbasi.

In the Punjab urdu daily *Pratap* was founded at

Lahore in 1919 by Mahashe Krishen and published from there under his editorship till 1947. It moved to Delhi after partition. Swami Shradhananda founded the Urdu daily, *Tej* at Delhi in 1923. Under the editorship of Deshabandhu Gupta the paper commanded great influence until 1951 when he was killed in an air crash in Calcutta where he had gone to attend, as its President, a meeting of the Standing Committee of All India Newspapers Editors Conference. Urdu daily, *Milap* was founded in 1923 by Mahashe Khushal Chand at Lahore. Like *Pratap*, *Milap* also moved to Delhi.

In the Central Provinces (now Madhya Pradesh) journalism passed through many vicissitudes. In 1910 Madhavrao Madhya started a Maratha weekly *Hitavada* which was published rather irregularly.

Foundation of daily Marathi journalism was laid by A.B. Kolhatkar who edited and conducted *Swadesh*, first from Nagpur and then from Bombay. In his engrossing style he created a new taste among the readers and carried political discussions right to the door of the masses. Another great Marathi journalist was G.A. Ogale who was first associated with *Desh Sevak* and later in 1914 started in Nagpur *Maharashtra* as a weekly. *Hitavada* was taken over by the Servants of India Society in 1913. N. A. Dravid became the first editor of the new *Hitavada* which was converted into an English language journal and continued as a weekly till 1926. In 1939 it became a daily. *Hitavada* and *the Maharashtra* can be said to be leaders of Madhya Pradesh journalism as they played an important part in making the electorate politically conscious in the early years of Montford Reforms. However, *the Daily News*, started in 1933, was the first English daily from Nagpur. It was edited by V.S. Venkataraman who earlier edited *Hitavada* weekly for twelve years. The *Daily News* was converted into Nagpur Times in 1939.

Among Hindi papers, *Nav Bharat* started publication in the thirties as a weekly. Later it became a daily. The editor of *Nav Bharat*, R.G. Maheswari, is regarded as the pioneer of Hindi daily journalism in Madhya Pradesh. *Lokmat*, started by a Calcutta businessman, also contributed to Hindi journalism in Madhya Pradesh. Barring these dailies Madhya Pradesh journalism has been largely of the periodical variety. Journals like *Subhachintak* of Jubbulpore, *Swarajya* of Khandwa and *Matribhumi* of Akole are well known for their contributions to periodical journalism. D.P. Misra edited *Sarathi* of Jubbulpore. *Karmaveer* was another popular journal edited by Makhanlal Chaturvedi who was well-known all over the country for his forceful writings in Hindi.

> "........ every issue of the paper presents an opportunity and a duty to say something courageous and true; to rise above the mediocre and conventional; to say something that will command the respect of the intelligent, the educated, the independent part of the community; to rise above fear of partisanship and fear of popular prejudice".
>
> Joseph Pulitzer

10
GANDHIAN ERA

10
GANDHIAN ERA

The war had profound material and intellectual impact on India. On the material side there were signs of prosperity in some areas with the setting up of new industries. On the intellectual side it was recognised that India's part in the war and the question of freedom of small nations did more to bring about a national awakening than any event since the Russo-Japanese War, which resulted in the victory of an eastern nation over a western.

On the conclusion of the War in 1918 the Government of India was again approached for the repeal of the Press Act of 1910. The initiative was taken by the Secretary of the State and earlier objections to vertain provision of the Act were considered. But nothing material happened. On the contrary, it was decided to postpone consideration of any change or modification of Press Laws until after the introduction of the Montague-Chelmsford Reforms.

Although the Montague-Chelmford Report was published in July 1918 the legislation was not placed in the statute book until 1919 when George V gave his consent to the Bill. In doing so he issued a Royal Proclamation surveying the constitutional progress since the Act of 1773, and announcing his intention to send his son, the Prince of Wales, to India to inaugurate the new Constitution and the Chamber of Princes (a duty eventually undertaken by the Duke of Connaught).

The reactions of the political parties to the Proclamation were duly reflected in the Indian press. While the Anglo-Indian press supported the Government's policy and the Moderates were willing to cooperate with the Government in making the reforms a success, the Nationalists were dissatisfied with the Reform Scheme which was condemned as "disappointing and unsatisfactory." The provisions of the Montague-Chelmsford Constitution envisaging a system of dyarchy are well known. Briefly, it transferred authority over twenty subjects, including education, public health, agriculture, excise and so forth to the Provincial Ministries headed by Indian Ministers in the provinces. The "Reserved Subjects" of which there were thirty-six, including law and order, finance, water supply, famine relief were administered by the Governors with their Executive Councils of British and Indian Ministers. At the Centre, the Governor-General was to be assisted by six Executive Councillors appointed by the Crown and they were to be in charge of Home Affairs, Finance, Education, Health and Land, Law, Railways, Commerce, Ecclesiastical Affairs and Labour. The Central Legislature was to consist of an Upper and a Lower House. In the provinces, the Executives were accountable to the elected legislators insofar as the Transferred Subjects" were concerned. It would be seen that the Cabinets were to consist of two halves — a system which many Indian nationalists thought, would definitely fail.

Absence of a recognised national language was one of the subjects agitating the nationalist opinion at that time. Gandhi has been advocating the case of Hindi. Many politicians and educationists also shared the view that Hindi should be the medium of instruction in the schools. It was at this time that Shivaprasad

Gupta, the millionaire philanthropist of Banaras founded his Hindi paper, the *AJ*, at Banaras on September 5, 1920. He wanted to have a newspaper in Hindi which would be a influential as *the Times* of London. As its policies were directed towards reaching the masses, the paper necessarily had to devote considerable spaces on educative matters. Selling price had to be as low as half an anna because of the poverty and poor purchasing power of the masses. Moreover, advertisers kept aloof from the papers printed in Indian languages. It was not realised that they reached a purchasing public which had hitherto been untapped by the larger advertisers. And when attempts were eventually made to reach this public the medium used was inappropriate.

On the political side, an indication of the extent of nationalist ambition can be gauged from the fact that the policy of *Aj* aimed at "striving for the complete independence of India by the spread of nationalism and the consolidation of the Indian people as a self-respecting, homogeneous whole, working for their goal by their own efforts." There was to be no dependence on the British Government but full advantage was to be taken of world forces and friendly contacts with other nations.

The Montague-Chelmsford Report was followed by the report of the Sedition Committee which was presided over by Justice Rowlatt. The Congress, at its Delhi session, declared that if the Rowlatt Committee's recommendations were implemented the Indians would be deprived of their fundamental rights. Nevertheless, the Rowlatt Bill was introduced in the Central Legislative Council and passed in February 1919. A disillusioned Gandhi, who attended the War conference in Delhi in 1918 where he supported the resolution on recruting for war, formed a Satyagraha Sabha in Bombay with a view to organising a country-wide demonstration. He urged all adults to undertake a 24-hour fast as a preliminary to suspension of all business on a specific date. Public meetings were to be held on that day throughout the country at which resolutions demanding withdrawal of the two measures were to be passed. The date was fixed for March 30 and later postponed to April 6.

In Delhi where the day was observed on March 30, a massive public meeting was held in the Jama Masjid. The police opened fire on a procession killing several persons. Gandhi was invited to Delhi for talks and he agreed to go there after inauguration of the satyagraha in Bombay on April 6. The Bombay satyagraha was a great success. An item of the programme was the sale of proscribed literature which included an unregistered weekly, *the Satyagraha*, published every Monday. Its first issue carried an article by Gandhi instructing satyagrahis on the methods they should adopt against the press laws.

On April 7, Gandhi left for Delhi and Amritsar. On reaching the Punjab, he was served with an order prohibiting his entry into the province. But as he insisted on his going on, he was removed from the train, detained at the Mathura police barracks and later put into a goods train and sent back to Bombay under police escorts.

Public feeling was roused by Gandhi's arrest and rose further to a high pitch following the Jalianwalabagh massacre and the atrocities perpetrated under the martial law regime in the Punjab. There was complete censor of news from the Punjab. But the happenings leaked out in no time in all their sordid details and all newspapers condemned the occurrence unequivocally. The Anglo-Indian papers stood in a category apart. They either condoned or found extenuating circumstances for the action of General Dyer and Sir Michael O'Dwyer. Some even tried to vindicate the acts perpetrated under the Martial Law in the Punjab.

The Press was purged again. *The Bombay Chronicle* topped the list of newspapers which were Victimised. Its editor, B.G. Horniman, was deported. The paper resumed publication after having deposited a security of Rs. 5,000 : its editor was sentenced to imprisonment and a fine and the paper suspended publication for a few days. The *Punjabee* suspended publication altogether. The *Hindu* and *Swadesamitran* of Madras were asked to furnish a security of Rs. 2,000 each and the former was banned in the Punjab and Burma. Similarly punished was *The Independent* of Lucknow. In Sind, two papers were penalised while two other suspended publication. *Pratap* of Lahore was prosecuted and its editor sentenced to 18 months rigorous imprisonment and to pay a fine of Rs. 500. Securities were also demanded from a number of other papers.

It was in this atmosphere that the Montague-Chelmsford Reforms were introduced. Sir Tej Bahadur Sapru, who was a member of the Viceroy's Executive Council in charge of law, took up the question of the repeal of the Press Act or its amendment. In March 1921, he constituted a committee with himself as the chairman. The committee's recommendations were as follows:

(1) The press Act should be abolished;

(2) The Newspapers (Incitement to Offences) Act should be repealed;

(3) The Press and Registration of Books Act, the Sea Customs Act and the Post Office Act should be amended where necessary to meet the conclusions noted below:

   (a) The name of the editor should be inscribed on every issue of a newspaper, and the editor should be subject to the same liabilities as the printer and the publisher, as regards criminal and civil responsibility;

   (b) Any person registering under the Press and Registration of Books Act should be a major as defined by the Indian Majority Act;

   (c) Local Government should retain the power of confiscating openly seditious leaflets, subject to the owner of the Press or any other person aggrieved being able to protest before a Court and challenge the seizure of any such document in which case the local Government ordering confiscation should be called upon to prove the seditious character of the document:

(d) The powers conferred by Sections 13 to 15 of the Press Act should be retained, Customs and Postal Officers being empowered to seize seditious literature within the meaning of Section 124-A, Indian Penal Code, subject to the review on the part of the local Government and challenge by any person interested, in the proper Courts:

(e) Any person challenging the orders of the Government should do so in the local court.

(f) The term of imprisonment prescribed in sections 12, 13, 14 and 15 of the Press and Registration of Books Act should be reduced to six months.

(g) The provisions of Section 16 of the Press Act, should be reproduced in the Press and Registration of Books Act."

At the Delhi session of the Central Legislature in 1922, the Newspaper (Incitement to Offences) Act of 1908 and Press Act of 1910 were repealed, as well as twenty-three other Acts and Regulations supplementing the ordinary criminal law, including the Rowlatt Acts.

The Legislature found it necessary to recommend legislation for the protection of Indian Princes. However, a meeting of the Chamber of Princes requested special protection for the Indian States, to replace that which had been taken from them by the repeal of the relevant provision in the Press Act. In the opinion of the Government, they were bound to accept the request on account of treaties existing with the Indian States. Therefore, the Princes Protection Bill was introduced. Feelings at the proposed measure were very high throughout the country and the Indian-owned Press vigorously condemned it. The Legislative Assembly reflected the opinion and refused leave for the introduction of the Bill. The Governor-General exercised the Extraordinary powers vested in him by the Government of Indian Act and certified that the Bill was essential in the interest of British India and recommended it to be passed in the form in which it was presented. The enactment of the measure, in the teeth of strong opposition from the public, provoked some very bitter and hostile comments. It is noteworthy that the Bill provided the first occasion for the exercise of the Governor-General 's power of certification.

Meanwhile, the country witnessed significant political developments. The Hunter Commission was appointed to inquire into the Martial Law excesses in the Punjab. During Marshal Law a number of prominent persons, including editors of newspapers, had been arrested. Feelings running high in the country over the Hunter Commission's investigations were further roused by its recommendations and the Government action thereon. The Special session of the Congress held in September 1920, adopted a resolution of full-fledged non-cooperation which included boycott of schools and colleges, law courts, legislatures and foreign goods. The Nagpur session of the Congress held in December changed the Congress creed to the "attainment of Swaraj by all legitimate and peaceful means". The Prince of Wales came to India in the following year despite Indian advice that the visit was inopportune. Boycott of the visit led to disturbances in Bombay between the Parsees who were in favour of welcoming the Prince and those who favoured the boycott. Early in 1922 an ineffectual effort was made to bring about an understanding between the Government and the non-cooperators. Gandhi listed some minimum demands and declared his intention to launch civil disobedience if they were not satisfied. The Chauri-Chaura incident of February 4, 1922, resulted in Gandhi suspending mass civil disobedience. But he was arrested for certain articles written by him in *Young India* and was sentenced to six years imprisonment.

In January 1924, Gandhi was operated on for acute appendicitis, and in the following month, he was released in order to enable him to convalesce in the place of his own choice. Spending sometime at Juhu, Gandhi left for Sabarmati Ashram towards the end of May and in September that year he undertook a fast for 21 days to bring about understaning between the Hindus and Muslims. In December that year, Gandhi presided over the 39th session of the Congress.

In his presidential address, he emphasised a number of significant points, namely, the need for religious and political tolerance, his decision to suspend non-cooperation and to concentrate, in the coming years, all the energies of the Congress on constructive work and the removal of untouchability.

In pursuance of this objective, the next five years were devoted to all-out effort on the part of Gandhi and the Congress to bring all elements together behind the combined effort for freedom irrespective of communal and political differences. The Congress session was preceded by a Unity Conference in September 1924 which was attended by members of all communities. The conference passed resolutions condemning those who took law in their own hands and proclaiming that all differences should be referred to arbitration and failing that to the Courts. While the conference did achieve greater unity than had hitherto been possible, it also brought to light a strong difference of opinion on the part of those belonging to different schools of thought. Then once againt an executive action by the Government provided common ground for various groups to meet. The Ordinance No. 1 of 1924 promulgated by Lord Reading on October 25, established a summary procedure of arrest and trial before Special Commissioners of persons whom, the Bengal Government was satisfied, belonged to associations whose object was revolutionery crime."

The bulk of the Indian Press unreservedly condemned the measure. However, Annie Besant was of the opinion that in the existing circumstances it was a regrettable necessity. With the Ordinance as the Chief Object of attack, Gandhi, C.R. Das and Motilal Nehru appealed to the nation recommending the Congress to suspend the non-cooperation programme except inso far as it related to the refusal to wear cloth not made in India and to authorise the Swarajya Party to carry on work in the legislature on behalf of the Congress. All sections of the congress were enjoined to encourage the use of home-spun khadi, to promote Hindu-Muslim unity and to remove untouchability.

Differences between the Swarajists and the Non-cooperators having been settled, an all-party leaders conference was convened in November to find a basis on which the parties might unite for the achievement of self-government. The conference could agree on one point only — and that was condemnation of the Bengal Ordinance. Committees were set up to consider the best way of reuniting all political parties in the Congress and to prepare a scheme of Swaraj, including a solution of the communal question. But the sub-committee appointed to examine the communal question was unable to arrive at an agreement while the Constitutional sub-committee recommended certain amendments in the Commonwealth of Indian Bill drawn up by Annie Besant and her colleagues.

The Swarajist majorities in Central Province and Bengal had, in the meantime, rendered the Montague-Chelmsford Constitution inoperative and the Governors in those provinces were using their special powers. In the Central Legislature, members of the Swarajya Party served on Select Committees and they cooperated in the passage of certain legislation (for example, The Steel Industry Protection Act, the first measure taken towards the adoption of protection). In April 1925, a convention which met at Kanpur with Tej Bahadur Sapru in the Chair, adopted Annie Besant's Commonwealth of India Bill.

Two events in the following year had an important bearing on the development of the press. One was the inauguration of the Government's beam wireless system of communication between Rugby and Kirkee. The System made the despatch of press telegrams cheaper than that of the cable company. But soon the government made the service over to the Imperial and International Communications (Successor of Marconi Company) and the rates for both wireless and cable transmission were made uniform. The increasing interest in wireless led to the formation of Indian Broadcasting Company.

Another event of far-reaching consequences was the flight of Sir Samuel Hoare (then Secretary of State for Air) from London to Karachi in sixty-three flying hours. This flight, terminating on January 5, 1927 opened Egypt to India air service.

About this time, the British Government came to the conclusion that it was desirable to supplement existing sources of news by a regular official service. Messages were to be transmitted by wireless and the service mooted in 1918, was known as British Official Wireless. The material was compiled by the British Foreign Office and relayed from Rugby. In India the distribution was in the hands of *Reuter*. The copy was made available to all newspapers at a nominal charge to cover the cost of distribution. Some of the smaller papers printed in English relied almost exclusively on this service, though it did not aim at being comprehensive; rather it amplified news of official or semi-official nature.

On March 8, 1926 the Swaraj Party walked out of the Central Legislative Assembly after Motilal Nehru had made a short speech in which he declared that Swarajists had cooperated with the Government and had helped to work the reforms for two and half years but in return received nothing but humiliation. This demonstration led to divided opinions and the Press reflected divergent views.

It was at this time the Govenment introduced the

Currency Bill, to give effect to one of the proposals of the Royal Commission on Indian Currency whose report had been published during the first week of August. The proposal was to stabilise the rupee at 16d. Since the measure affected the economic structure of India those sections of the Press influenced by mercantile interests urged that the bill should be opposed with every weapon at the disposal of the nationalists. Accordingly, when the bill was being discussed on August 23, the Swarajists returned to the Legislative Assembly. The House decided to circulate the Bill for opinion, whereupon the Swarajists again left the Assembly.

As the Indians were taking more and more interest in public affairs it became clear to nationalist leaders and industrialists, like Annie Besant, M.R. Jayakar, Puroshottamdas Thakurdas, G.D. Birla, Phiroj Sethna, Walchand Hirachand and others felt that unless there were some national news distributing organisations, their views on the policies which were not in harmony with those of the existing agencies, might go by default. The *Associated Press* became an associate of *Reuter's*. The fact that *Reuter News Agency* and *Associated Press* were receiving money for supplying news to the Government officers, had the effect of withholding nationalist confidence in the neutrality of that organisation. Consequently, it was decided to set up a nationalist news agency named *Free Press of India* with S.Sadanand as Managing Director. The Government's Currency Bill provided the first important controversial news which the agency handled. Through the correspondents all over the country it was able to give wide publicity to views of those who were hostile to the measure.

An apparent atmosphere of stagnation prevailed in the political sphere as India was awaiting the Government's announcements regarding the Parliamentary Commission which was to examine the working of the Montague-Chelmsford Reforms. The announcement regarding the setting up of a statutory Commission was duly made on November 8, 1927. It led to an outcry, as the personnel of the Commission were restricted to the members of the British Parliament. Nationalists were more disappointed than the Moderates. While the former had been saying for the past two years that only Round Table Conference would meet their demands the Liberals had been expecting some acknowledgement of their spirited cooperation and they felt that the exclusion of the Indians from the Commission was tantamount to an insult to India's self-respect. Those willing to cooperate with the Commission, headed by Sir John Simon, consisted of the leaders of the Justice Party, a few Liberals, a section of Muslims and a section of Sikhs. The Congress, at its Lahore Session, not only declared that the Commission should be boycotted at every stage and every forum but that mass demonstrations should be organised throughout India, that vigorous propaganda should be carried on to make the boycott effective and successful, and that the elected members of all legislative bodies should refuse to help the Commission and should abstain from attending meetings of the legislatures except for certain specific purposes. An overwhelming majority of the Indian-owned Press whole-heartedly supported the policy. But of more far-reaching consequences was the adoption of a resolution declaring that the goal of Indian people was complete national independence; Hitherto, the object of the Congress was the attainment of dominion status and the independence resolution was adopted afer considerable discussion.

Moreover, the Press, by no means, was unanimous in its approval of the new goal which the Congress had set for itself. There was an organised boycott of the Simon Commission which was greeted with black flag demonstrations whereever it went and Simon in vain held out assurances that Indians would be associated with the work of the Commission. By a majority of six votes the Central Assembly adopted a resolution declaring that it should not associate itself in any way or at any stage with the work of the Simon Commission. Just as the resolution was being debated a reporter of a nationalist daily newspaper dropped an attache case from the Press Gallery and partially stunned Sir Basil Blackett, the Finance Member. The incident caused some excitement in the nationalist Press.

At this time, a book which raised a storm of protest in India was published— *Mother India* by Miss Katherine Mayo, an American author. Gandhi condemned it as a "drain inspector's report". Newspapers throughout the country condemned the book not only because of its contents but also because Miss Mayo had received considerable assistance from the Government in collecting materials for it. The book dealt with child marriage and allied social topics. The writer dwelt almost exclusively on the unsavoury aspects of certain Indian customs and thereby roused the entire Indian Press which condemned her work as a scandalous libel.

Hindu-Muslim feelings were roused to a high pitch of bitterness in which Hindu beliefs, customs and practices were criticised in the Muslim Press and by Muslim writers. As a counterblast, Rajpal, a Hindu writer published a book "*Rangila Rasul*" reflecting adversely on the character of Prophet Mohammed, which incensed Muslim feelings. The author was tried and sentenfeed, in the first instance, to 18 months imprisonment. The sentence was reduced to six months and finally the author was acquitted by the Punjab High Court. The case roused country-wide interest not only because of the subject matter of the book but Sir Malcolm Hailey, the then Governor of the Punjab, was said to have indicated in a public speech what the judgement should be before it was delivered. Sir Shadilal, who was the Chief Justice, lodged a protest. Rajpal was stabbed to death soon after while he was sitting outside a book-selling shop. Within a few days of pronouncement of judgement, another alleged attack on the Prophet Mohammed was published at Amritsar. In view of the intensification of Hindu-Muslim feelings in the Punjab and the different interpretation of the law it was decided to transfer the hearing of the second offence to a Division Bench of the High Court. The Bench held that such an attack on the founder of Islam would, prima facie, fall under Section 153 A of the Penal Code and the accused would duly be sentenced.

Experience had proved that Section 153 A of the Penel Code was capable of more than one interpretation. To remove this ambiguity the Government of India decided to amend the law. The Select Committee of the Assembly, set up to examine the proposed measure, re-worded the Clause defining the offence in the Act as follows:

"Whoever, with deliberate and malicious intention of outraging the religious feelings of any clan of His Majesty's subjects, by words, either spoken or written, or by visible representations, insults or attempts to insult religion or religious beliefs of that class, shall be punished with imprisonment of either description for a term of which may extend to two years, or with a fineor with both.,"

Most Hindu members of Assembly were not convinced that the proposed amendment of the law was necessary; but it was felt that it might appease public opinion and, therefore, should be accepted. Muslim members, recent attacks on the Founder of their religion still fresh in their memory, wanted to safeguard themselves from any repetition of these episodes. A member of their party moved an amendment to make the offence contained in the bill non-bailable. When the bill was put to vote, sixtyone members voted in favour and twentysix against the measure.

Political opinion in England was dismayed by the extent of boycott of the statutory commission. There were many genuinely interested in the welfare of India and Britiain who deplored the deterioration in relations, the more so as proceedings of the reforms committee, presided over by Sir Alexander Muddiman, seemed to indicate that it would not be difficult to reach an agreement. The Viceroy, Lord Irwin, sought to reassure Indian opinion by admitting that "wisdom or unwisdom" of excluding Indians was a question on which every man was entitled to his own opinion. "But", he said, " what no man is entitled to say — for it is simply not true— is that His Majesty's Government sought to offer a deliberate affront to Indian honour and Indian pride." He declared that whether Indian assistance was offered or withheld, the enquiry would proceed, and the report would be presented to Parliament and on such report parliament would take whatever action it deemed proper.

INFLUENCE OF COMMUNISTS

The political situation was rapidly deteriorating. While John Simon and his colleagues were finalising their recommendations the Indians, by and large, were suspicious of Government intentions. But what really alarmed the authorities was the growing influence of the Communists among the industrial labourers in large towns. In 1926 there had been about 203 strikes involving over a half of a million people, compared to 129 strikes in the previous year. In nearly one-third of the strikes the workers succeeded in obtaining concessions. A view widely held at this time was that the Commintern was assisting Communist agitators in other countries. Apprehensive of the influence of the Communist politicians, if they were allowed to proceed unchecked, the Government in 1928 introduced in the Legislative Assembly a Public Safety Bill with the object of empowering the Governor General to deport from India any British or foreign Communists agents who might be found to be seeking to overthrow the Government in British India. The bill, as amended by the Select Committee, was put before the Assembly but was rejected at the introduction stage by the casting vote of the Assembly President Vithalbhai Patel. A second attempt by the Government to introduce a revised bill was also fruitless as the President held the view that it was against the rules of the business of the House that any question should be asked or any resolution moved in regard to any matter which was under adjudication by a court of law having jurisdiction in any part of His Majesty's dominion. The authorities were convinced that the situation had worsened. As evidence of this they cited the outrage which took place at the Assembly in Delhi when a bomb was thrown from the gallery on the floor of the House. The official inquiry into the outrage led to the discovery of what was known as "Lahore Conspiracy Case."

Soon after the bomb episode the Viceroy announced that it had become imperative for the Government to be empowered with the powers proposed in the Public Safety Bill without further delay. He had accordingly decided to avail himself of the authority conferred upon the Governor-General under section 72 of the Government of India Act and accordingly issued an ordinance. Events followed thereafter in quick succession. The Meerut Conspiracy Trial of three journalists among others charged with Communist conspiracy, commenced early in 1929, and a procession led by Lala Lajpat Rai in Lahore to protest against the Simon Commission was lathi-charged and he himself was struck on the chest and had barely recovered from his injuries when he passed away. Among those arrested was The arrested three journalists, Lester Hutchinson, a Britisher, who had edited a political periodical in Bombay, named the *New Spark*, M.G. Desai, the former editor of *The Spark* (the parent of the New Spark) and Kishore Lal Ghosh.

Responsible Indian politicians were not slow in their desire to answer the challenge thrown by Lord Birkenhead, the Secretary of State, at the time of the Simon Commission, Birkenhead had said tauntingly that Indians were quite incapable of agreeing on any workable political framework. He said that he had twice invited critics in India to put forward their own suggestions for a constitution, and that this offer was still open. Efforts were made in different quarters to formulate an agreed scheme and in August 1928 a report was published signed by eight leaders including Pandit Motilal Nehru, as the leader of the Congress Party, Sir Tej Bahadur Sapru, leader of the Liberals, Sir Ali Imam, a former member of the Governor-Generals Executive Council. This All Parties' Report, known as Nehru Report, was supported by the Moderates. But Jawaharlal Nehru disagreed with the report as he was not prepared to compromise on the Independence issue. Motilal Nehru made it known that he would not preside over the forthcoming session of the Congress in Calcutta if he could not secure a majority for the resolution in favour of the All Parties' Report. The resolution was finally adopted with a rider that if the British Government did not agree to that Constitution within a year, the Congress would revert to the goal of independence. Jawaharlal Nehru wrote in his "Autobiography";

"It was an offer of a year's grace and a polite ultimatum. The resolution was no doubt a come-down from the ideal of independence, for All Parties' report did not even ask for full Dominion Status. And yet it was probably a wise resolution in the sense that it prevented a split when no one was ready for it, and kept the Congress together for the struggle that began in 1930. It was clear enough that the British Government were not going to accept the All Parties' Constitution within a year. The struggle was inevitable and, as matters stood in the country, no such struggle could be at all effective without Gandhiji's lead."

Gradually, the supporters of the All Parties' report began to get disenchanted. Disappointed that certain demands which they had put forward were not agreed to, the section of Muslims led by Jinnah withdrew their support. The majority of the Muslims were thus in the opposition. This development resulted in the Hindu Mahasabha declaring that since the Muslim leaders had refused to accept the report, Mahasabha had now reverted to its original stand of opposition to any special treatment in any matter to any community. This was a reference to the provision in the Report granting concessions to the Muslims in the matter of extra-representation in the legislatures and Cabinets where the community was in a minority.

The Nehru Report has thus lost its importance. Motilal Nehru and his followers, however, still urged that a Round Table Conference between the representatives of the British Government and of political India should meet to discuss the ways and means of implementing the reforms suggested in the Report.

In Great Britain, a Labour Government, headed by Ramsay MacDonald came into power in 1929. The then Viceroy, Lord Irwin, after consultating with the new Government, announced that a Round Table Conference with representatives of British India and the Indian States would be held before giving shape to the reform proposals based on the Simon Commission Report which had not been submitted at the time. The reaction was favourable in certain quarters. Meetings were held all over the country assuring the Government of a sympathetic response from the nationalist leaders. Irwin held talks with important leaders like Gandhi, Motilal Nehru, Vithalbhai Patel, Tej Bahadur Sapru and Jinnah to follow up the "Delhi Manifesto" as it was called. But the outcome was zero. The Congress at its Lahore session, presided over by Jawaharlal Nehru, formally accepted complete independence for India as its goal. The resolution read as follows:

"This Congress endorses the action of the Working Committee in connection with the manifesto signed by party leaders, including Congressmen, on the Viceregal pronouncement of the 31st October relating to Dominion Status, and appreciates the efforts of the Viceroy towards a settlement of the national movement for Swaraj. The Congress, however, having considered all that has since happened, and the result of the meeting between Mahatma Gandhi, Pandi Motilal Nehru and other leaders and the Viceroy, is of opinion that nothing is to be gained in the existing circumstances by the Congress being represented at the proposed Round Table Conference. This Congress, therefore, in pursuance of the resolution passed at its session at Calcutta last year, declares that the word "Swaraj" in Article 1 of the

Congress Constitution shall mean complete independence; and further declares that the entire scheme of the Nehru Committee Report to have lapsed, and hopes that all Congressmen will henceforth devote their exclusive attention to the attainment of complete independence for India. As a preliminery step towards organising a campaign for Independence, and in order to make the Congress policy as consistent as possible with the change of creed, this Congress resolves upon a complete boycott of the Central and provincial legislatures and committees constituted by Government and calls upon Congressmen and others taking part in the national movement to abstain from participating directly or indirectly in future elections and directs the present Congress members of the legislatures and committees to resign their seats. This Congress appeals to the nation zealously to prosecute the constructive programme of the Congress, and authorises the All India Congress Committee, whenever it deems fit, to launch upon a programme of civil disobedience including non-payment of taxes, whether in selected areas or otherwise, and under such safeguards as it may consider necessary."

CIVIL DISOBEDIENCE

A programme for fresh Civil Disobedience was drawn up and the Working Committee, which met in Ahmedabad in February 1930 authorised Gandhi to lead the movement. On March 12, 1930 Gandhi started Salt Satyagraha. He reached Dandi on April 5 and was arrested on the same day and taken to Yarawada jail. The arrest touched off disturbances in Bombay and Calcutta, rioting at Sholapur and police firing.

Expectedly, the Press mirrored the various points of view. The extreme nationalist Press supported the campaign in editorial and by displaying news of the movement. The Liberal and the Anglo-Indian Press on the other hand unreservedly condemned Congress activities. The "illicit" Congress bulletin was widely circulated in Bombay and beyond. Notwithstanding all the attempts of the authorities to discover the staff of publication, they remained anonymous throughout the campaign.

Great excitement prevailed all over the country. Also present was the possibility of grave disorders. The terrorists in Bengal raided and looted the armoury at Chittagong. As a result, the Bengal Ordinance was introduced on April 19 empowering the Government to take summary action in connection with the suspected terrorists. Six other Ordinances were issued in quick succession arming the authorities with powers for dealing with intimidation and instigation. Among the measures was the "Indian Press ordinance 1930" to provide for the better control of the Press.

Under the terms of the ordinance. Magistrates were empowered, in their discretion, to demand securities of not less than five or more than two thousand rupees from any person keeping a printing press who was required to make a declaration under Section 4 of the Press and Registration of Books Act, 1867. From the publishers of newspapers who were required to make a declaration under Section 5 of the Act, the magistrate could, demand a security of less than five hundred rupees or more than two thousand rupees. Power to declare such securities forfeited was conferred when it appeared to the local Government that any matter published was likely to have a tendency, directly or indirectly, whether by inference, suggestion, allusion, metaphor, implication or otherwise:

(a) to incite to murder or to any offence under the Explosives Substances Act, 1908, or to any act of violence, or

(b) to seduce any officer, soldier, sailor or airman in the Army, Navy or Air Force of His Majesty or any police officer from his allegiance or his duty, or

(c) to bring into hatred or contempt His Majesty or the Government established by law in British India or the administration of justice in British India or any Indian Prince or Chief under the suzerainty of His Majesty, or any class or section of His Majesty's subjects in British India, or to excite disaffection towards His Majesty or the said Government or any such Prince or Chief, or

(d) to put any person in fear or to cause annoyance to him and thereby induce him to deliver to any person any property or valuable security, or to do any act which he is not legally bound to do, or to omit to do any act which he is legally entitled to do, or

(e) to encourage or incite any person to interfere with the administration of the law or with the maintenance of the law and order, or to commit any offence, or to refuse or defer payment of any land-revenue, tax, rate, cess or other due or amount payable to Government or to any local authority, or any rent of agricultural land or anything recoverable as arrears of or along with such rent, or

(f) to induce a public servant or a servant of a local authority to do any act or to forbear or delay to do any act connected with the exercise of his public functions or to resign his office, or

(g) to promote feelings of enmity or hatred between different classes of His Majesty's subjects, or

(h) to prejudice the recruiting of persons to serve in any of His Majesty's forces, or in any police force, or to prejudice the training, discipline, or administration of any such force".

On one security being forfeited any printer making a fresh declaration had to deposit with the magistrate before whom such a declaration was made, a further amount of not less than one thousand or more than ten thousand rupees. If this further security was forfeited the local Government might, by notice in writing, forfeit the further security, the printing press and all copies of the offending publication to His Majesty. When these forfeitures were declared the local Government might direct a magistrate to issue a warrant to seize and detain the forfeited property and to enter any premises for the search of such property. Appeal could be made to the High Court to set aside such orders within two months from the date of their execution. Such applications were to be heard by a Special Bench of the High Court composed of three judges, or where the High Court consisted of less than three judges, of all the judges.

Alarmed by the prevailing condition in the country with a campaign of civil disobedience on the one hand and exceptional measures in the shape of ordinances on the other — a number of nationalists resigned from the Assembly. The Liberals deplored the decision taken by Gandhi but they were equally apprehensive of repressive measures. As a matter of fact, the council of Liberal Federation urged from immediate repeal of the press ordinance and the release of all political detenues who had not been found guilty of violence.

In the meantime, many prominent leaders, including Gandhi and Jawaharlal Nehru, had been arrested. The Government resorted to large-scale arrests as the movement gained momentum. True, the movement did not bring the Government machinery to a grinding halt as was expected by the leaders, it definitely created many formidable problems. The boycott of British goods and the groups of picketers posted outside shops selling British wares were not difficult to tackle. But the campaign was not confined to youthful demonstrators. The Hindu mercantile community throughout the country, especially in Bombay, supported the Congress cause, many for class interest as many advantages accrued to them as a result of the boycott of British goods and the consequent stimulus given to the sale of Swadeshi products. Then there was tremendous enthusiasm among women to join the movement responding to Gandhi's call.

At a meeting of the Working Committee in June, composed largely of substitutes who were taking the place of imprisoned leaders, a resolution was adopted calling upon troops and police to disobey Government orders. In consequence of this incitement to disaffection, the whole Committee was proclaimed an unlawful association and the acting President Motilal Nehru and several others were arrested.

The Report of the statutory commission had just been published. Though the recommendations were made obsolete by future events it is pertinent to point out that the Round Table Conference, which changed the direction of Indian Constitutional discussion, was the outcome of the recommendations of Sir John Simon. It is significant to record that Indian liberal opinion was completely dissatisfied with the recommendations in the Report and the advanced nationalist opinion was unanimously hostile. Actually, the recommendations of the Commission were simply ignored.

Never before had the Press played so important a part in the national campaign. Enthusiasm was kindled and maintained by the vigorous action of the nationalist newspapers. Whenever the Government saw a cause of action the ordinance was invoked and number of nationalist newspapers suspended publication, while others forfeited securities, and some other editors were arrested. They included S.A Brelvi of *the Bombay Chronicle*. Security was demanded from *Ananda Bazar Patrika*, *Amrita Bazar Patrika*, *Liberty* and *Free Press Journal*. These developments dealt a blow to the Free Press of India which had been founded in 1927. With the closing down of newspapers and the apprehension on the part of others that publication of *Free Press* telegrams would lead to proceedings being taken against them, that organisation was put to considerable financial loss. Therefore, the management of the organisation, with the support of leading members of the Indian mercantile community, launched an English newspaper in Bombay on June 13, 1930, named the *Free Press Journal*. The new publication immediately attracted notice as it made an attempt to break through the orthodox newspaper make-up. It employed a new kind of lay-out by displaying matter in bold types and with banner headlines.

Though the Round Table Conference was to meet in London in the autumn of 1930 there were doubts about its prospects because of non-participation of the Congress. The two prominent Liberal leaders, Tej Bahadur Sapru and M.R. Jayakar, tried to persuade the Congress leaders who were in Yaroweda Jail, to attend the RTC. Their attempts failed as the Congress leaders' terms for withdrawing of the C.D. movement were not acceptable to the Government. The stalemate continued with the pressing on with the preparations for RTC and the Congress continuing its campaign for Civil Disobedience. When it was definitely known that the Congress would not take part in the RTC, the nationalist Press began to cast doubt on the standing of the Indian personnel and also on the significance of their deliberations in London. There were debates whether pro-Congress newspapers should refuse to print any account of the conference proceedings; but this was found to be a wholly impracticable suggestion. *Reuter* had made all arrangements for full and comprehensive service of RTC news which the Anglo-Indian and Liberal papers would have, in any event, published. *The Free Press* of India had also, notwithstanding its national bias, made special arrangements for the coverage of RTC proceedings, and "lobby" developments. The people in general were also interested to know what was happening in London. Therefore, in addition to the services maintained by *the Reuter* and *the Free Press*, the leading newspapers were represented at the conference by special correspondents. The *Hindu*, the *Madras Mail*, the *Times of India*, the *Bombay Chronicle*, the *Statesman*, the *Leader*, the *Amrita Bazar Patrika* and the *Pioneer*— all sent their representatives. In addition, two prominent journalists were delegates to the conference. The were C.Y Chintamoni, the editor-in-chief of the *Leader* and B. Shiva Rao who was connected with *Young India*. F.W. Wilson, the editor of the *Pioneer* which also gave its support to Indian liberal viewpoints, also went to London to cover the conference.

Observing the impasse created over the RTC because of non-cooperation of the Congress the Government released the Congress leaders and withdrew the notification declaring the congress to be an unlawful association. After this gesture by the Government the Working Committee authorised Gandhi to seek an interview with Lord Irwin. On various days between February 17 and March 5 Gandhi had private interviews with the Viceroy; the ultimate result being the well-known Gandhi-Irwin Pact. The terms of settlement, included, among others, withdrawal of Civil Disobedience, repeal by the Government of the ordinances and special measures and participation of the Congress in the Round Table Conference.

After the Pact, Gandhi went to London to take part in the RTC towards the end of 1931. Differences arose, however, in the Minorities Committee subsequently over Ramsay MacDonald's Communal Award and Gandhi dissociated himself from the decision.

About this time trouble was brewing in NWF Province and United Provinces. Khan Abdul Ghaffar Khan and Dr Khan Saheb were leading demonstrations of Khudai Kidmatgars in NWF province. In UP Jawaharlal Nehru launched a no-rent campaign among the agriculturists and had been arrested.

Returning to India on December 8, 1931 Gandhi held consultations with the Congress Working Committee on the developments which had taken place during his absence. He cabled to the Viceroy Lord Willingdon (Irwin's successor) drawing his attention to the Frontier and UP ordinances, the shootings in the Frontier and arrest of his colleagues and the Bengal Ordinance and asked whether the viceroy expected to meet him. The Viceroy replied that he was willing to meet Gandhi and discuss the way in which the spirit of cooperation could be maintained; but he pleaded his inability to discuss the measure the Government of India had taken in Bengal UP and NWFP. In his reply, Gandhi said that constitutional issues had receded to the background in the face of the Ordinances and the action taken by the Government which he denounced as "legalised Government terrorism". He forwarded a resolution of the Working Committee to the effect. The Viceroy deplored the attitude taken by Gandhi and the Congress and declared that no advantage would accrue from an interview "held under the threat of resumption of Civil Disobedience". Gandhi, in reply, regretted the decision of the Viceroy and the Government. While accepting full responsibility on behalf of the Congress and himself for the consequences of Civil Disobedience Gandhi assured the Government that the campaign would be conducted " without malice and strictly non-violent manner."

RULE BY ORDINANCE

This exchange of views has been dealt with at some length in order to give a background to the excitement which animated the Press, as well as public and private discussions. The atmosphere might be compared to that which existed prior to a declaration of war. Immediately it was known that a resumption of Civil Disobedience Movement was imminent and the Government pressed into operation the machinery which it had already prepared to meet any possible emergency. Four Ordinances were promulgated— the Emergency Powers Ordinance, conferring certain special powers for the maintenance of law and order and, in particular, for widening the operative section of the Press Act so as to permit action against the publication of matters calculated to encourage the C.D movement; the Unlawful Instigation Ordinance, directed against the no-tax campaign, the unlawful Association Ordinance, aimed at Congress buildings and funds and the prevention of Molestation and Boycotting ordinance, directed against picketting and boycotting of public servants.

A substantial section of public opinion, while deploring

the C.D Campaign, condemned the Government for its policy of "ruling by Ordinances". By the middle of the year the movement had definitely declined and it had been hoped that the Ordinances would be allowed to lapse. The Government, however, felt that any modification of its policy might lead to a revival of the Civil Disobedience on a large scale. Therfore, on June 30, a consolidated Ordinance, called the Special Powers Ordinance, 1932, was promulgated, embodying most of the powers contained in the four ordinances that the Indian Press (Emergency Powers) Act, 1931, wa also to be applicable to any book, newspaper or document which tended, directly or indirectly:

1. "to seduce any officer, soldier or airman in the military, naval or air forces of His Majesty or any police officer from his allegiance or his duty, or

2. to bring into hatred contempt His Majesty or the Government established by law in the British India or the administration of justice in British India or any Indian Prince or Chief under the suzerinty of His Majesty, or any class or section of His Majesty's subjects in British India or to excite disaffection towards His Majesty or the said Government or any such Prince or Chief, or,

3. to put any person in fear or to cause annoyance to him and thereby induce him to deliver to any person any property or valuable security, or to do any act which he is not legally bound to do, or to omit to do any act which he is legally entitled to do, or

4. to encourage or incite any person to interfere with the administration of the law or with the maintenance of law and order, or to commit any offence, or to refuse or defer payment of any land-revenue, tax, rate, cess or other due or amount payable to Government or to any local authority, or any rent of agricultural land or anything recoverable as arrears of or along with such rent, or

5. to induce a public servant or a servant of a local authority to do any act or to forbear or delay to do any act connected with the exercise of his public functions or to resign his office, or

6. to promote feelings of enmity or hatred between different classes of His Majesty's subjects, or

7. to prejudice the recruiting of persons to serve in any of His Majesty's forces, or in any police force, or to prejudice the training, discipline or administration of any such force."

The effect of this Ordinance was to bring the Government's powers into line with those it had at its disposal under the Indian Press Ordinance of 1930. The only difference in substance was that, whereas under the terms of the Ordinance of April, 1930, the maximum first security demanded from printers and publishers were two thousand rupees, under the terms of the Indian Press (Emergency Powers) Act of 1931, the Maximum first securities were one thousand rupees

Between 1932 and 1946, the struggle for independence passed through many vicissitudes. Ramsay MacDonald gave his Communal Award on August 17, 1932, and Gandhi who was in jail, decided to go on a fast in protest against Seperate Electorate for the Depressed Classes. There was consternation all over the country and after protracted negotiations a substitute formula was evolved reserving for the Depressed Classes 148 seats in the various legislatures, with provision of primary elections in which Depressed classes would vote exclusively and return four candidates for each reserved seat, out of which general electorate would elect one. As a result, Gandhi broke his fast on Septemebr 26. The Government reciprocated by removing all restrictions on Gandhi in respect of visitors, correspondence etc, to enable him to pursue his campaign for the removal of untouchability. Gandhi remained in Jail and on January 4, 1933, the anniversary of his arrest, public meetings were held throughout the country.

There were more arrests. Nevertheless, the Congress session was held in Calcutta on March 31, 1933. On May 8, 1933 Gandhi undertook a self-purificatory fast and he was released on the same day.

Meanwhile, the *Free Press of India* had been enlarging its publishing activities. By now it was sponsoring an English daily in Madras (the *Indian Express*) and an English daily in Bombay (the *Free Press Journal*) as well as Gujerathi and Marathi newspapers. Moreover, plans were being laid for the establishment of Free Press newspapers in all the large cities of India. When the project became known to the newspapers in Calcutta, subscribers in the city questioned the propriety of a news agency publishing a newspaper which would enter into rivalry with the news agency's clients. Competition among Calcutta newspapers were already unprofitable and the latest development was one which the Calcutta Press felt they could not regard with equnimity.

Hitherto, the nationalist newspapers in Bengal had been supporters of the *Free Press* services and if they were now to withdraw their support as a protest, the ideals of agency with whose aims they were in sympathy would have disappeared, and they *Associated Press of India* would have regained its monopoly. In the circumstances, the Calcutta Editor of the *Free Press*, B. Sen Gupta, decided to sever his connection with the Free Press and to set up an independent organisation rather than take the risk of extinction. Thus the *United Press of India* (UPI) was born.

There were brief intervals of understanding between the Congress and the Government, particularly in the period between 1937 and 1939 when, as a result of an assurance that the Governors would not interfere with the day-to-day administration of a province outside the limited range of his special responsibilities, Congressmen decided to return to the legislatures and assume the responsibilities of office in the provinces. Throughout this period, however, the Press Emergency Powers Act of 1931 remained in force and was applied with greater or less severity, according to the political circumstances. The record of prosecutions in the fifteen-year period exceeded the number of prosecutions under the 1910 Act. Well over a thousand newspapers were victimised in Bombay, Bengal, Delhi, Madras, the Punjab and the United Provinces. Bombay led with 596 demands for security while the Punjab came second with 280. Bengal led with 48 forfeitures of security, Punjab coming second with 37.

> "One of the object of a newspaper is to understand the popular feeling and give expression to it; another is to arouse among the people certain desirable sentiments; and the third is fearlessly to expose popular defects."
>
> Mahatma Gandhi

11
WORLD WAR II AND 'QUIT INDIA'

World War II broke out on September 3, 1939. Though India was far away from the war theatre in Europe the Viceroy unilatarally associated India with the Britain's declaration of war on Germany without even consulting the provincial members or the Indian leaders. Not that the public were unware or uninterested in Indian developments. The Indian nationalists were strongly anti-fascist. But to them much more absorbing than war were the domestic political developments viz, the rise of the Muslim League, the struggle between the right and left wings of the Congress, the fate of the provincial Ministers etc. The discernible feeling was that it was Britain's affair, not India's. India could only interest herself when freedom had been won. The old idea that Britain's embarrassment might be India's opportunity was widespread. There was a general approval of the cause coupled with a widespread reluctance to do very much about it. The slogan, "No taxation without representation" was changed into "no popular war effort without responsible government."

Yet the Congress was prepared to cooperate in war effort provided some minimum conditions were met, viz, a promise of post-war Constituent Assembly to determine free-India's political set-up and immediate formation of some sort of responsible government at the Centre. According to the Congress, such conditions were essential if Indian opinion was to be mobilised in favour of war. But Lord Linlithgow, in his statement of October 17, 1939, mainly reiterated the old offer of Dominion Status in a distant future and promised post-war consultations with representatives of several communities to amend the 1935 Act and setting up, for the present, of a purely consultative group of Indian politicians and representatives of the princely States with no executive power whatsoever. On the demand for an elected Constituent Assembly he remained silent. The Government was, clearly, not in a mood to yield. Frustrated, the Congress resolved not to cooperate with the British war effort. The Congress Ministries in the State resigned.

At the outbreak of the war, the Government had promulgated the Defence of India Act which, among other things, provided for precensorship of materials for publication in the Press relating to certain matters. The penalty of imprisonment was extended to five years. The Official Secrets Act was amended to provide a maximum penalty of death, or transportation, for the publication of information likely to be of use to the enemy. The Press Emergency Powers Act was also similarly amended to provide against the conveying of confidential information to the enemy or the publication of any prejudicial report which amounted to commission of a prejudicial act as defined in the Defence of India Rules.

The attitude of the Congress, in the initial months of the war, was indecisive; At the Ramgarh Congress in March 1940 a resolution was adopted for launching civil disobedience "as soon as the Congress organisation is considered fit enough for the purpose, but left the timing and form of the movement entirely to the personal direction of Gandhi. Within the Congress two distinct trends of opinion were there. Gandhi and the right-wing dominated High Command counselled restraint, tried for some kind of agreements with the British and

World War II and 'Quit India'

later unwillingly sanctioned low-key movement of a limited nature. But the entire left urged for militant anti-war and anti-government action. Though Congressmen were expecting a big move there was no immediate proposal for civil disobedience, Gandhi hastened to point out soon after the Congress Ministries had resigned .. Gandhi himself expressed doubts occasionally as to whether "Ahimsa" allowed direct support to war. He had, in fact, advised Poland, France and Britain to have recourse to non-violent resistance. But the Working committee made it clear on June 17, 1940 that it was fully prepared to back the war effort if only the British gave some concessions on the two key demands mentioned earlier-- post-war independence pledge and an immediate national government at the Centre.

In August 1940 when the "Battle of Britain" raged over the skies of an isolated island Secretary of State Amery and the Governor-General Linlithgow were prepared for some concessions to win Indian support. But Winston Churchill, the Prime Minister of the National Coalition, whittled down the proposal. Linlithgow's offer of August 8, 1940 included Dominion Status in an unspecified future, a post-war body to frame a Constitution, immediate expansion of Viceroy's Executive to include some more Indians and a War Advisory Council. The Viceroy's Executive was enlarged to give Indians a majority for the first time and a National Defence Council was set up. However, the Congress considered the "August offer" as disappointing and Gandhi at last sanctioned Civil Disobedience of an ineffective kind. The sole issue was freedom of speech and the right to make public anti-war pronouncements. Individual Congressmen, nominated by Gandhi himself (starting with Vinoba Bhave on October 17 and Jawaharlal Nehru on October 31) courted arrest by making anti-war speech. The movement petered out by the autumn of 1941 although about 20,000 had gone to jail. According to some historians, this was perhaps the weakest and most ineffective of all Gandhian movements.

So far, the Government saw little need to use specific powers to restrict the press since the nationalist press was wholly anti-fascist. But the Government's attitude changed as soon as Gandhi launched his "individual Satyagraha". On October 26, 1940 the following notification was issued:

"In exercise of the powers conferred by Clause(b) of sub-rule(1) of Rule 41 of the Defence of India Rules, the Central government is pleased to prohibit the printing or publishing by any printer, publisher or editor in British India of any matter calculated directly or indirectly, to foment opposition to the persecution of the war to a successful conclusion or of any matter relating to the holding of meetings or the making of speeches for the purpose, directly or indirectly, of fomenting such opposition as aforesaid; Provided that nothing in this order shall be deemed to apply to any matter communicated by the Central Government or a provincial Government to the Press for publication."

Sir Reginald Maxwell, Home Member of the Government of India, invited representatives of Indian and Eastern Newspaper Society to an informal discussion on this order. Debdas Gandhi, acting President of the Society, B. Shiva Rao and B.J Kirchner met the Home Member on October 31, 1940. Explaining the scope of the orders Maxwell pointed out that they did not involve any new restriction on the Press, but amounted only to an exercise of existing powers in relation to a particular class of matter. While he gladly acknowledged the general helpful attitude of the press towards the prosecution of war, the new orders were intended, he observed, to prevent the exploitation of newspapers for encouraging anti-war propaganda.

In the discussions that followed the Home Member's remarks, reference was made to the Policy of the Government underlying these orders and to certain possible difficulties and abuses in regard to their enforcement. It was pointed out by the representatives of the Society that if there was any intention to impose a strict ban on the publication of even actual news the object of the Government was likely to be frustrated. The desirability of trusting to the sense of responsibility of newspapers as regards the manner of presentation of news was stressed; and it was further pointed out that the object of the government deciding to restrict newspapers to news contained only in official communique. It was, therefore, suggested that the matter should be left to the good sense of the newspapers acting in consultation with Press Advisers. The Home Member promised to give consideration to the points and suggestions made in the course of discussion. Actually, however, no orders were issued withdrawing the restrictions. To consider all these restrictions an emergent conference of editors of newspapers from all over India was summoned to be held in Delhi on November 10, 1940. The conference was attended by about fifty editors or representatives of newspapers.

In his forthright speech, the President of the Conference K. Srinivasan, Editor of *the Hindu*, wondered that when the entire press, without a word of dissent, helped the Government in their propaganda for war effort in all possible ways the government chose to issue orders under the Defence of India Regulations" which if conformed to, would reduce the position of an editor to that of an inanimate automation. The conditions that were sought to be imposed by that order were such that no self-respecting editor could submit to them".

Srinivasan pointed out that "government have, without qualification, acknowledged the help they have so far received from the Press throughout the period of war. But the continuing drift in the policy of the Government and consequent worsening of the political situation have upset the equllibrium of those in charge of administration, and as a result we have been served with an order which, it is said, is aimed at preventing exploitation of newspapers by the sponsors of the Satyagraha Movement. A little introspection on the part of the authorities would have shown them that it is they themselves who are attempting to exploit the newspapers to help them to control the political movement in the name of efforts to win the war. The charge that the Satyagraha movement was pro-Hitler and, therefore, all publicity relating to it is fomenting anti-war activity is manifestly unjust and cannot be accepted. We must make it plain that we cannot and will not be parties to the suppression of all normal political activity in the name of war.

"It may be said in reply that for the duration of the war we must allow ourselves to be governed by methods associated with dictatorship and all talk of liberties of the citizen or the Press in a crisis is nonsense. May I remind those who may be tempted to adopt this line that in the summer of this year, when an invasion of Britain seemed imminent after the French collapse, Major Attlee declared in the House of Commons that under all circumstances the press would be free to express its views without official interference? But we have not, in this country, a National Government based on the will of the people, which, according to another Cabinet Minister, Sir John Anderson, is the surest safeguard of the liberties of the Press as of the individual. The absence of a national Government at the Centre and administration under Section 93 of the Government of India Act in seven provinces are the greatest handicaps to a successful war effort. In the conditions which are prevalent today in this country restrictions on the Press devised by an irresponsible Executive are bound to be destructive of free expression of opinion based on the publication of impartial and true reports appearing in the Press. It is a hopeful sign that the authorities in Delhi have recognised the necessity for securing the cooperation of the Press and are now prepared to meet us in overcoming our difficulties. We may at the outset reiterate that it is far from our intention to create difficulties for the Government or impede their war effort. Our sole concern is to conduct a newspaper free to express opinions frankly, and to that end factual representation of events in the widest sense must be allowed. We must have a body analogous to the Ministry of Information in England which will take counsel and act in cooperation with a body of responsible journalists in Delhi as well as at all provincial centres. The Government must have full confidence in and trust us to conduct ourselves properly as responsible members of the public.

"We, in India, are painfully aware of the many differences in the political sphere. But I am glad to feel that in regard to the liberties of the Press differences of outlook or opinion are not likely to divide us. A free press with a full sense of responsibility must be allowed to function, and it is our business to suggest to the Government the right and only method of approaching us to help them in winning the war."

The government saw reason. Within twentyfour hours, in a somewhat dramatic gesture, the notification issued under D.I. Regulations was withdrawn. On December 11, 1940 the government issued the following communique:

The government recently felt it necessary to make it plain, by an Order under the D.I. Rules, that they could not permit the publication of any matter calculated to foment opposition to the successful prosecution of the war or the open support of any movement designed to that end.

"In doing so, they intended no reflection upon the press, whose consistent support, since the outbreak of the war, in the struggle against the totalitarian Powers they readily and gratefully acknowledge.

"As the result of friendly conversation in Delhi with representatives of leading newspapers, who have given them an assurance that they have no intention of impeding the country's war effort and that any deliberate and systematic attempt by newspapers to do so would be viewed with disapproval by the Press as a whole, the Government now feel that the matter well be left to discretion of editors, in consultation with Press Advisers in cases of doubt.

"They are, therefore, pleased to withdraw the order in question.

"They are further pleased to accept a suggestion that a small advisory committee of representatives of the press, resident in Delhi, shall be set up to advise the Government on any matters affecting the press, and they will recommend to provincial governments, the constitution of similar advisory committees in the provinces."

This came to be known as Delhi Agreement.

Soon after this major achievement the conference of editors was converted into All India Newspaper Editors Conference (AINEC). A system of Press Advisers, orginally designated Press Censors, was set up in all the provinces with the Chief Press Adviser at the Centre. The arrangement was that the editor should have the benefit of the advice of the Press Adviser in the matter of publication of all news coming within the purview of D.I. Rules. But soon the Delhi Agreement came under severe strain as the overzealous Press Officers exceeded their brief and sought to maintain a rigorous control over the press. All India news published in one region was banned in another. Authenticated news was severely censored to the point of becoming misleading. Headlines were dictated and detailed instructions were issued on the position to be given to a news item and the type in which they should be set. Even the proceedings of the legislatures were censored and the full reporting of Civil Disobedience cases in the law courts was not permitted. Restrictions were also imposed on comments and criticisms of the Government and the Government officials. All powers assumed by the Government were fully exercised and the civil and military censors constituted under D.I. Rules suppressing events and views of political significance on the ground that such publications impeded the effective prosecution of war.

UNWARRANTED RESTRICTIONS

It was difficult for the editors to stomach all these unwarranted restrictions. In the following months, there were complaints of breach of agreement both from the Press and the Government. A few newspapers like the National Herald of Lucknow, Sainik of Agra, Hindustan Times of Delhi and Istiqlal of Quetta were penalised for breach of Government instructions. But in large number of cases Press Advisory Committees succeeded in avoiding needless clash between the Press and the Government.

The AINEC remained firm in its stand about supporting the Gandhian movement and asked the Government ordinarily not to ban publication of Gandhi's statements. In view of the fact that the Government had withdrawn the notification of October 1940 and the Government's assurance that they have no desire to suppress Gandhi's statements and were not disinclined to give them their special consideration, the AINEC assured Gandhi it would welcome the reappearance of Harijan weeklies whenever Gandhi in his judgment thought it fit to restart them. In the opinion of the AINEC, the temporary disappearance of the weeklies had left a void in Indian journalism.

The AINEC reaffirmed the determination of the Press in India to strive for the freedom of the country without fear or favour and consequently give legitimate publicity to news about political movement in the country. It was reiterated that since the newspapers were totally opposed to the totalitarian doctrines of Nazism and Fascism and had no intention of hindering Britain's war effort against her enemies, the Government should give the Delhi Agreement a fair trial.

But difference persisted between the AINEC and the Government over the Satyagraha movement and publication of Gandhi's statements. The Indian press could not accept the Government's interpretation that the "Satyagraha campaign" was intended for the sole purpose of impeding the war effort. The editors were worried about the health of Gandhi. They took note of the fact that Gandhi had just kept his proposed fast in abeyance; it had not been abandoned. "It is conceivable that if the Government should continue to suppress his statements he may take the view that life under such circumstances is not worth living. Indian papers, quite frankly, will not accept any responsibility for compelling him to take such a decision."

In its memorandum to the Government in December 1940 the Central Advisory Committee said:

"In the situation which is developing, nationalist papers feel entitled to regard Gandhiji's statements as exceptional and cannot fairly be expected to become willing parties to their suppression. It must be borne in mind that they are not bound to refer everything to Press Advisers, nor is there any obligation on their part to accept their advice. It is open to an editor to say, "I have accepted the advice of the Press Adviser in nine cases out of ten; but in the tenth the advice tendered is unsound and therefore I shall take the risk of publication." Every editor knows what that risk is in the existing circumstances. Government should not regard acceptance of press advising as a matter of course. No editor can or will allow his judgment to be subordinated to that of an outside authority. That would mean the imposition of rigid censorship, not the offer of press advice."

The AINEC suggested that the Government should use this opportunity for making a fresh attempt to solve the political deadlock. It was made clear that the "Press is anxious for a political settlement, without which the internal situation is bound to deteriorate. Its general support of war was based on two considerations; one is a sincere desire for a British victory, the other, an equally ardent hope that it will mean freedom for India.

In spite of Civil Disobedience and the imprisonment of large number of influential leaders, the Press continues to be friendly in its attitude towards war. If that attitude is to be positive and enthusiastic, India's freedom must be guaranteed and concrete steps taken in such a way as to eliminate the present bitterness and suspicion."

However, the Government remained non-committal on the issues raised by the editors. The Chief Press Adviser to the Government, Desmond Young, in his reply, dated January 30, 1940 reiterated that " Government have no wish to impose any further restriction on the Press or depart from the spirit of Gentleman's Agreement. At the same time, he pointed out "neither the Government of India nor the Government of any country engaged in a life and death struggle with a foreign power can permit anything which will prejudice the successful conduct of the war". In this connection he referred to the resolution the House of Commons had passed by 297 votes to 11 approving of effective Government measure against the Daily Worker of London for its habitual publication of matters calculated to impede the war effort and assist the enemy."

As regards statements by Gandhi, Young said, "Government have no desire to suppress them unless they are calculated to impede the prosecution of war or provide the enemy with propaganda material, and will certainly give their propaganda special consideration in view of the respect in which Gandhi is held and the interest which attaches to anything he writes."

Political situation in the country continued to be very fluid and confusing. Barring M.N. Roy group which felt that the war was anti-fascist and therefore demanded unconditional support, the entire Left was in favour of militant anti-war struggle. Subhas Chandra Bose was unambiguous in his stand that Britain's difficulties should be made into India's opportunity. He presided over an Anti-Compromise conference held alongside the Ramgarh session of the Congress which bitterly criticised

Gandhian moderation. Socialists were in an increasingly militant mood with Jaya Prakash Narayan contemplating armed struggle while in jail in 1941. Though the relations between the Socialists and the Communists had already worsened there was no major political difference till late 1941 so far as attitude to war was concerned." The about-turn in Comintern Policy after the Nazi-Soviet Pact of August 1939 was a serious embarrassment for the Communists in Europe but an asset for their comrades in India, allowing an easy synchronization of "Internationalists" support to Soviet policies with nationalists hostility to Britain's war— a situation which would be exactly reversed after Hitler's invasion of Russia on June 22, 1941", writes Sumit Sarkar in his Modern India.

The Left, however, failed to sustain the movement because of British repression. Subhas Bose led a Satyagraha in Calcutta in July 1940 demanding removal of Holwel Monument (a memorial to British victims of the alleged Black Hole). At least, for once the Muslim students took part in large numbers in a movement linked with the honour of Siraj-ud-daulah, the last independent Muslim ruler of Bengal. But the Hindu-Muslim unity apart, the whole thing obviously had very limited significance. Bose escaped from home internment in January 1941 and used the Communist underground network in his flight through Afghanistan and Russia to Germany.

The Indian situation qualitatively changed in the latter half of 1941 following Hitler's invasion of Russia and Japan's entry into the war. In a swift move through the South East Asia from December 1941 Japan drove the British out of Malaya, Singapore and Burma and pushed the war at the doorstep of India. Upto December 8, 1941 there were Indian leaders who felt that the war was remote and that India could remain a detached spectator of a grim contest between two rival systems (Fascism and Democracy) of world polity. Now they had to change their opinion. Very few knew that Subhas

World War II and 'Quit India'

Bose's Indian National Army (INA) was also marching towards India helped by the Japanese. As a matter of fact, both the Congress and Communist leaders had built up a resistance movement against the advance of the INA, though the Congress later took advantage of the INA's sacrifice to win the elections.

The Government of India grasped the opportunity to seek unstinted cooperation of the Press in the war efforts and to advise them to bury all differences over political issues. Addressing the sixth meeting of the Standing Committee of the AINEC in Calcutta on December 18, 1941 Sir Akbar Hydari, the first Indian Member of Information and Broadcasting with the Government of India, in a subtle speech appealed to the press to cooperate in bringing home to the people of India the perils of war, with the possibility of air raids on certain parts of the country becoming imminent. He said, "Gentlemen, I appeal to you. If you cannot forget our internal differences I appeal to you to let them stand over for the present, whether they be between India and Britain or between Hindus and Muslims, postpone them. We all stand for a certain way of life which is now threatened by the advocates of brutal force and materialism. In the face of that threat I would say to those of you who, for political reasons may be, have lukewarm in your support of the war, abandon your attitude of benovolent neutrality, for there can be no neutrality now that face to face with danger and with evil."

Translating his appeal into practical terms Sir Akbar said," In the city of Calcutta, 60,000 volunteers are wanted for the beneficient humanitarian work of the A.R.P. It is a work which has no political implications, which can be performed without acceptance of any particular constitutional or political form, and which may result in the saving of many lives. And yet the response so far has been most disappointing... not because the citizens of Calcutta are lacking in civil concern, but simply because the vital necessity and duty of undertaking this work has not been brought home to them by the Press. At the moment it is impossible to forecast how close the war will come to this city .... But would it not be criminal negligence on the part of each one of us to fail to assist in making adequate preparations against this damage? If we are caught unprepared, we shall not be able to excuse ourselves at the bar of history by saying that we did not realise that A.R.P. was our job. Will you, gentlemen, make it your special business to bring home to the citizens of Calcutta, without delay, their personal responsibilities for A.R.P.? Here at least is a matter over which we can indeed must -- unite without hesitation if we put aside our differences now and work together against a common enemy. I am convinced that the same spirit of unity which will have assisted us in the hours of danger and anxiety, will avail, after the war, to secure a settlement which will be honourable and profitable to all."

In his reply, the AINEC President Srinivasan emphasised the need for close consultations between the Government and the press and reiterated that "the press in India was animated by a single purpose, namely, that we would exercise our independent judgment of all issue and not allow ourselves to be exploited by anyone for the furtherence of a particular cause."

He urged upon the Government to make a gesture which would provide psychological background for getting Government and the people together in a common endeavour to serve and safeguard the best interests of the country.

The editors made no secret of their views that Gandhi should withdraw his Satyagraha movement taking into consideration the gravity of the international situation. But they firmly believed that an interim solution of the political deadlock was urgently needed. "The release of Satyagraha prisoners is undoubtedly a step in the right direction ....But the mere release of prisoners can only provide the atmosphere and cannot serve by itself as an adequate gesture of goodwill. Far more is necessary to convince the people that this is their war and victory will mean freedom for all, including India. As an earnest of that freedom Britain should be prepared to install immediately in the seats of power and authority, both at the Centre and in the provinces, the natural leaders of the people." (AINEC papers).

However, differences with the Government continued to persist over various issues like restrictions over daily Pratap of the Punjab, ban on the publication of certain Congress resolutions and publication of news relating to conduct of troops whose misbehaviours with the public were being frequently reported in the Press.

Meanwhile, the internal situation worsened further as war came nearer to India. Singapore fell on February 15, 1942, Rangoon on March 8, the Andaman islands on March 23. The British, at long last, felt the need to make some gestures to win over Indian public opinion. The U.S President Roosevelt took up with Churchill in Washington in December 1941 the question of Indian political reform. Two Liberal Indian leaders, Sapru and Jayakar, appealed for immediate Dominion Status and expansion of the Viceroy's Executive into a national government. Chiang-kai-Shek, during his visit to New Delhi, expressed sympathy for Indian aspirations for freedom.

In the first week of March 1942, Sir Stafford Cripps persuaded the war Cabinet to agree to a draft declaration promising post-war Dominion Status with right of secession, a constitutions-making body elected by provincial legislatures, with the individual provinces being given the right not to join it and with States being invited to appoint representatives.

The Declaration was not published immediately. Cripps came to India on March 23 to negotiate on its basis with the Indian leaders. This was not to the liking of the Governor-General Linlithgow who threatened to resign. But Churchill explained that "It would be impossible, owing to unfortunate rumours and publicity, and the general outlook, to stand on a purely negative attitude and the Cripps Mission is indispensible to prove our honesty of purpose .... If it is rejected by the Indian parties ... Our sincerety will be proved to the world."

Plagued throughout by suspicion, ambiguities and misunderstanding, Cripps Mission failed to deliver the goods. Cripps had gone beyond his brief during his talks with official Congress negotiators -- Nehru and Azad. Gandhi deliberately remained in the background throughout Cripps stay in India.

Talks eventually broke down on the question of control over defence. Linlithgow thought that Cripps was conceding too much real power to the Congress. Cripps blamed the Congress for the failure. As a matter of fact, the mission failed because of British bluff and double-dealing. From the very beginning bulk of the Congress leadership and ranks were not very enthusiastic about it. Things, in fact, were now moving rapidly towards the total confrontation between the Government and the Congress. Gandhi who had described the Cripps' proposal as a post-dated cheque on a crushing bank was in a militant mood. Leave India to God or to anarchy, he repeatedly urged the British-- "the orderly disciplined anarchy should go, and if, as a result, there is complete lawlessness I would risk it". On August 9 the Congress, at its Bombay session, passed the famous "Quit India" resolution and followed up its call for mass struggle on non-violent lines in the widest possible scale, under Gandhi.

QUIT INDIA, 1942

As India's struggle for freedom took a decisive turn the Government swung into action immediately. Fresh Notification under D.I. Rules was issued suppressing all news relating to Congress activities. The Notification prohibited "the printing or publishing by any printer, publisher or editor of any factual news (which expression deemed to include reports of speeches or statements made by members of the public) relating to mass movements sanctioned by the AICC or to the measures taken by the Government against the movement, except news derived from, and stated in the newspapers which published it, to be derived from (a) official sources, or (b) the Associated Press of India, the UPI or the Orient Press of India, or (c) a correspondent regularly employed by the newspaper concerned and whose name stand registered with the Magistrate of the district in which he carries on his work".

Over twenty leading daily newspapers adopted unprecedented and extreme course of suspendin publication in protest against "Increasing and humiliating restrictions imposed by the Central and provincial governments which made it impossible for any newspaper to function with self-respect and consistency, with due and conscientious discharge of the responsibilities to the public."

The retaliatory mood of the Press was manifest in the speeches delivered at the second session of the AINEC held at Bombay on October 5, 1942. In a hard-hitting speech B.G. Horniman, Chairman of the Reception Committee, warned the Government that editors also have their measures of retaliation. "We have what are called sanctions which we can implement on any stand we make in this matter. Suppression of news is a game to be played by two parties. If the Government suppress news that are inconvenient to them we can also suppress news which are convenient to them. It is an essential factor in their carrying on the war effort. If we are to take up that position, it will be very inconvenient to them. Unless we are prepared to keep our measures of retaliation in preparation and let it be known that we are prepared to retaliate I do not think we will get any satisfaction at all. Suppression of news, as I said, we can do more effectively .... If they (Central and provincial governments) find all their propaganda, all their communiques and speeches on Indian political situations, whether from Delhi or from Whitehall, not published, I think they will take a very much more moderate attitude. We are capable of making a complete blackout of every Government propaganda and communique."

The President of the Conference K. Srinivasan also unequivocally condemned the new restrictions and stated that the Govenment's failure to consult him before issuing their Press Note of August 8 and the subsequent notification regarding pre-censorship constituted a gross breach of Delhi Agreement. He made it clear that "there is no question of our willing submission to any proposal which, in our opinion, is derogatory to the dignity of the profession or in any way prevents us from functioning as responsible newspapers".

In its main resolution, the conference expressed its opposition to any scheme of pre-censorship and said that the Press should be free to publish without pre-scrutiny objective accounts of any incident in connection with the movement or disturbances. The Conference at the same time called upon Editors to exercise restraint in regard to such reports and also avoid exaggerated reports of misuse of powers by Government servants. Deliberate departure from this general policy was to be dealt with by Provincial Governments in consultation with the Advisory Committees. This position was accepted by the Government and this came to be known as Bombay Agreement. Most of the newspapers, who had suspended publication after the August notification, were now able to resume publication.

Nevertheless, in some "extreme" cases action was taken against an offending newspaper, more often than not, against the advice of the Press Committees. The AINEC, as a body, came into conflict with the Government when it tried to use its extraordinary powers to exclude from publications facts relating to public agitation over Prof. Bhansali's fast. This was direct violation of the Gentlemen's

World War II and 'Quit India'

Agreement between the editors and the Government. As a protest the Conference asked all newspapers to suspend publication for a day and to exclude from their papers all Government House circulars, the New Year Honours list of 1943 and speeches of members of the British Government, the Government of India and the provincial governments, with the exception of passages containing decisions and announcements. Many Indian newspapers observed Hartal on January 6, 1943 and the retaliatory measures were also strictly observed. In the meantime, Prof Bhansali called off the fast and on January 12, 1943 the Government withdrew the prohibitory order and the ban on publication of official news was reciprocally withdrawn. (Prof. Bhansali was neither a detenu nor a prisoner. As a Gandhian, he undertook the fast to protest against the behaviour of troops towards civilians in two villages in the Central Provinces).

Strong protests against the Press restrictions were also vioced by the Press Association, New Delhi. This Association of Press Correspondents, accredited to the Government of India, held an emergency meeting in Delhi on August 19, 1942 under the presidentship of Usha Nath Sen and recorded its "greatest concern" over restrictions placed on the publication and dissemination of news both within and outside India. A memorandum submitted to the Government by the Association catalogued numerous restrictive rules and regulations imposed since the commencement of the war and said that the "summary manner in which they (restrictions) have been imposed and the way in which they are operating have created the impression that the Press cannot act freely and independently and is being reduced to the position of a controlled press. While restrictions are necessary to prevent information of military value from falling into the hands of enemy, they should not be made to serve the purpose of political censorship.

Sharply criticising the provision of press advising the memorandum cited instances to prove that "Press Advising" had become pre-censorship from a political angle." Restrictions on political matter are such as to render the presentation of a balanced picture of the situation in India extremely difficult. Particularly in messages going abroad, undue preference is given to the Government point of view. Opinions from abroad condemning the Congress movement have been liberally distributed in India whereas statements such as President Roosevelt's full definition of the Atlantic Charter and recent Chinese Press comments regarding the Indian situation have been denied publicity by the authorities. Permission was refused for the publication of Gandhi's letter to Marshal Chiang Kai-Shek. "Press-advising" and military censorship constitute, in fact, double censorship resulting in delays in transmission, arbitrary deletion of passages, and occasionally even killing of entire messages. In quite a number of instances "press-advised" message of a political nature have subsequently been amended by military censors, even though they may have contained no statements relating to troops or operations. There has been prohibition of messages for countries overseas giving bare details of certain governmental measures for controlling the disturbances. For instance, messages relating to the grant of wide powers to military officers of the rank of Captain were not passed for transmission abroad."

Referring to attempts made by Press Advisers to exercise control over the entire range of news supplied by agencies, the memorandum said," The United Nations are interested in India as a vital base of operations against the Axis Powers. Excessive interference limiting the scope of messages concerning the disturbances is bound to result in a dangerously misleading picture of the Indian situation being given to the Allied countries. Internally, Press reports are judged by the Indian public in the light of personal knowledge of incidents in particular area. One-sided reports destroy public confidence in the Press and deal a blow to the professional credit of the correspondents. The decision of a large number of newspapers to close down indicates their desire to escape public censure for being purveyors of wrong and misleading version of events."

The memorandum urged upon the Government to review the system of registration of correspondents, the limitations placed on the number and character of messages, the functioning of "Press-advising" and military censorship, both of outgoing and incoming messages and all other restrictions imposed on the Press and on correspondents.

BENGAL FAMINE:

The year 1943 witnessed a terrible famine in Bengal. Rising prices and shortages with the coming of a large number of allied troops led to fears that the food reserves of the country were being depleted to feed the army. Bureaucratic mismanagement of the war reached its climax in the Bengal Order to seize all country boats and destroy them. This gravely affected the transportation of rice from the rural markets to the towns. This was a kind of "scorched warth" policy sought to be imposed by a callous bureaucracy who did not know that in many parts of Bengal during the monsoon house to house communication required boats. "To deprive people of East bengal of boats is like cutting of vital limbs". Wrote Gandhi in the Harijan of May 3, 1942.

The food crisis was caused mainly by the stoppage of rice imports from Burma and South East Asia. Rationing measures were extremely belated and inadequate and confined to a few big cities. In the terrible summer and autumn of 1943, lakhs trekked to Calcutta to starve to death on its streets begging no longer for rice but just for the rice-water. About three million perished in Bengal in a basically man-made famine. Starvation and mal-nutriton led to major epidemics of malaria, cholera and small-pox that took a heavy toll of lives. Lord Wavell, who succeeded Linlithgow as the Governor General, himself complained bitterly in private of London's indifference towards Indian food problem.

Though this was one of the greatest tragedies of the century not much news about famine came to light because of severe restrictions on the Press. When the famine was taking a heavy toll of human lives, the provincial government in Bengal tried to fight the calamity with false assurances about tackling the situation, and did not hesitate to make huge profits on the purchase of foodstuffs from the Punjab. The Government of India did not permit the foreign correspondents to cable abroad even the bare facts of deaths and hospital admissions due to starvation issued daily in Calcutta by the Director of Information to the Bengal Government. Some accounts of the prevailing distress were permitted to be cabled provided the bare horrible facts were toned down by the descriptions of Government measures to alleviate the distress. The principal motive was to keep the British and the American people in the dark about the situation. However, it goes to the credit of *The Statesman* to draw the attention of the people both in India and out of it to the "maladministration" by publishing descriptions and pictures of the horrors of famine. A British-owned paper, the Statesman drew the ire of the authorities for its courage to take the lid off the famine situation. On August 13, 1943 *Amrita Bazar Patrika* came out with a sarcastic editorial castigating the authorities for issuing false statements. The editorial captioned "A Food Millennium".

"Why should there be starvation, this all pervasive hunger and misery, bodies lying unclaimed in public thoroughfares, emaciated human beings searching for food in filthy dustbins and hundreds of men and women running to and fro for food—Why should there be heart-rending scenes of social wrong and inequity enacted in the midst of bounteous plenty? Is it then a dream, an aberration, a phantom of the monster that devours the food resources that are Bengal's? Or is it that His Excellency the Governor's Council of Ministers is frittering away these resources thoughtlessly or putting them in a hidden pool lest, as Mr Amery once suggested, the people of Bengal should bring disease and estilence by over-eating?"

These and such other editorials were punctuated by telling photographs depicting" When Man and Beast Fight for Food", "Hunger and Misery" etc. which became too faithful to be tolerated by the persons in authority and so came on the *Amrita Bazar Patrika* a suresptitious order which was also not to be published or, in any manner, referred to. The *Patrika*, however, continued to give full publicity to the famine tragedy without any Editorial for fifty days continually.

On October 8, 1943 an Order under D.I Rules was issued imposing precensorship on the *Amrita Bazar Patrika* in respect of news and articles relating to famine situation as also the general order of the same date under Clause (b) of sub-rule (i) of Rule 41 of the D.I.R prohibiting the publication of any reference in the province to the Order on the Patrika.

A former Chief Reporter of *The Statesman*, Kedar Ghosh, in his "Reminiscences of the Reporter" recorded an interesting anecdote about supression of an exclusive news item relating to the Government's "Denial Policy" which, if published unmutilated, would have lessened the severety of Bengal famine to a great extent by alerting the people of the Government's dangerous move.

He wrote: "One evening, on my routine rounds (soon after the outbreak of World War II) I went to a luxury hotel in Calcutta to nose around for important personalities among the latest arrivals. None of the names on the register smelt newsy. I did not like to draw a blank day and was hanging around. Rumours floated by. One seemed particularly interesting to the newsman in me. Some hotel executives were talking about the negotiations that had been going on between the Bengal Government and a Calcutta business firm for a contract under the "Denial Policy".

The British Army had withdrawn from Burma by then, the Japanese had bombed Calcutta, and the Indian National Army was marching into Kohima. The enemy must be denied food on Indian soil, and it had been decided to buy up all the rice from the border and coastal districts and remove it beyond the reach of the invading Army.

The tip was sufficient to set me on the chase. I hurried to the Secretariat and got the confirmation of the story from the Commerce Department. The copy was sent to the Press Censor for scrutiny, but it bore my name typed in the top left-hand corner. Consultations at the topmost level followed, and ultimately, the copy was squeezed out of the Censor's reluctant grip, greatly mutilated in the process.

The inevitable happened next morning. The man responsible for the story was summoned to Writer's Buildings, and this time the Commerce Secretary, Mr Kripalani, again a hard-boiled Indian Civil Service man, was the prosecutor. He coaxed and cajoled me, and after some time, gave it up.

The 1943 Bengal famine, the worst in recent memory, would have perhaps been averted and the man responsible prevented from creating it, had the story about the 'Denial Policy' been published at the early stage of negotiations.

It forewarned people about what was coming but the warning was not sufficiently in advance. The mischief had already been done. The agencies of the business firm concerned immediately went into action and the coastal and border districts of the province were swept clear of foodgrains. Not only that. Boats and most other types of country-craft were seized and withdrawn. As it transpired, the enemy did not come to be denied food on Indian soil; it was the sons of the soil who were denied food and were sacrificed at the altars of bureaucratic muddle-headedness and of the mammons of unrighteousness among traders and others. At least one million people died—died the death of cattle. Many cursed the authorities. Some might have cursed the Press: who knows?"

However, the Standing Committee of the AINEC which examined the *Amrita Bazar* article, took serious exception to the Government order and said," the Government have taken a needlessly alarmist view of the general feeling in the country and call attention to a very real danger which, it is the duty of all concerned to consider seriously and do everything in their power to provide against. The Standing Committee further felt that the second order of the Government banning the publication of all references to the original order was even more reprehensible and further protested against the prohibition of the publication of reference to the Bengal Order in other parts of India.

Several other newspapers were also subjected to restrictions on various issues. The Chief Press Adviser Kirchner took exception to "indecent" cartoons (a) designed to bring the Government of India into hatred or contempt, (b) those which are prejudicial to war effort, especially the ones suggest differences between the United Nations and (c) those which are vulgar or in bad taste."

On August 21, 1943 the *Hitavada* of Nagpur published news of the resignation of J.R. Blair, Chief Secretary to the Government of Bengal. The Editor A.D. Mani was immediately served with an Order under D.I. Rules, asking him to furnish within three days the name and address of the informant. The Standing Committee emphatically protested against the action of the Central Provinces Government as "an unwarranted interference with the well-established convention governing the relations between an editor and his correspondents. The Committee objected to the use of D.I. Rules to compel an editor to disclose the source of his information and requested the Government to withdraw the order. The Committee congratulated A.D. Mani on "the courage with which he had vindicated the highest tradition of the profession." Similar orders were also issued by the Bihar Government on *Patna Times* and some other Patna-based newspapers. On September 15, 1943 the *Sind Observer* wrote an editorial captioned" Ambedkar on Empire" which was based on an interview with Dr Ambedkar. The interview itself was published in *Sind Observer* and other papers on September 11. The Government of Sind objected to the editorial and issued an order under Indian press (Emergency Powers) Act of 1931 demanding a security of Rs 2000. The Sind Press Advisory Committee had considered this article and opined that it was not prejudicial report actionable under the law and was not calculated to excite the disloyalists and impede the war efforts. Read as a whole, the article was innocuous. The Standing Committee of the AINEC also held the same opinion and urged the Government of India to prevail upon the Sind Government to withdraw the Order.

There were other instances of arbitrary action by the authorities against the Press. For example, the Central Provinces Government had ordered the prosecution of the Editor, Assistant editors and the publisher of the *Hitavada* and *Nagpur Times* under Ordinance III of 1944 with previous consultation with the Provincial Advisory Committee. The AINEC specially deplored the arrest of Assistant editors as they are not legally responsible for what was published in the newspaper. Pre-censorship orders were passed on the *National Call* and the *Hindustan Times* for publishing Sarojini Naidu's statement at the Delhi Press Conference on January 25. The AINEC strongly protested against these actions and reiterated that "Press advice is not obligatory on editors and its rejection does not by itself constitute an offence." Also there were complaints of drastic and unjustified actions against *Sansar Samachar, People's War,* the *Journalist* and *Forum* under the *Indian Press* (Emergency Powers) Act in the form of demanding and forfeiting security.

Times were, doubtless, turbulent when Linlithgow was the Governor-General. But he tried his utmost to make a balance between the needs of the war and the needs of the Indian Press, and succeeded to a great extent. Despite the pinpricks the press had experienced from the bureaucrats at provincial levels the overall relations between the Press and the Government were satisfactory. The Press was particularly happy with Linlithgow for his contribution to the establishment of consultative machinery which, to a great extent, reduced the causes of clash between the Press and the Government to a great extent. For the Indian Press it was, perhaps, one of the finest moments when Linlithgow paid rich tributes, wholly deserved, to the integrity and public spirit of the Indian press before leaving the country. In his farewell address to the Central Legislature, Linglithgow observed: "Misunderstanings there may have been from time to time. But I remain grateful to this great institution for its fairness, its eager anxiety to serve the public, its concern to observe, and if possible, to improve, the best traditions of journalism, and I would not like to leave India without paying this public tribute it, to it, and to that hardworking bdoy of intelligent and able men by whom India is so well served in the Press."

By 1944 the tide turned in favour of allied forces. The Axis Powers were on the retreat. The British regained their control over their colonies in South East Asia. The campaign of INA, which appeared on the borders of Assam, ended in a failure though INA remained a source of inspiration for the people. Domestic political situation was also less turbulent than before. Taking stock of this changed situation Syed Abdullah Brelvi, the AINEC president, made a strident demand for abolishing all Press restrictions. Presiding over the third annual session of the Ainec in Madras on January 10-11 in Madras Brelvi said, "Since we held our last session in Bombay the situation has changed considerably. The Bombay Resolution was passed to meet special circumstances created by disturbances. The special circumstances having ceased to exist a revision of our existing arrangements with the Government is essential. The Press has no desire to impede war efforts. That is the basis of Delhi Agreement. It is also the basis of Delhi Agreement that the Press will not be a party to the suppression of legitimate political activities. There is nothing in the present political situation in the country to warrant any restrictions on the Press except these necessitated by purely military considerations. On the contrary, the situation demands that the Press should be absolutely unfettered to ventilate legitimate grievances regarding, for instance, the treatment of prisoners and detenus especially as unfair advantage has been taken of the Bombay Resolution by some provincial Governments to prevent this being done."

About this time the American Society of Newspaper editors mooted a proposal that the forthcoming Peace Conference should guarantee freedom of the Press throughout the world. The Society carried the matter a step further and put forward a proposal for a News Charter for the world ensuring the removal of political, economic and military obstacles to the freedom of world information in peace time. The US Secretary of State, Stettinus, revealed that the US plans for exploratory talks with other nations to secure international understanding guaranteeing that "there shall be no barrier to interchange of information among all nations." A delegation of US editors toured various countries to confer with "appropriate governmental bodies, Press associations, newspapers and radio executives regarding the "American sponsored programme for free exchange of information." The need for a World News Charter had been brought home to the American editors by the realisation that the freedom of the Press and free exchange of world information could most effectively guarantee peace. Hitler, by controlling news and radio services, prepared the German people for the war as they were prepared for the first Great War through the German News Agency, *Wolf Bureau*. The militarists of

Japan also followed similar tactics. The Americans themselves were victims of monopoly of news agencies in the purveying of news enjoyed by their respective Governments. Pointing this out, Kent Cooper, executive head of the *Associated Press of America*, said," What is not generally known and what must be fully understood, if there is to be success in purifying the flow and counterflow of international news and information, is that what the Nazis did is only an extreme form of what has gone on steadily throughout most of the world under our very nose." He complained that even as during the years immediately preceding this war, "in many countries rarely world news from the United States could be found unless it were an item dealing with a Chicago gangster killing or a Hollywood divorce case." (AINEC papers).

The AINEC welcomed the US editors move for Guarantee of freedom of the Press written into peace treaties in definite and unequivocal language. But at the same time it emphasised the need for political freedm without which "a news Charter, even if embodied in peace treaties, will not be worth the paper on which it is written." We stand for freedom of the Press. We stand for the emancipation of the readers as well as other channels of information from monopolistic control either of Government or of private agencies. While we shall cooperate with our American friends in the task they have set out to accomplish, we cannot forget that we have an urgent problem of ours to solve and we must insist that in the meanwhile, the Press in India should be placed on the same footing as the Press in Britain and in the United States .... The laws which fetter the freedom of the journalists (in India) are as formidable as they are numerous. It is true that the Press Act of 1910 of odious memory was repealed in 1922. But, unfortunately, not a few of its sinister provisions continue to be embedded in the Press Act and the Princes Protection Act, not to speak of the onerous provisions of the Indian Penal and Criminal Procedure

Acts and Customs, Post Offices and Registration of Books Act. The time has come when we should demand the immediate repeal of the Press Emergency and the Princes Protection Acts and the necessary amendment of the Penal and Criminal Procedure Acts and other Acts so as to make the Press Law in this country no more restrictive than is the Press Law in the U.S.A. or Great Britain."

The Conference adopted resolutons calling attention to the defective functioning of the Consultative machinery and also demanding revision of the Press Laws of the country so as to bring them in line with the laws in the United Kingdom and the United States. It also endorsed the American demand for guarantee of Press freedom in the Peace Treaties.

The conclusion of the war raised the question whether the consultative machinery was to be continued or scrapped. The Government held that the system should function in accordance with the Constitution of the AINEC. They also addressed the provincial Governments recommending to them the continuance of the Press Advisory Committees set up during the war or the establishment of such committees where they did not at present exist. The Government also expressed their unwillingless to enlarge the scope and functions of the Committees.

The question of removal of all controls for the "legitimate growth" of the Press was again raised in the fifth session of the AINEC held at Allahabad on February 16-17, 1946. The Conference was of the view that "as the war emergency has practically ceased, the continuance of the controls in regard to the publication of newspapers, supply of newsprint, import of machinery and grant of foreign exchange constitute an unnecessary interference with the rights of the Press and the administration of these controls, give room for serious complaints of discriminations, favouritsm and corruption."

The Conference demanded that in the future

Constitution of India, a specific declaration for the freedom of the Press, capable of being enforced in the courts of Law, should be included in the declaration of Fundamental Rights.

NEHRU'S VIEWS

Jawaharlal Nehru, who inaugurated the Conference, dwelt at length on "news suppression and freedom of news" and elaborated his personal views on these two issues and many others. On "news suppression" Nehru maintained that newspaper editors should avoid not only distortion but also suppression of news. He regretted that in India " there was not only a good deal of suppression of news by the authorities, but suppression of views as well. A sense of fear pervaded the newspaper offices. They did not dare to publish some particular news because they feared they might get into trouble ... If news was suppressed by the authorities, no newspaper could function properly, for by this a newspaper lost importance. People ceased to believe what a newspaper said or people imagined that what newspapers said was not whole truth. It was an odd thing," he said.

Nehru asked the newspapers not to be influenced by any external factors. Obviously, they had to face the continual desire of the authority to suppress news and facts. Referring to the Bengal famine Nehru said that people died by thousands and yet there was no mention of it in the papers. It was most astounding. One newspaper (*The Statesman*) ultimately broke through the cordon and news gradually came through. He also discouraged suppression of news on the ground that it inevitably made people get a false ideas of the situation and when real facts were disclosed, people were surprised and upset.

Nehru urged the newspapermen to insist on complete freedom of news, criticised the news services which were not satisfactory as the news services only covered cities and certain types of people. The rural India was forgotten, he said. Nehru also referred to the possibility of setting up a federation of a larger number of countries in the East through the development of news contacts with countries like Egypt, Iraq, Iran, Singapore and so on. He predicted that the future of Indian journalism lay with Indian language newspapers.

Tushar Kanti Ghose, Editor of *Amrita Bazar Patrika*, who presided over the session, referred to action, taken against *Natational Herald* of Lucknow, *Sansar* of *Banaras*, *Searchlight* of Patna, *Forum* of Bombay and *Swadhinata* of Calcutta and remarked sarcastically," the World War II came to an end in August 1945 but war-like spirit of the authorities did not desert them."

He pointed out that in all these cases the Press (Emergency Powers) Act was brought into requisition. "The Government are as willing to resort to ordinary law and procedure to punish an alleged offender as they were during the war". Even the flow of news was not free and despatch of news reports were interfered with by district and telegraph authorities. As many as 113 war-time ordinances had been repealed in whole or in part by Ordinance No. 1 of 1946. This was apparently very reassuring. But close scrutiny of the Government's gesture revealed that in most cases the substantive ordinances were allowed to remain intact, though with cetain amendments. It validated all and every act done under the Ordinances. And more, it did not propose to afford relief to sufferers from previous ordinances. Criticising this hypocritic policy, Ghosh commented, "to take away with one hand what has been given with the other has been the traditional policy of the powers that be in this country. We find the same spirit of niggardliness in the so-called repealing ordinance."

Ghosh put forward eight demands which included, among other things, withdrawal of D.I. Rules, repeal of war-time ordinances along with the Press (Emergency Powers) Act and Princes Protection Act, suitable amendment of laws relating to sedition, contempt of court and criminal Procedure Code so that the "laws affecting the Indian Press may be on a par with similar laws in the U.S.A. and the U.K. and all other democratic countries", and lifting of ban on the publication of newspapers, articles, books or political writings. But the Government of India pleaded their inability to reform Press Laws on the plea that "certain restrictions are found necessary even in peace time and it is impossible, in the circumstances, to reconsider these restrictions."

However, one could not miss the marked change in the attitude of the Government towards the Press after the war. The Government agreed, for the first time, to self-regulation by the organisations of newspapers themselves, thereby avoiding much of the rigours and bitterness caused by controlling measures. The first problem tackled under the system was the scarcity of newsprint which became acute during the war. Mainly to deal with this problem an association of newspaper employers, called the Indian and Eastern Newspaper Society (IENS) had already been formed in 1939. The Society managed to increase the allotment of newsprint from ten per cent made by the Government to thirty per cent. In the editorial side the most important development was the establishment of AINEC which rendered yeomen's service for a long period before it was split.

During the war years the British tried to deal with the Indian problem by sending Cripps Mission to India which failed. In September 1944 Gandhi and Jinnah met for talks on the basis of Rajaji formula. There was criticism of the meeting from the Hindu and Sikh minorities in Punjab and Bengal. However, the talks produced no result.

The Simla conference held on June 25, 1945 was attended by 21 representatives of various parties — Congress leaders had been released earlier for their participation. The proposals envisaged an Executive Council with parity of representation for Muslims. The conference ended in failure largely due to the insistence of the Muslim League that the Muslim members of the Council would be chosen exclusively by them. This would have been disastrous for the Congress which claimed to represent all minorities.

Meanwhile, two developments of far-reaching consequences took place. In November 1945 a British move to put the INA men on trial immediately sparked off massive demonstrations all over the country. The trial had a profound impact on the Indians. Congress leaders like Jawaharlal Nehru were critical of Subhas Bose as he was associated with "Fascists"; but even recognised his flaming patriotism. Three officers of the INA were charged with waging war against the King Emperor: they were Col. Shah Nawaz, Captain Shegal and Lt. Dhillon. A defence committee was formed and Nehru himself was one of its members. The trial was notable for the brilliant advocacy of Bhulabhai Desai. But as expected the accused were sentenced to transportation. The C-In-C subsequently remitted their sentence and the three toured the country as heroes.

The British became more concerned and extremely nervous about the INA spirit spreading to the Indian Army. The disaffection in the British Indian Army during the winter of 1945-46 culminated in the great Bombay Naval mutiny in February 1946. These were, perhaps, the two most significant developments that convinced the British that India could not be held in bondage any more. The announcement of British Cabinet Mission to India was made on February 19, one day after the naval mutiny broke out. The Mission consisting of Lord Pethick-Lawrence. Secretary of State for India, Sir Stafford Cripps and A.V. Alexander arrived in India in March, 1946 to discuss with the Indian leaders and the Viceroy the terms and conditions of an orderly and smooth transfer of power to Indian hands and arrangement for framing India's future Constitution by Indians themselves. But the Mission failed to bring the Congress and the Muslim League together because of Jinnah's intransigence. In the circumstances, Gandhi was obliged to advice the Mission to furmualate the plan on their own which might form the basis of discussion between the differing parties. On May 16 the Cabinet Mission announced its plan which was as reasonable a compromise as could be devised to break the impasse. In brief, it was a compromise, on the one hand, between the "almost universal desire outside the supporters of the Muslim League, for the unity of India" and on the other, "very genuine and acute anxiety of the Muslims lest they should find themselves subjected to a perpetual Hindu majority rule". Pending the framing of a Constitution by a national Constituent Assembly, whose members would be elected by the newly-elected members of the provincial assemblies, the Viceroy would proceed with the formation of interim national Government. Reacting favourably to the plan Gandhi described it as "the best document the British Government could have produced in the circumstances". But Jinnah criticised the plan for its "commonplace" and exploded arguments and insisted that Pakistan was the only solution. Frustrated, Jinnah declared August 16 as "Direct Action Day". The immediate upshot of the call was communal carnage in Bengal, then ruled by Muslim League, and Bihar where thousands of innocent people, both Hindus and Muslims, became victims of medieval mob fury.

Meanwhile, the Viceroy coaxed Jinnah to let the Muslim League join the interim National Government. But the Muslim League came in only to wreck the Government from within so as to demonstrate that there could be no national government of "two nations".

In all these developments, Press was a direct participant. Ballabhbhai Patel, who was Minister for Home and Information in the new Government, appealed for the cooperation of the Press, counselled them to observe due caution in regard to reports and comments on communal disturbances and announced the Government's intention to set up a Press laws Enquiry Committee.

Addressing the Standing Committee of the AINEC on

October 13, 1946 Patel assured the editors that the "Interim Government is most anxious to have cooperation of the Press in the difficult task that lies ahead of us. We shall scrupulously respect freedom of the Press; in fact we shall help it to exercise its legitimate functions: and we have every confidence that the Press on its part, will assist us in administering the affairs of the country during the strenuous times through which we are passing, because of the change-over from foreign rule to Independence. It will be your responsibility to guide and reflect public opinion during this formative period. I am sure you will discharge it with credit to your calling and benefit to yor motherland."

While underscoring the need for "unfettered freedom" of the Press in the presentation of news and expression of views, he reminded the Press of its obligation to preserve the integrity of the State and support the legitimate activities of a popular government. "It must, when occasion demands, help the government in defeating the forces of disruption. Negatively as well as positively, the press should discourage unruly elements. When feelings run high and tempers are frayed, it is the duty of every responsible person to desist from saying or doing things which are likely to inflame passions. Incitement to violence will, of course, not be tolerated. But there are forms of writing containing veiled incitement which do great harm. I do hope and trust you will avoid both."

Patel lauded the Central Press Advisory Committee for formulating certain guidelines for the Press in respect of news and comments on communal disturbances. These were:-

(1) During riots, reports should not contain anything to indicate the community of either victims or assilants;

(2) While every endeavour should be made to ensure that reports are factually correct and are received from sources known to be reliable, such reports

as give details in defance of the law are calculated to inflame public feelings or to create communal hatred should be treated with the greatest circumspection;

(3) Reports of speeches, statements of news directly inciting people to violence should be avoided;

(4) Care should be taken in editorials to avoid expressions calculated to encourage or condone violence or arouse communal bitterness.

The friction between the Congress and the Muslim League created a rift in the ranks of the Press as well. The disturbances which occurred with disastrous frequency evoked sinister echoes in sections of the Press. Popular feelings were seriously inflamed by what appeared in the Press and various attempts were made through local codes and coventions to allay a mischief which law and public opinion were unable to restrain. In Bombay and Delhi well-defined voluntary codes were put into operation. When the malady was spread all over India local remedies were not of much avail. The section of the Press which was in sympathy with the Muslim League was not willing to be restrained by Codes evolved by the AINEC. The Government of India then called a conference of the editors in Delhi when an ad hoc committee consisting of members of both sections was set up. It amended the AINEC Code by enlarging it.

At an emergency meeting of the Standing Committee of the AINEC held in December 1946 Patel explained the circumstances under which an adhoc committee came into being. There was a suggestion that a special session of the Conference should be summoned to deal with the communal situation, so as to give some specific lead to the Press; but in view of the tension in the country the suggestion was not pressed. When the Standing Committee met in Delhi in February 1947 it was overwhelmed with complaints and cross-complaints over inflamatory writings in the Press and repressive actions on the part of the provincial governments, specially Bengal and Punjab. The Committee passed a resolution urging self-restraint on the part of the Press and justice on part of the Government.

PARTITION OF INDIA

The partition of the country under the Mountbatten plan threw the country into a convulsion. The bloodshed on the border coloured the ink of communally-minded journalists elsewhere and the Government found it necessary to bring back the D.I. Rules in the shape of Public Security Laws. These laws armed the local governments with powers of pre-censorship, suppression and confiscation. The AINEC evolved a fresh Code relaxing the restrictions in some respects but tightening them where the safety of the State was involved. The Government accepted the Code as a working arrangement.

Before closing this chapter it has to be mentioned that the war was a blessing in disguise for the people of India and the Press as well. It goes without saying that while the war hastened the process of transfer of power it had opened up new avenues of employment for educated youngmen in the newspaper industry which recorded phenomenal development. The war enormously expanded the circle of reading public. The benefit had been shared by the English language newspapers along with their Indian language contemporaries. The Indians gave striking evidence of their business capacity in almost every branch of industry and commerce, including the newspaper industry. However, this development was viewed with misgivings by many who feared that with the growth of capitalism in the newspaper industry, journalism would cease to be a mission and that it would assume the character more and more of a profession. It was felt that with timely action and team spirit the Indian Press could be saved from the fate that had overtaken American journalism which had come to be largely controlled by newspaper trusts and cartels.

Doubts were there among a section of journalists about the shape of things to come in the newspaper industry in free India. Addressing the fifth session of the AINEC at Allahabad in February 1946, Tushar Kanti Ghosh, President, said, "It is only by our united efforts that we can protect the Press from the assaults of a power-intoxicated bureaucracy. Even when the country will be free, I do not believe that the Press will have no more difficulties to overcome. Party spirit and intolerance born out of it, even totalitarianism in another form, may emerge as a danger to the Press. We will, therefore, have to exercise constant vigilance as the price of liberty. The team spirit that was evident among Indian newspapers as a whole has been our great asset. Let us not incontinently dissipate that asset in the false belief that now that the war is over, it will be all smooth sailing for us." Speaking almost in the same vein Devdas Gandhi said, while addressing the sixth session of the AINEC in Madras in April 1947 as its President, "I shall not disagree with the view that the Press must keep its powder dry to defend itself against encroachments on its rights which may in due course develop even from the side of popular Government."

These statements turned out to be prophetic as would be evident from the developments in the post-independence era.

" I would rather have a completely free Press with all the dangers involved in the wrong use of that freedom than a suppressed or a regulated Press."

Jawaharlal Nehru

12
INDEPENDENCE AND AFTER

Independence on August 15, 1947 marked the end of the glorious struggle of the Indian Press for freedom, which, to a great extent, was synonymous with the people's struggle for political freedom, and the beginning of a new era promising a democratic policy where the Press can breathe freely. Most of the proprietors and editors of the nationalist Press were, directly or indirectly, associated with the freedom struggle. They underwent the same type of privation as the political freedom fighters. The rapport between the nationalist Press and the Congress at the Centre and in the provinces reduced the area of confrontation, for the time being, at least. "The old conflict between the Press and the State has vanished overnight", claimed the AINEC President Devdas Gandhi. Besides, Independence saw almost total withdrawal of British journalism from India. Most of the British-owned newspapers changed hands having lost their relevance in the changed political situation.

The Press creditably adjusted itself to this change, even going to the extent of observing "restraints" in view of the post-partition communal orgy in the sub-continent. This was perhaps the first test of earnestness of the

Indian Press to voluntarily place the interest of the country above everything else. The Press was prepared to cooperate with the State in the immense task of maintaining peace and sacrifice some of the liberties in the matter of factual reports of events. Bearing in mind the need for the cultivation of harmonious relations between the various sections of the people and the paramount obligation of the Press to contribute in a positive way to the restoration and maintenance of peaceful conditions in the country the AINEC in October 1947 framed the following seven-point Code for the Press:

(a) All editorial comments, expression of opinion, whether through statements, letters to the editor, or in any other form, shall be restrained and free from scurrilous attacks against leaders and communities, and there shall be no incitement to violence;

(b) News of incidents involving loss of life, lawlessness, arson etc shall be described and reported in strictly objective terms and shall not be heavily displayed;

(c) Items of news calculated to make for peace and harmony and to help in the restoration and maintenance of law and order, shall be given prominence and precedence over other news;

(d) The greatest caution shall be exercised in the selection and publication of pictures, cartoons, poems etc.

(e) Figures of casualties and names of communities shall not be mentioned in the headlines;

(f) The source from which the casualty figures are obtained shall always be indicated and no figures shall be circulated or published without fullest verification;

(g) Nothing shall be published that is in conflict with the safety of the State.

However, the Provincial Press Committees were free to come to any working arrangements, not inconsistent with the above, with provincial governments.

The Government of India accepted the voluntary Code as a "working arrangement in the belief that it will help in the supreme task of restoration and maintenance of peaceful conditions in the country."

Recommending the new Code to be adopted by all editors Devdas Gandhi, in a circular addressed to all members said," You will note that the Code is recommended for adoption throughout India and takes the place of previous Codes and Conventions." He requested the editors to see that the fullest effect was given to the Code and hoped that Provincial Press Advisory Committees and provincial Governments would treat the new Code as the basis of their dealings with the Press so far as the present emergency was concerned.

The country experienced a trauma when Gandhi fell to the bullets of Nathuram Vinayak Godse in Birla House, Delhi, on January 30, 1948. The first political assassination in free India, and that too of the apostle of non-violence sent shock waves throughout the world. The Indian Press rose to the occasion as one man to condemn this dastardly act and demonstrated its maturity in paying homage to the departed great in a befitting manner. The *Hindustan Standard* of Calcutta excelled all others by leaving the editorial column blank. While placing on record the deep sense of grief and sorrow over the tragic martyrdom of Gandhi the Press took a special note of the fact that Gandhi worked ceaselessly as a journalist for nearly fifty years. In his work as an editor and as a writer he set up standards of precision, veracity, fearlessness and fairness to opponents which have served as a model to all those who belong to the profession", said a resolution adopted by the AINEC on April 19, 1948. It was a truism, to say the least.

However, Gandhi's death had a salutary effect on

the communally-surcharged atmosphere in the subcontinent which eased to some extent.

GENEVA CONFERENCE:

A very important event during the year, so far as the Press was concerned, was the UN Conference on freedom of information held in Geneva in March-April, 1948. This conference was called in pursuance of the resolution passed in February, 1946 by the General Assembly of the UN, that the latter could not achieve the purpose for which it had been created unless the poeple of the world were fully informed of its aims and activities, that freedom of information was a fundamental human right and was the touch-stone of all freedoms to which the UN was consecrated, and that, finally, understanding and cooperation among nations were impossible without an alert and sound world opinion, which, in turn, was wholly dependent on freedom of information.

The conference passed 43 resolutions and three Conventions on (a) freedom of information (b) gathering and international transmission of news and (c) the institution of an international right of correction of false and distorted reports likely to injure friendly relations between States. Freedom of expression apart, the Conference also discussed the shortage of newsprint and difficulties in regard to the supply and improvement of physical facilities due to distinction between soft and hard currencies.

On news agencies, the conference expressed the view that the countries where national news agencies were not sufficiently developed, provisional measures might appropriately be taken by governments to encourage their development as independent news agencies and that at no time should the development of foreign news agencies by unfair and abnormal means be allowed to prejudice the normal development of national news agencies.

Although the conference considered the need for a

Code of Conduct for the journalists and the requisite machinery for its implementation it preferred to refer the question to United Nations Sub-committee on Freedom of Information and the Press. In view of the fact that freedom of information carried with it duties and responsibilities the conference laid down that the freedom would be subject to necessary penalties, liabilities and restrictions clearly defined by law, but only with respect to the following: (a) matters which must remain secret in the interest of naional safety (b) expressions which incite persons to alter by violence the system of Government or which promote disaster; (c) expressions which are obscene or which are dangerous for youth and expressed in publications intended for them; (d) expressions which are injurious to the fair conduct of legal proceedings; (e) expressions which infringe literary or artistic rights; (f) expressions about other persons which defame their reputations; (g) legal obligations resulting from professional, contractive or other legal relationships including disclosure of information received in confidence in a professional or official capacity; and (h) the prevention of fraud.

INDIA-PAKISTAN AGREEMENT:

An inter-dominion conference was held in May 1948 at Calcutta to discuss certain outstanding issues affecting both Pakistan and Indian Union. An agreement was arrived at which, among other things, referred to the part that had to be played by the Press. It said:—

"Both Governments recognize that the whole-hearted cooperation of the press is essential for creating a better atmosphere and, therefore, agree that every effort should be made in consultation of the representatives of the Press, wherever possible, to ensure that the Press in each Dominion does not:

(a) indulge in propaganda against the other Dominion;

(b) publish exaggerated versions of the news of a character likely to inflame, or cause fear or alarm to the population or a section of the population in either Dominion;

(c) publish material likely to be construed as advocating a declaration of war by one Dominion against the other Dominion or suggesting the inevitability of war between the two Dominions."

The AINEC President whole-heartedly endorsed the three points and called upon the editors to make their best effort to see that their newspapers conform to the principles enunciated in those points. "The Press can do no greater service than by the exercise of the utmost restraint at the present moment and by going out of their way to foster good feeling between the two Dominions," he said.

There was another inter-dominion conference in New Delhi in December 1948 when the Calcutta Agreement of April was reviewed. A revised agreement was arrived at which, in addition to the Press, covered the media of books, broadcasts and film with special stress on the need for discouraging propaganda for the amalgamation of India and Pakistan or of portions thereof and of warmongering.

At the instance of the Governmment a special appeal was issued by the President calling upon the Press to cooperate on the lines of December Agreement. The revised agreement also provided for the appointment of an inter-Dominion information Consultative Committee including representatives of the Press.

Earlier in March 1947, the Government of India had set up an Enquiry Committee to report on the Press Laws in force in the country. The Committee was directed to review the Press Laws of India with a view to examining "if they were in accordance with the fundamental rights formulated by the Constituent Assembly of India".

The Committee recommended, inter alia, repeal of the Press (Emergency Powers) Act, 1931, and the

Independence And After

incorporation of some of its provisions in the general statutes laying down the law of crime.

It also reecommended:

(1) certain minor amendments in the press and Registration of Books Act;

(2) The repeal of the Indian States (Protection against Disaffection Act, 1922 and the Indian State (Protection) Act, 1934;

(3) The repeal of the Foreign Relations Act and the enactment, in its place, of a more comprehensive measure on the basis of reciprocity;

(4) The modification of Section 124-A of Indian Penal Code and exclusion of the application of Section 153-A of the advocacy of peaceful change in the socio-economic order;

(5) Section 144 of the Criminal Procedure Code not to be applied to the Press, separate provision being made, if necessary, in case of emergency;

(6) Amendment of the Telegraph Act and the Post Office Act to provide for the review by responsible Ministers of the Government of the actions and orders of subordinate officers.

The Committee further recommended that all actions taken against the Press in the exercise of the emergency powers should be preceded by consultations between the provincial Governments and the Press Advisory Committees or similar body.

But the bonhomie between the press and the new rulers did not last long as the latter lost no time to show their teeth as true successors of the oppressive alien rulers. The hitch occurred on the two issues of (a) Public safety Legislation and (b) absence of freedom of the press as a fundamental right in the Constitution and amendment of the Constitution to put "resonable restriction" on freedom of expression. Opposing the

Public Safety Legislation, the AINEC said that "such legislation militates against free expression of public opinion and is not only open to abuse, but has been actually abused by the executive authority in some provinces."

While recognising the need for the executive to be clothed with special powers under conditions of national emergency and while calling for a due sense of responsibility in stabilising India's newly-won freedom the AINEC demanded that legislation conferring such wide powers should be revised, particularly in the direction of providing suitable safeguards including, above all, judicial review of executive action. It also demanded that all actions taken under emergency measures should be reviewed in consultation with the representatives of the Press. But the Central Government stuck to its old position that some restrictions were necessary in view of the state of undeclared emergency. However, Home Minister Patel assured the AINEC that the "special powers would not be used arbitrarily."

Friction also developed over the question of recognising freedom of the Press as a Fundamental Right. The Constitution of India has defined the "freedom of speech and expression" as a Fundamental Right under Article 19 (i) (a). No special provision was there in the Fundamental Rights on freedom of Press as such, but it is included in the freedom of speech and expression. A new set of problems arose over the exercise of this right. Certain newspapers, against whom action had been taken, with or without the advice of the Press Advisory Committees, successfully appealed to the High Courts and the Supreme Court which over-ruled actions of the executive on the ground that they were ultra vires of Article 19 (2) of the Constitution which laid down that "nothing in sub-clause (a) clause 1 of the Article shall affect the operation of any existing law insofar as it related to, or prevents the State from making law relating to libel, slander, defamation, contempt of court or any matter which offends against decency, morality or which under-mines the security of, or tends to overthrow, the State".

Apart from the law, the court decisions placed the authorities in an invidious position. Nevertheless, the Government of India decided to amend Article 19 (2) of the Constitution. The journalists all over the country made strong protests. Without paying any heed to their protests the Government of India introduced an amendment which was passed in 1951. The amendment provided that the freedom of speech and expression could be curbed by such" reasonable restrictions" as the liegislature may deem necessary to impose in the interest of the security of the State, friendly relations with foreign States, public order, decency, morality, or in relation to contempt of court, defamation or incitement to an offence. In 1963, a further amendment provided for restrictions "in the interest of sovereignty and integrity of the country".

This amendment, despite protests from the journalists and votaries of Press freedom, brought, for the first time since Independence, the Press and the Government on a confrontation course. The AINEC, at its Bombay session on June 24, 1951, adopted resolutions condemning the amendment as a threat to freedom of expression; it directed all newspapers and periodicals to publish prominently the following: "Freedom of expression is our birthright and we shall not rest until it is fully guaranteed by the Constitution." It called upon newspapers or the country to suspend publication on July 12, 1951, as a mark of protest. It called upon every candidate standing for election to pledge to work for and secure the repeal of the amendment of the Constitution; and finally, it resolved to suspend the working of all committees functioning in an advisory, consultative or associate capacities with the Government.

Only a few newspapers responded to AINEC's call and still fewer published the pledge. In the same year, the representatives of AINEC and the Indian Federation of Working Journalists (IFWJ) separately met the Home Minister, C. Rajagopalachari, in Delhi when he explained to them the purport of the Press (Objectionable Matters) Bill which, although more comprehensive than any earlier legislation affecting the Press, made all actions by the Government against the Press subject to judicial scrutiny. The Press (Objectionable Matters) Act became law in the same year, after some amendments suggested by the editors had been incorporated.

The Preamble of the Act looked innocuous as it was to provide against the printing and publication of incitement to crime and other objectionable matters. Also there were other improvements. While the Act of 1931 was permanent statute, this Act was a temporary one to remain in force for a period of two years. The new Act provided for a judicial enquiry by a Sessions Judge before security could be demanded from a printing Press or forfeited to the Government; and the person against whom a complaint had been made, could demand the matter to be determined with the aid of a jury, and had a right to appeal from the order of the sessions judge to the High Court.

The Act was followed by the repeal of four central and five State Acts and provisions in hitherto State Acts relating to printing, publication and distribution of any newspapers, news-sheets, books or other documents, whether by providing for the pre-censorship thereof or for the demand of security from the printer or publisher or another manner declared void.

"The enactment of the measure goes back in principle on the recommendations of the Press Laws Committee of 1921 and 1948 in as much as both committees favoured the dispersal of the provisions against the Press through the Indian Penal Code and Criminal Precedure Code so as to sustain the principle that the ordinary law of the land, rather than special enactments, should govern the control of the Press. The two views represent two distinct schools of thought, and broadly speaking, it may be said that while American opinion favours special laws, the convention in Britain is to secure control of the Press through the application of the general laws of the country. The American Press Commission clearly held that the freedom of the Press does not mean that the general laws of the country should be inapplicable to the Press or that special laws should not be adopted to govern certain types of utterences.

The real gain to the Press accruing from the enactment of the Press (Objectionable Matters) Act of 1951 was that all executive actions were made subject to the decisions of a Court of Law. The gain was not inconsiderable, for while action taken under the Press Act of 1910 and the Press (Emergency Powers) Act of 1931, ran into thousands, under the present law action has been taken between February 1, 1952, and October 31, 1953, in 134 cases; out of 86 cases in which security was demanded, security was ordered to be taken in 16 cases, 47 cases were pending. Applications were rejected in 20 cases, two cases were withdrawn and in one case warning was administered. In the other 48 cases, there were orders of forfeiture under Section 11. At the same time, it is a point to consider that over a wide area of the Press, the mere thought of prosecution has acted as a deterrant against the full exercise of the freedom of the Press." (History of Indian Journalism p 177).

The AINEC persisted in its opposition to the measure even after it was enacted. The IFWJ also recorded its protest and urged for a comprehensive enquiry into the working of the Press. Soon the Government of India announced its intention to set up a Press Commission and the controversy about the amendment of the Constitution and the newly-enacted Press law subsided. Composed of the representatives of the leading newspaper organisations, the Press Commission started its work on October 11, 1952 under the chairmanship of Sri Justice G.S. Rajadhyaksha. The Commission which examined the question of further extension of the Press

(Objectionable Matters) Act was divided. The majority sought to rely on internal control of the Press by a Press Council and expressed the desire that the Government should drop the Special Act after two years if the Press Council succeeded in checking those who indulged in the publication of obectionable matter. The implementation of this recommendation by the Government was a landmark in Indian democracy. The Act of 1951, which was extended up to February 1956, was allowed to lapse thereafter and it was also formally repealed by a subsequent Repealing Act of 1957.

FIRST PRESS COMMISSION

The first Press Commission made a comprehensive study of the problems of the Indian Press and submitted a valuable report in 1954. The Commission found that at the end of 1952 there were 330 dailies, 1189 weeklies and 1733 journals of other periodicities in existence. The dailies had a combined circulation of a little over 25 lakh copies. Finding that the circulation of newspapers was low, the Commission observed that "there was an immediate potential for a large increase in readership, much greater in the rural areas than in urban area." It found that the reasons preventing interested households from going in for newspapers were primarily "the cost and lack of distribution facilities."

The Commission recommended a socially-responsible role for the Indian Press and envisaged a continuation, in new circumstances, of a role which the nationalist section of the Press had pledged during the long years of independence movement. It stressed not only "the need for maintenance of professional standards with regard to accuracy, comprehensiveness and objectivity but also the objective towards which journalism should strive." The Commission observed. "In our view it is only a clear perception of the objective, which can give a meaning and significance to the vocation of journalism. The ultimate goal of Indian Society has been very clearly defined in the Directive Principles embodied in the Constitution. This is to secure and protect a social order in which justice— social, economic and political — shall inform all the institutions of national life". The goal was more explicitly defined later, during 1976, when Parliament adopted 42nd Constitutional Amendment which, inter alia, amended the Preamble to describe the Indian State, as a "Soverign Socialist Democratic Republic" (in place of "Sovereign Democratic Republic").

The Commission also dealt at length with issues like the role of the Press in maintaining communal harmony; Constitution and Press laws; right to information and Official Secrets Act; precensorship, defamation, disclosure of sources of information; contempt of legislature; composing and printing, ownership pattern of newspapers and periodicals, status of newspaper editors, functions of domestic news agencies, journalism training etc.

Between February 1956 and December 1975, there was no comprehensive or specific Press laws of the Union of the nature of the Press (Emergency Powers) Act, 1931 or the Press Objectionable Matters Act, 1951. But piecemeal attempts were made to control and punish prejudicial publications by introducing or amending the criminal laws.

Meanwhile, the Government sought to curb Press freedom through the backdoor by enacting the Newspaper (Price and Page) Act, 1956 which, though an ameliorating measure, had an indirect restrictive effect. The enactment of Newspaper (Price and Page) Act, 1956 and its annulment by the Supreme Court in 1962 illustrated how the freedom of the Press might be interfered with by the Government indirectly.

The Act was made with the seemingly laudable object of preventing unfair competition among newspapers through price under cutting and to protect the smaller newspapers from unfair competition of the bigger newspapers having larger financial resources. Another object was to prevent monopoly of the few commercial groups owning big newspapers.

The Supreme Court turned down both these contentions.

After the expiry of the Press (Objectionable Matters) Act, 1951 Parliament enacted the criminal law Amendment Act, 1961 imposing restrictions upon the freedom of expression and of Press as well as the freedom of Assembly and of movement, on grounds of security of the State and public order.

During the Chinese aggression in 1962 the Government proclaimed emergency which was followed by Defence of India Ordinance. The Ordinance was embodied in the Defence of India Act on December 12, 1962. The Act empowered the Central Government to make rules in respect of a number of matters including —

(i) the prohibition of publications or communication prejudicial to the civil, defence or military operations;

(ii) the prevention of prejudicial reports;

(iii) the prohibition of printing or publishing any prejudicial matter in any newspaper; demanding security from any press which is used for printing such matter and forfeiture of such security; closing down any press which continues in such activity even after forfeiture of security.

A Press Council, patterned after the British Press Council, was set up in 1966 under the Press Council Act, 1965 enacted in implementation of the Press Commission recommendations. The object of establishing the Council was to preserve the freedom of the Press and to maintain and improve the standards of newspapers in India. It was to form a Code Conduct to prevent writings which were not legally punishable but were yet "objectionable".

The Press Council Act was followed by the enactment of three other measures affecting the Press. These were: The Civil Defence Act of 1968, the Criminal and Election Laws (Amendment) Act of 1969 and the Indian Penal Code Amendment Act of 1969.

Independence And After

Events flowed rapidly during the 20-year period from 1950 to 1970. The Government's failure, because of various constraints, to meet the rising expectations of the people created serious problems and generated tensions. The whole country was in turmoil over the reorganisation of States on linguistic basis. Emotions ran high over claims and counter-claims. Many States witnessed linguistic riots. Soon after the reorganisation of States the Goa problem came up with the Portuguese authorities vainly trying to brutally suppress the liberation movement. After the liberation of Goa in 1961 India had to face Chinese aggression in 1962. The betrayal of the Chinese, who had apparently established "Bhai Bhai" relations with India a couple of years before the war, a too much for Jawaharlal Nehru to bear mentally and physically. He suddenly fell ill at the Bhubaneswar Congress session in 1962 and ultimately passed away in 1964. A year after Nehru's death Indo-Pak border became live when Pakistan declared war on India in 1965 and met with an ignominious defeat. Lal Bahadur Shastri who was the Prime Minister at that time, had gone to Tashkent in the USSR where he signed a joint-declaration with the Pakistan President Ayub Khan. Soviet Russia acted the peace-broker. Shastri did not come back home as he died at Tashkent a few hours after signing the Declaration. Nehru's daughter Indira Gandhi, who succeeded Shastri took some drastic economic measures like bank nationalisation and abolition of Privy purse to revamp the country's economy and the sagging morale of the people. Political situation underwent dramatic changes with the split in the Congress over the election of V.V. Giri as the President of India. Pakistan, still licking the wounds of 1965 war, again attacked India following the outbreak of a revolution in East Pakistan in 1971 under the leadership of the Awami League leader Mujibur Rahman. A state of emergency was declared in the country to meet the situation. Pakistan was again humbled by the Indian Army. The outcome of the 14-day war was the emergence of independent Bangladesh. The development was a shot in the arm of Indira Gandhi's Congress which returned to power following a spectacular victory in 1971 elections. During this period the newspaper industry also recorded a fast growth. The number of newspapers in the country increased from 8026 in 1960 to 11036. The number of daily newspapers had gone up from 465 in 1960 to 695 with a circulation of 82.99 lakh. The circulation of daily newspapers in 1970 recorded an improvement of about 8.1 per cent over the previous year. With 695 dailies India remained the second largest publisher of daily newspapers in the world.

A special study made by the Registrar of Newspapers of the growth of Hindi and English newspapers during the period from 1964 to 1969 showed that number of Hindi dailies increased from 159 in 1964 to 208 in 1969 and their circulation increased from 8.65 lakhs to 11.91 lakhs. During the same period the number of English dailies hd gone up from 62 to 74 and their circulation had increased from 15.41 lakhs to 19.53 lakhs. That is to say, English dailies numbering a little more than one-third of the total number of Hindi dailies commanded more than 64 per cent of the total circulation of Hindi dailies.

The all-round growth of the Press augured well for the Indian democracy the success of which depended on the blossoming of as many ideas as possible. Elaborating the concept the first Press Commission observed: "Democratic society lives and grows by accepting ideas, by experimenting with them and where necessary, rejecting them. It is necessary, therefore, that as many as possible of these ideas which its members hold are freely put before the public."

But in the discharge of its functions as the watch-dog of public interest the Press got into the hair of the Government. In 1950 while addressing the AINEC Jawaharlal Nehru declared," I have no doubt that even if the Government dislikes the liberties taken by the press and considers them dangerous, it is wrong to interfere with the freedom of the press. I would rather have a completely free Press with all the dangers involved in the wrong use of that freedom than a suppressed or a regulated Press." But Nehru's daughter had altogether different ideas about the Press. During her rule the Press gave full support to all the measures taken by her Government to safeguard the unity and integrity of the country. But on the questions of bank nationalisation, abolition of privy purse, appointment of a Chief Justice of Indira's own choice superseding three senior judges of the Supreme Court and such other economic and political issues there was hardly any unanimity and each newspaper had its own views about them and it expressed them freely. During her rule the newspapers were broadly divided into two groups— "independent and uncommitted" Press and "committed" party Press. With all their imperfections, the majority of the non-party Indian newspapers had no preconceived line on political affairs of the country, and therefore, they often differed with each other in their editorial comments on many national controversies. This was not to the liking of Indira Gandhi who only wanted a "committed" Press which would render unqualified support to all measures taken by her Government and also by her personally as the Congress leader.

As a matter of fact, from the day Indira Gandhi came back to power in 1971 mid-term poll on radical Socialist plank her Government's intolerance of Press freedom became strident. The three charges made against the Press by her Government were (a) the Press reflected only the monopoly business and was unrepresentative of the public opinion; (b) it consistently opposed the Government's economic policies; and (c) during the mid-term poll of 1971 it failed to reflect the electoral trends. Indira dismissed the Indian Press as of no consequence as it "represents hardly five percent in the country".

"As the Government's policies turned more and more radical, its confrontation with the press developed a sharper edge. In the post-split Indira Gandhi era, that cnflict degenerated into veritable feud. A rigid control on newsprint distribution and import of machinery has been turned into an instrument blatantly to discriminate against the bigger newspapers on the plea of helping the smaller and weaker units among them. In addition, the Damocles' Sword of the measure for the diffusion of newspaper ownership hangs over the head of the Press," wrote D.R. Mankekar in his 'Press Under Pressure'.

NEWSPAPER ECONOMICS

Meanwhile, in April 1972 a fact finding committee was set up, with Dr Bhabotosh Datta as the Chairman, to enquire into the economics of newspapers. The Committee was to evolve norms for different elements of expenditure from the point of reasonableness combined with efficiency and examine the prevailing levels of expenditure with reference to such norms; and to record its findings in regard to the effect of restriction on newsprint supplies to different categories of newspapers and the fair prices to be charged by newspapers of different categories.

The report of the Committee, submitted in January 1975, brought to light many hitherto undisclosed aspects of newspaper economics. The Committee found that during the period under review from 1967 to 1973 the share of metropolitan dailies in total daily circulation fell from 46.5 per cent in 1967 to 39.1 per cent in 1973, the non-metropolitan dailies correspondingly increased their share from 53.5 per cent to over 60 per cent. This showed that the provincial and local papers are successfully competing with and holding their own, against the metropolitan daily papers. During the period under review, most of the Urdu papers in the country were small circulation papers and served local population only.

The report said: "If ther is a strong case for making primary education and adult literacy universal and free and providing text books free of cost, there is also a case of doing whatever is possible for increasing the number of newspaper readers and for providing newspapers at a reasonably low price. In a country with a population of nearly 60 crores (in 1975), of whom nearly 40 crores are adults and in a country with universal adult suffrage, the fact that the number of copies of newspapers sold is not even one crore is distressing. Even if there are five readers per copy of a daily newspaper the total number of newspaper readers will not be more than five crores. It should be a clearly recognised policy in planning for socio-economic improvement that cheap newspapers should be available to a much larger number of readers than at present."

The Committee made a numbr of recommendations on newspaper production and capital equipment, profitability newspapers undertaking, news and advertisement ratio, norms of expenditure and fair prices and Monopoly and Restrictive practices by some newspaper groups.

On the question of de-linking and diffusion of ownership, the Committee was of the opinion that "if newspapers are accepted as a public service it is essential that profits earned from newspapers should be ploughed back into this newspaper enterprise itself. Pending the adoption and requisition of legal measures, it will be desirable to take steps for checking the use of newspaper profits for non-newspaper purpose." If diffussion of ownership becomes really what it is intended to be, the shareholding must be widely distributed among large numbers including of course, employees outside the groups of original owners. Thus, it may be expected, will put an end to the practice of high-salaried appointments to the members of the owner groups.

Referring to the proposal for setting up a newspaper Finance Corporation, the Committee said, "It is necessary, however, to see that the creation of a Newspaper

Finance Corporation does not lead to the emergence of the newspaper industry as a "sick" industry. If the financing is not done on strictly economic considerations, it becomes a form of subsidy, which will raise a question about discrimination and favours.

"In any case", the Committee asserted, "If it is undesirable to have a Government-controlled Press, it is undesirable also to have a large element of subsidy to the Press from the Government, unless it is given to weaker sections and unless the purpose is to maintain competition rather than restrict it. If Newspaper Finance Corporation becomes a necessity, it should not be an agency for discriminatory assistance," the report said.

INTERNAL EMERGENCY

However, the relations between the Press and the Government reached its nadir and the Press came under severest pressure after the Allahabad High Court judgment in June 1975 which held the Prime Minister guilty of malpractices in 1971 elections to the Lok Sabha. Indira Gandhi persuaded President Fakruddin Ali Ahmed to proclaim internal Emergency on June 25, 1975. Leaders like Jaya Prakash Narayan, Morarji Desai, Charan Singh, Chandra Sekhar, Atal Behari Vajpayee, Madhu Limaye, besides thousands of other opposition activists, had been rounded up. It was a happening of historic dimensions. But the media was forced to black it out.

Under the Defence and Internal Security of India Rules censorship was ordered. Crude methods were applied to muzzle the Press. "Conscious that its implementation of Censorship may take time, and in the mean while Delhi papers at least may come out with screaming headlines about the cataclysmic events, Government resorted to blatant illegality. Power supply to newspapers (in Delhi) was cut off. According to Delhi Electric Supply Undertaking oral instructions were received by them from the Lieutenant Governor of Delhi that this be done. Most Delhi newspapers were, therefore, unable to bring out their editions on June 26, 1975". (White Paper on Misuse of Mass Media during the Internal Emergency, p 8).

Soon after the declaration of emergency Vidya Charan Shukla was appointed the Minister for Information and Broadcasting in place of I.K. Gujral. Shukla established strict control over various media units of the Ministry. At a meeting on July 26, 1975 Indira Gandhi herself laid down the broad policy in respect of media. At this meeting it was proposed to abolish the Press Council, fuse the four news agencies into one, review the advertisement policy, withdraw the housing facilities given to journalists and deport the foreign correspondents not willing to fall in line. "Shukla immediately went into action to execute these policy guidelines. In the process, the country witnessed misuse of mass media inconceivable in a democracy. The distinction between party and government disappeared. Akashvani and Doordarshan became propaganda instruments of the ruling party and peddlers of a personality cult. Even media such as the Press and films otherwise outside the control of government were made to dance to the tune called by the rulers by a ruthless exercise of censorship powers, enactment of a set of draconian laws which reduced press freedom to nought and an unabashed abuse of authority in the matter of disbursing advertisement, allocation of newsprint and release of raw stock for films." (White Paper on Misuse of Mass Media, HV)

The newspapers were divided into three categories—friendly, neutral and hostile. Indira Gandhi showed her utter unconcern for the credibility of the print media. While addressing a conference of AIR Station Directors on September 9, 1975, she said, "Quite honestly, I don't understand what it (credibility) means. Who has credibility? The newspapers who had day in and day out printed falsehood? Where every prediction has turned out to be false"?

This distorted view of the Press held by the Prime Minister underlined all the decisions taken by the Government to control the media. In all 253 journalists were arrested and put behind bars. Forty-three correspondents, two cartoonists and six photographers were disaccredited. Seven foreign correspondents were expelled from the country and entry of twenty-nine foreign correspondents was banned. Government advertisements were withheld from about one hundred newspapers and periodicals. Request for advertisement of twelve newspapers and periodicals was rejected. Eighteen newspapers and periodicals were banned. Normal facilities available to accreditated correspondents were withdrawn. Censorship was not imposed in a uniform manner. "News items cleared by Censor at one place were found objectionable in other regions and penalised. High Court rulings permitted publications of item unlawfully censored. Pre-censorship was imposed on publishing proceedings of courts and representations against such illegal use of censorship provisions were not entertained. Pre-censorship was frequently used to harass editors who did not toe the official line, with the purpose of compelling them to fall in line. News which was critical of Maruti and Sanjay Gandhi came in for particularly unfavourable notice. Similarly, news relating to reporting of crime and news which depicted failure on the economic front was also censored and the publishers were often subjected to punitive action." (White Paper on Misuse of Mass Media, p.3).

Even oral ban was imposed on quotations from Rabindranath, Gandhi, Nehru, Nazrul and others. Besides, the four news agencies —*Press Trust of India*, *United News of India*, *Hindustan Samachar* and *Samachar Bharati*— were merged into one single news agency named Samachar. The hand of Government continued to shape and guide the formation of *Samachar*. "Furthermore a serious legislative assault was mounted on the Press. A series of constitutional and statutory enactments were pushed through which made Press freedom in this country totally illusory. The Prevention of Publication of Objectionable Matter Act, which imposed draconian curbs on the Press, was passed. By including it in the Ninth Schedule of the Constitution, this Law was made immune to judicial scrutiny. By another Law, the Press Council was abolished. The ostensible reason given in the statement for objects and reasons was that the Press Council of India had not been able to frame a Code of Conduct. A third Law repealed the Parliamentary Proceedings Act of 1956 depriving the Press of the immunity it enjoyed in the matter of coverage of parliamentary proceedings. Ironically, the relevant Bill was introduced by Feroze Gandhi, husband of Indira Gandhi, in the Lok Sabha to protect newspapers from legal action on grounds of libel etc. for the publication of faithful accounts of parlimentary proceedings. This piece of legislation is popularly known as Feroze Gandhi Act.

However, gagging of the Press was Indira Gandhi's undoing. Many felt that she could have stayed in power, in spite of emergency, if only she had not resorted to Press gagging. This resulted in all sorts of gossips and rumours which snow-balled to create unenviable conditions for her.

Lok Sabha was dissolved. Arrested leaders were released. People unequivocally recorded their disapproval of the emergency by voting Indira Gandhi's Congress out of power in 1977 elections.

The Janata Party, a conglomerate of Congress (o), Bharatiya Lok Dal, Jan Sangh and Socialists, secured absolute majority in the Lok Sabha and Morarji Desai was sworn in as the Prime Minister on March 24, 1977.

FETTERS REMOVED

Soon after assumption of office by the Janata Government all the fetters imposed on the Press during the Emergency were removed. On April 9, 1977 the Prevention of Publication of objectionable Matters Act was repealed. The Parliamentary Proceedings (Protection of Publicaion) Act was not only re-enacted restoring the privilege but was buttressed and expanded, giving it Constitutional protection, by inserting Article 361 A in the constitution by the Constitution (44 Amendment) Act, 1978. Along with this the Press Council Act was passed and the Press Council revived.

A one-man committee was set up under the Chairmanship of K.K. Das to enquire into the abuse of mass media and to present a white paper to Parliament. The white paper was placed before Parliament on August 1, 1977. (Briefly reported earlier).

The committee on the "Misuse of Mass Media" was preceded by another committee set up to examine the structure of the news agency "*Samachar*" which came into being during the internal Emergency through the merger of four news agencies then existing. The committee, headed by Kuldip Nayar recommended:

1. That *Samachar* be dissolved and in its place there should be two news agencies: *VARTA* AND *SANDESH*. They in turn should set up jointly an organisation for entire national services which may be called *NEWS INDIA*. The whole set up should be created under an Act of Parliament which should be reviewed after ten years.

2. *VARTA* would be charged with the responsibility for organising and developing Indian Language Services but would include services in English.

3. *SANDESH* would work in the English language and strive to expand coverage in terms of areas and subjects and to achieve high standards of efficiency and

4. Two domestic Agencies should join to set up an organisation for international services which may be named *NEWS INDIA*. Two members of the committee—Mr. C.R. Irani and Mr. A.K. Sarkar—submitted a dissenting note strongly opposing

the creation of monopolistic agencies for Indian Language or international services, and urging for restoration of *PTI* and *UNI* as fully competing news agencies "primarily in the English Language for the simple reason that this is the language in which service is demanded, but with the provision for both to branch into regional language depending on the demand."

Eventually, the four agencies were restored to their pre-emergency position and they started their separate operations in April 1978. However, the name *VARTA* was used by the *UNI* to christen its Hindi news service and *PTI's* Hindi News Service was named "*BHASA*".

SECOND PRESS COMMISSION

Yet another laudable step taken by the Janata Government was the constitution of the second Press Commission. Announcing the decision the then Minister for Information and Broadcasting L.K. Advani, stated in the Rajya Sabha on May 18, 1978 "a series of steps have already been taken during the last one year to strengthen freedom and independence of the Press by way of setting right several aberrations of the Emergency. Although these steps paved the way for the revival of a free and independent Press, it is considered that the time has come for an in-depth examination of the entire state of the Press in the country with a view to determine further steps that need to be taken to restore it to full vigor and health. As its role in educating public opinion has been firmly established, it is essential to safeguard the freedom and independence of the Press against pressures of all kinds. All this points to the need for re-examining the place, status and functioning in a democratic set-up more so, in view of the recent experience when the Press was subjected to a series of legal and administrative assaults.

The Commission was headed by Justice P.K. Goswami, a retired Judge of the Supreme Court. But the Commission's work was interrupted by the fall of Janata Government under the weight of its inner contradictions. Despite its good work in respect of restoration of Press freedom the Government did not come up to the expectations of the people because of its non-performance and faction-feud. Its obsession with punishing Indira Gandhi who was arrested and sent to Tihar Jail for 24 hours on October 3, 1977, was also not appreciated. Later Indira was expelled from the Lok Sabha. The Janata Party eventually split with Charan Singh-Raj Narayan group breaking away and forming a new party. Jagjivan Ram made a futile bid to revive the Janata Government. Charan Singh became Prime Minister on July 16, 1979.

Soon after the split in the Janata Party the leaders who were champions of Press freedom during the emergency started threatening the Press after coming to powers. The trait of intolerance was as marked in them as it was in the Congress rulers during the emergency days. The attention of the Press Council of India was drawn by allegations that the Press in the Country was under increasing pressure from political leaders and that a climate of intolerance was being fostered in the country. In particular, some remarks by certain political leaders including Raj Narain, Devi Lal and Karpoori Thakur were brought to the notice of the Council whereby they were alleged to have threatened to boycott and burn such newspaper as did not toe their line. The council on September 3, 1979 passed the following resolution:

"Of late, reports have appeared in the Press that certain responsible public men have made statements like burning certain news papers etc. Allegedly using such language as might constitute threat to the freedom of the Press. Some others are reported to have allegedly justified the use of Government advertisements in newspapers as a weapon to pressurise them.

While the Press Council is most anxious that the Press should be completely objective and responsible in its reporting, such statements coming from prominent leaders are bound to have demoralising effect on the newsmen in particular and the Press in general, and are likely to inhibit the Journalists in reporting various events and news freely and objectively apart from expressing legitimate and bonafied comments.

While the Council would like the newspapers to express their views fearlessly on sensitive internal and national issues, it has been noticed that a section of the Press has failed to maintain the dignity and decorum expected of it particularly in covering the recent political crisis. The Council feels greatly concerned with these unfortunate developments and unanimously resolved at its meeting held on September 3, 1979, to appeal to all concerned to refrain from making statements which tend to undermine the freedom of the Press and interfere with the role expected of it in a democratic policy. At the same time, the Press is also expected to maintain high standards of public task and professional responsibility. ("PCI Annual report: 1979; p.p. 9-10".)

However, Charan Singh Government was short-lived. It lasted only 24 days. Charan Singh resigned as the Congress withdrew its support on August 20, but continued as caretaker Prime Minister. President dissolved the Lok Sabha on August 21, 1979. In the elections that followed Indira Gandhi Congress returned to power securing two-third majority. Indira became Prime Minister again.

The Press Commission headed by P.K. Goswami, which functioned till January 1980 decided to tender its resignation with the change of Government at the center. Two weeks after Indira Gandhi took over the reins of administration the minister for Information and Broadcasting informed the commission that the new Government would like to continue the Commission based on more comprehensive set of terms of reference. This, you will appreciate, will be possible if the Commission is reconstituted. It is in this context that the Government has regretfully decided to accept your resignation. The commission was reconstituted with Justice K.K. Mathews, retired Judge of the Supreme Court, as the Chairman. Ther terms of reference were not significantly different except that there was more stress on responsibility as a concomitant of Press freedom in a developing democratic society. Some new items were included viz, the citizen's right to privacy, growth of small and medium newspapers, the flow of news to and from India and the proposal for a new information order.

It would be interesting to note that when the second Press Commission was constituted the circulation of newspapers had gone up to 132.29 lakhs in 1979 from a little over 25 lakhs (an increase of 423.9 per cent) at the end of 1952. In the case of weeklies, the circulation had increased from 30.20 lakhs in 1956 to 129.4 lakhs in 1979, an increase of 327.94 per cent. The circulation of other periodicals had gone up from 50.24 lakhs in 1956 to 202.96 lakhs in 1979, an increase of 303.98 per cent. But despite this growth the circulation of newspapers relative to population continued to be very low. In 1975 the diffusion rate of dailies per 1000 people was only about 15.4 copies although the literacy rate increased from 16.67 per cent in 1961 to 36.17 per cent in 1981. It was found that about 76.6 per cent of all newspapers were published from bigger cities, including metropolitan cities, State capitals and other cities. Only 23.4 per cent were published from towns and other places with a population up to one lakh. As far as the circulation was concerned, the dailies coming out from bigger cities (totalling 144 in 1979) claimed 93.3 per cent of the total circulation of dailies in the country.

The Commission dealt in great details with the subjects like the role of the Press, Constitution and laws, pressures on the Press, right to privacy, role of Press Council; the Press as an industry; the Press as a public utility; training and research etc, and made its recommendations most of which remain unimplemented

Independence And After

even today. For example, the Commission recommended the establishment of a Newspaper Development Commission which would promote development of the Press as a whole, as distinct from individual newspaper. Nothing has been heard about it so far. The Commission also favoured delinking and diffusion of ownership and control for achieving the "goals of our State which run counter to the vested interests of the owners of those newspapers who have large interests in other business".

The Commission was convinced that the prescription of a price-page schedule with a news-to-advertisement ratio was "absolutely essential for promoting fair competition among the existing units and for providing a fair chance of success to newcomers in the interest of diversification of the source of dissemination of information so as to provide for expression of a broad spectrum of views." However, members of the Commission differed among themselves on this issue.

The Commission emphasised on the need for expansion of training and research in journalism and recommended that "while it is pointless for each University to institute a journalism course there should be at least one university or professional training facility of high standard in every major linguistic region. The Commission recommended "establishment of a National Council of Journalism Training, preferably to be sponsored by the Press Council of India. When an apex body for journalism training emerges it will be fitting for it to concern itself with the promotion and coordination of communication research, with particular reference to newspapers. Such a National Council for Journalism Training and Communication Research might be sponsored jointly by organisations of newspaper publishers and editors, Press Council and the proposed Newspaper Development Commission with support from AIR\Doordarshan." This rcommendation has also been put into cold storage.

Other important recommendations are given below in brief:

ROLE OF THE PRESS:

The role of the Press in the developing and democratic society should neither be that of an adversary nor an ally of the Government. To be a mindless adversary or an unquestioning ally would be to abdicate judgement. A free Press should be in our view a constructive critic.

Editors should insist on their right to have the final say in the acceptance or rejection of advertisements, specially those which border on or cross the line between decency and obscenity, legitimate claims for a product or service and the proferring of magical remedies. The editor's authority should extend not only to the contents of advertisement but also to the proportion of space devoted to them. The editor should also have the right to veto a particular positioning of advertisement that he may regard as undesirable.

There should be strict enforcement of the provision in the Indian Penal Code with regard to communal incitement. Journalists have to be on guard against attempts by authorities or by landlords to pass off agrarian revolts against exploitation as Naxalite or other politically motivated violence.

The Press must address itself to the question of what contribution it is making to the strengthening of the morale fabric of society and discouraging the trend towards conspicuous and exessive consumption which a developing country can ill afford. The Press will have to bring to light and extend support to genuine public grievances, it should take a forth-right stand against unconstitutional methods of agitaion.

CONSTITUTION AND LAWS

No useful purpose will be served by inserting a separate provision in the constitution on freedom of the Press as that concept is already embodied in Article 19 (a) and by inserting such provision no particular benefit can be conferred on a non-citizen like a company.

Journalism is not merely an industry, it is a public service and a profession. The Press has a social responsibility and accountability to the public. The theory that the freedom of the Press knows no restraint is gone.

Power of pre-censorship should be invoked only in case of extreme necessity in the national interest. Section 5 of the official secrets Act, 1923 may be repeated and substituted by other provisions suited to meet the paramount need of national security and other vital interest of the state as well as the right of the people to know the affairs of the state affecting them.

From the point of view of freedom of the Press it is essential that the privileges of Parliament and State Legislatures should be codified as early as possible.

PRESSURE ON THE PRESS

Public opinion should assert itself to restrain misguided elements among the public from exercising their disagreement with newspaper reports through physical violence against the premises or property of the newspaper or its editor or employees rather than sending a rejoinder for publication or making a complaint to the press council or availing of a remedy provided under the law of land.

Political parties and trade union leaders should not for political reasons utilise their following among newspaper employees or hawkers to hinder the publication and/or distribution of any newspaper.

Editorial functioning should be insulted from proprietorial pressure irrespective of whether such pressure is exerted on behalf of private business interests or on behalf of governmental authorities.

The Press should be able to resist not only external pressure but also inducements which would undermine its independence from within. Journalists should be on guard against the temptations to enjoy favours, whether from Government authorities, employers, advertisers or others.

RIGHT TO PRIVACY

The Indian Penal Code (Amendment) Bill, 1978, which incorporated the recommendations of the Law Commission in respect of invasions of privacy and which lapsed with the dissolution of the last Lok Sabha, may be reintroduced in Parliament as early as possible.

Ligislation incorporating a general right to privacy may not be advisable.

The Press Council could appropriately be entrusted with the task of taking cognizance of complaints of unfair publication relating to matters concerning privacy.

Sensitive private facts relating to the health, private behaviour, home life or personal or family relationships should not be published except when it is in public interest to do so if the publication of these facts is likely to cause distress, annoyance or embarrassment to the person or persons concerned. Disclosure of remote criminal proceedings should be avoided.

The Press should not be unduly inhibited in performing its important function of giving news in the public interest as distinct from news that may pander to prurient or morbid curiousity. But a correct balance has to be struck between the citizen's claim to privacy and the public's right to information.

THE PRESS AS A PUBLIC UTILITY

The underlying principle that governs, or should govern, the Press is that the gathering and selling of news and views is essentially a public trust. It is based upon a tacit contract with the public that the news shall be true to the best of the knowledge and belief of those who offer it for sale, and that their comment upon it shall be sincere according to their lights.

A journalist who sells, or is a party to selling, news that he knows to be false or only partly true, or who

Independence And After

trims opinions so as to make them palatable, is more guilty than a tradesman who gives short weight or a manufacturer who offers adulterated goods. The spreading of false statements is more harmful than the sale of material wares under false pretences. The journalist who betrays his trust is more blameworthy than a dishonest tradesman. Journalism, as the basis of the newspaper industry holds a special position because its raw material is really the public mind and its trades chiefly in moral values. In a sense the trusteeship or moral responsibility of the Press is akin to that of ministers of religion, statemen and leaders of public thought. In another sense it is subject to industrial and marcantile conditions that do not effect these other trustees in the same degree.

When newspapers are controlled by other big businesses they become vehicles of expression of the ideology of their owners and the selection., presentation and display of news in such newspapers would be dictated by that ideology. The newspaper industry in their hands becomes involuntarily the cultural arm of other businesses and industries and takes a vested interest in maintaining the existing socio-economic system. The newspapers controlled by them may be selective in their presentation of news and views in return for benefits conferred in respect of their other business interests ...odd exceptions apart, commercial newspapers do not normally find a word to say in sympathy with the legitimate demands of the working class. They become naturally antagonistic to the implementation of certain key Directive principles contained in party IV of the Constitution. Legislative measures intended to ensure that the ownership and control of the material resources of the community are so distributed as best to subserve the common good, or that the operation of the economic system does not result in concentration of wealth and means of production to the common determent (Article 39 of the constitution) run counter to their business and other economic interests. If all major newspapers come to represent a similar if not the same view-point as is not unlikely when all of them belong to large private business enterprises a view-point which is against the interests of big business may not receive a fair deal in their columns ... It is enough for our purpose to say that legislative measures needed for achieving the goals of our State run counter to the vested interests of the owners of those big newspapers who have large interests in other business.

It is precisely because the businessmen owning or controlling big newspapers have not acted on the advice of the First Press Commission of creating trusts for their management that we are obliged to seriously consider the question once again and seek other remedies.

However, there was sharp difference of opinion between the chairman and six members of the commission on the one hand and four other members, namely S.K. Mukherjee, Rajendra Mathur, Girilal Jain and H.K. Paranjape on the other. The majority of seven favoured govenmental regulation of newspaper ownership and management, while the minority of four opposed it.

Notwithstanding the concern voiced by the Press Commission about 'Pressures' a number of State Governments tried to curb Press freedom on the pretext of preventing 'scurrilous' writings. In 1982 the Government of Bihar, headed by the congress chief Minister Jagannath Misra, had sought to amend the Indian Penal code and Criminal Procedure Code to refrain newspapers from publishing 'scurrilous' reports. The bills (popularly called Bihar Press Bill) were introduced in the State Assembly in July 1982. But faced with stiff opposition from newspapermen all over the country the Government withdrew the bills. The Bihar Government probably took the cue from the Tamilnadu Government which had an identical statute. But noticing the reactions among the journalists the Government of Tamilnadu also shelved the measure. "A difficult and complicated situation had arisen because of the proposed introduction of Andhra Pradesh Press Bill. There was a very strong opposition to the proposed Bill from the Press, ultimately resulting in the victory for the Press in seeking to maintain its independence. The Government had very appropriately not proceeded with the matter any further". (PCI. Annual Report, 1985, p. 1). A similar attempts to introduce 'Pre-censorship' were also made unsuccessfully in Punjab and Assam.

However, there were forces bent on creating insecure conditions for newspapermen. Incidents of assaults on newsmen and attacks on newspaper offices grew in number. Murders of a number of journalists, like the editor of *Madhya Yug* of Banda, *Blitz* correspondent A.V. Narayan, Editor of *Preet Lari*, Sumeet Singh and editor of *Encounter*, Pingali Dasaratham of Andhra Pradesh, attacks on the editor of *Matrubhumi*, lathi-charge on Andhra Pradesh newsmen outside the State Assembly; devastating fire in the *Gujarat Samachar* complex, which caused extensive damage to *Gujarat Samachar* office and completely damaged the *Western Times Press* and assaults on the non-striking employees and distributors of *Ananda Bazar* Group of newspapers sent shock waves through the Press world. Functioning of newsmen became all the more difficult in conditions surcharged with tensions created by riots and communal strife. Terrorism in Punjab following the Blue Star Operation in Amritsar Golden Temple undertaken by the Government of Indira Gandhi and her assassination on October 31, 1984 lent a new dimension to the concept of 'pressure' on the press. However, "the Press had very responsible role to play and it showed commendable restraint. By employment of necessary comments and agreements for lessening and toning down the tension, the press, by and large worked strenuously far driving home the great need of the hour, namely, maintenance of law and order, suppression of communal disturbances and positive efforts towards safeguarding the unity and integrity of the country: (PCI Annual Report, 1985, p. 111).

So far as the recommendations of the second Press Commission were concerned no steps had been taken by the Government of India to implement them. The commission in the majority report had suggested that the legislature was competent to enact the proposed law under Article 19 of the constitution to make it "mandatory for persons carrying on the business of publishing a newspaper to sever their connections with other businesses". But the 'action taken report' on the recommendations of the second Press commission, laid on the table of Parliament on May 14 1986, said: "The Government appreciates the recommendations made by the commission but feels that in view of the legal, constitutional and other complexities involved, the matter may be referred to an expert committee for examination and report". On the issue of price-page schedule the action taken report' suggested that an expert committee be set up to go into the question. Nothing has been heard since then. The Government, perhaps, preferred to play safe in view of the sensitive nature of the two recommendations.

DEFAMATION BILL

"It is noteworthy that perhaps due to the chastening effect of March 1977 electoral verdict following the period of emergency and censorship, the press was left free of legislative intervention for more than eight years from January 1980 when Indira Gandhi returned to power. There was once again a confrontation when the Rajiv Gandhi Government introduced in parliament in August 1988 a Defamation Bill" (Q.N.S. Raghavan, The Press in India, p 162)

The bill put the onus of proving the truth of the statement and to establish also that the statement was made for the public good on the person accused of having made a defamation statement.

Eye brows were raised and the motive of the Government was suspected as the Defamation Bill was brought forward after "disclosures and allegations in the Press about Kick-backs received by or on behalf of Prime

Minister Rajiv Gandhi and /or the Congress (I) from Nobel Industries of Sweden in a contract for the purchase of the Bofors Gun for the Indian Army. This scandal was to cost Rajiv Gandhi dearly: as leader of the Congress (I) he could secure for his party less than 40 per cent of the popular vote in the elections held for the Lok Sabha in November 1989, as against the unprecedented share of about half of the votes that the party received when he led it in the December 1984 elections within weeks of his succeeding his assassinated mother as Prime Minister. The difference was due to absence of the sympathy factor that had been at work in 1984, as well as to the adverse impression created by the Bofors Scandal. The Defamation Bill was hurriedly introduced by the Rajiv Gandhi Government in the Lok Sabha on August 29, 1988 and was passed the next day. In a remarkable display of unity, newspaper employees, who had been looking to the Government for securing improved wages and working conditions, joined hands with their employers in demonstrations all over the country against the Defamation Bill as an attack on press freedom. The rallies were climaxed by a march in the capital along Rajpath to Parliament House in which newspaper publishers marched alongside representatives of All India Newspaper Employees Federation, the Indian Federation of working jornalists, National Union of journalists and the Editors Guild. Doubtless, recalling the ruling party's experience in 1977 when the voters' verdict was in part against the emergency regime of Press censorship, Prime Minister Rajiv Gandhi thought it wise to drop the Defamation Bill. It was not proceeded with the Rajya Sabha". (Raghavan, the Press in India, p. 163).

During the tenure of Rajiv Gandhi another bill seeking to amend the Press and Registration of Books Act was introduced in Parliament in December 1988. The bill sought to arm district magistrates with powers to carry out inspection checks of newspapers establishments to verify circulation claims, and to raise the amount of fine that could be levied on newspapers for violation of the Act from Rs. 500 to 5000. The amending legislation had also empowered the appropriate authority to cancel the concessional rate of postage for newspapers if they consisted mainly of advertisements. This bill was also abandoned.

About the same time the Government of Karnataka, under the Chief Ministership of R.K. Hagde, sought to introduce two apparently well-intentioned measures which had direct bearing on the functioning of the print media. These were : Karnataka Freedom of the Press Bill 1988 and Karnataka Legislative (Powers, Privileges and Immunities) Bill 1988. The Freedom of the Press Bill sought to ensure free functioning of the press and laid down three basic provisions. These were: (a) Immunity from disclosure of source of information; (b) right of access to public documents and (c) penalty for causing hurt etc. With the intention of preventing any journalist from performing his duties. The Karnataka Legislative Bill sought to codify the privileges enjoyed by the Karnataka Legislators and *inter alia* sought to lay down punitive punishments for contempt thereof by the Press vis-a-vis the inherent freedom of speech and expression under Article 19 (2). But as the bills came under fire from almost all sections of the Press and various other quarters the Karnataka Government referred the two bills to the Press Council of India for in-depth examination.

The council welcomed both the bills as steps in the right direction and felt that it would be "eminently desirable" if the Parliament adopted the two measures. However, the matter ended there.

There was a hue and cry over the Jammu and Kashmir special powers (Press) Bill, 1989 which the J & K Government introduced in the State Assembly in August 1989 with the intent to regulate the Press in the State.

The Bill provided for "regulation and control of printing or publication of certain matters in the interest of public orders and security of state. It also "provided for regulatory action for the purpose of preventing or combating any activity prejudicial to the maintenance of public order; for prevention of activities prejudicial to the smooth and peaceful running of business establishments, or for prevention of activities prejudicial to the smooth and peaceful running of employment in essential services". The Bill caused a storm of protest all over the country because of sweeping powers of pre-censorship vested in the administration. The State Government referred the matter to the press council. After hearing the state Government in October 1989 the council took the view that the state Government "has sufficient powers in its armoury in the form of existing legislation, state and central, which can be used to deal with gross misconduct by the Press over the entire ground in respect of which fresh powers are sought under this bill". It further held that pre-censorship was inherently inimical to freedom of the Press and therefore advised withdrawal of the 'superfluous' bill and the formation of a Press advisory council in the State to promote dialogue. The J&K Government withdrew the legislation.

The political scenario in the country underwent swift changes since the defeat of the Congress in 1989 Lok Sabha poll. Viswanath Pratap Singh was sworn in as the Prime Minister of the National Front Government on December 2, 1989. But this Government lasted only a little over eleven months. It was not unexpected. In fact, the death knell of the Government was tolled on December 1, 1989. Chandra Sekhar, the founder-President of the Janata Party, was an aspirant for the office of the Prime Minister. But he did not have the support of other party leaders who chose to plump for Viswanath Pratap Singh. Correctly sensing the situation Chandra Sekhar himself proposed the name of Devilal as the Leader of the Janata Parliamentary Party. This he obviously did to anticipate Viswanath Pratap. But to his utter surprise and dismay, Devilal let him down by proposing the name of Viswanath Pratap for the office. The proposal was promptly supported by others. Chandra Sekhar saw in this whole game a "conspiracy", felt humiliated and openly vowed to "retaliate". He lay low waiting for the opportune moment to strike back. Soon Devilal, the Deputy Prime Minister, fell out with Viswanath Pratap on the issue of his son Omprakash Chauthala who had managed to become the Chief Minister of Haryana through the back-door. The Government was thrown into a crisis when the Prime Minister sacked his deputy (Devilal) rather unceremoniously. The Jat leader organised a massive "Kisan rally" in Delhi to show his political might. As a counter-move Viswanath Pratap played the "Mandal" card (27 per cent job reservation in Central Government Services for backward Classes) which stoked the fire of caste conflict all over the country. Meanwhile, the difference between the Bharatiya Janata Party and the National Front over Ayodhya "Ram Temple" issue snowballed in to yet another serious crisis when the BJP leader L.K. Advani, who was driving round the country in his "Ram Rath", was arrested at Samastipur in Bihar by the police of Laloo Prasad Yadav's Government. In protest, BJP withdrew its support reducing the National Front Ministry into a minority. Earlier, Devilal also joined hands with Chandra Sekhar to split the party. Eventually, the Government fell having lost the trial of strength in the Lok Sabha on November 7, 1990.

The break-away group of the Janata Party, headed by Chandra Sekhar, formed a minority Government on November 10, 1990 with the support of the Congress from outside. Within four months serious misgivings grew between Chandra Sekhar and Rajiv Gandhi mainly over two issues: (one) facilities extended to US war planes to refuel in Indian airports during the Iraqui-Kuwaiti war and (two) police surveillance of Rajiv Gandhi's house at 10. Janpath, New Delhi. On March 6, 1991 Congress withdrew its support and Chandra Sekhar Government collapsed. However, Chandra Sekhar continued as caretaker Prime Minister till June 20, 1991.

Mid-term elections to the Lok Sabha were held in May and June. The poll process was disturbed by the assassination of Rajiv Gandhi at Sriperambudur in Tamilnadu on May 21, 1991. However, the Congress scrapped through the poll and P.V. Narshimha Rao took over as the Prime Minister on June 21, 1991. But governance was not a very smooth-sailing affair for Rao. In spite of bold steps taken to liberalise the economy by dismantling the "licence-pemit raj", the government was buffeted by waves of social and political unrest in many parts of the country in the wake of the demolition of the controversial mosque on December 6, 1992 at Ayodhya. Another factor contributing to the general unrest and disenchantment with the rulers was the disclosures of a series of "scams" and scandals. The Press exposed a good many skeletons in Rao's cupboard. Credibility of the government dipped to an all-time low as scandals involving ministers and people in high places came to light.

Corruption was not a new phenomenon in India. But it had assumed serious proportions during the rule of Narashima Rao. Below are given in brief outlines of a few of the sensational cases of corruption exposed by the Press:

1. **The Airlines deal of 1991** : Kickbacks of Rs 200 crore were alleged in Rs 2500 crore deal. The US and French authorities furnished evidence but the file just gathered dust.

2. **The ABB (Asean Brown Bovary) loco deal of 1993:** The then Railway Minister Jaffer Sharief was accused of having favoured ABB in $ 190 million deal ignoring lower bids of Bharat Heavy Electricals Ltd. The matter was not persued.

3. **The Securities Scam of 1992:** Joint Parliamentary probe into the multi-crore scam indicted Rameshwar

Thakur, Minister of State for Finance and B. Shankaranand, Petroleum Minister. Shankaranand also quit being indicted by the C.B.I for diverting Rs 132 crore from Oil India Development Board to the Syndicate Bank for investment in the stock markets.

4. **The sugar scam of 1994:** The Union Minster of State for Food, Kalpanath Rai, had to quit the Council of Ministers after being indicted by the Gyan Prakash Committee for bungling sugar imports.

5. **The Jain 'hawala' rcket of 1995:** The CBI issued notices to ten Union Ministers, former Ministers and Presidents of three political parties in September 1995 for involvement in the Rs 65 crore scam. It came to light through the disclosure of the dairies maintained by the industrialist Surendra Kumar Jain which meticulously documented a trail of "hawala" pay-offs to political heavy-weights and public servants. The immediate fall-out was the resignation of a number of ministers in Rao's cabinet.

6. **JMM pay-off case:** On March 27, 1996 the CBI registered a case in Delhi High Court against Jharkhand Mukti Morcha MPs— Suraj Mandal, Sibu Soren, Simon Marandi and Sailendra Mahato --- under the Preventive Detention Act.. They were charged with accepting huge amounts of money in return for their support to Rao government during the no-confidence motion in the Lok Sabha in July 1993.

7. **Urea Scam:** In November 1995 National Fertilizer Ltd contracted to buy two lakh tonnes of urea from a little-known Turkish firm, Karsan Ltd, to be supplied before May 4, 1996, at a landed cost of $ 190 a tonne against the international price of $ 240 a tonne. NFL paid full advance of Rs 133 crore in violation of norms, but not a gram of

urea reached Indian shores. Kickbacks of $4 million were alleged to have been paid during the period of December 1995 to January 1996 (when Rao was the Prime Minister) to Prime Minister's son Prabhakar Rao, his relative Sanjeeva Rao and former Fertilizer Minister Ram Lakhan Yadav's son Prakash Chandra. Pay-offs were made through the Dubai-based hawala operators. The CBI arrested C.K. Ramkrishnan, a former Managing Director of NFL and D.S Kanwar, a former Executive Director, Marketing of NFL, and Sambasiva Rao, Karson's Hyderabad-based agent.

The Press, by and large, boldly perfomed its role of watchdog, without fear or favour, alerting the people of the virus of corruption eating into the vitals of the body politic. With all these dirty loads on its head a debilitated Congress Party, having ben split twice during the course of one year from May 1995 to May 1996, fought a losing battle in the Lok Sabha elections in May 1996. The press predictions of a "hung parliament" with no party getting absolute majority, after the poll, came true. The non-Congress parties fought the elections mainly on the issue of corruption. The Congress and its allies (Indian Union Muslim League, Kerala Congress (M) and AIADMK) were practically routed having captured only 141 seats; BJP and its allies (Shive Sena, Samata Party and Haryana Vikash Party) got 194 seats and the Third Front (Janata Dal, CPI, CPIM, DMK and ten other) bagged 179 seats and the remaining 22 seats went to independents.

The 11th Lok Sabha had a character uniquely its own. The "backward castes" who have been steadily gaining political power in local and State Governments since the early sixties, now occupied an unprecendented number of seats in the Lok Sabha. The growth of the regional forces was reflected in the Lok Sabha— a number unparalleled in Indian parliamentary history. The strength of farmers who have seen a steady increase in their numbers in the past five houses— had this time jumped from 33 percent to almost 52 per cent giving the Lok Sabha a distinctly rural flavour. It had truely become a "microcosm of the nation", as Subhash Kashyap, a former Secretary-General of the Lok Sabha, described it.

The days of national parties and the hold of upper castes were apparently over. The backwards were not only represented in sheer numerical strength but they also formed an articulate lobby in Parliament. An analysis of the results clearly showed that the people voted as members of castes and sub-castes. The decline of the Congress was due to lack of a charismatic leader, "Mandalisation" and Mandirisation" of the polity which had broken society into groups and sub-groups and Rao's inability to translate economic liberalisation and national security as alternatives.

It was a 'hung parliament'. But since the BJP and its allies formed the single largest group President Shankar Dayal Sharma invited the leader of the group, Atal Behari Vajpayee, to form the government on the condition that he will prove his majority in the Lok Sabha by May 31, 1996. Vajpayee accepted the offer to form the government and was sworn-in on May 16, 1996. For the BJP it was a political gamble. The party hoped that the Congress (I) would split after its crushing defeat, that the National Front and the Left Front, known for their fractious and ever-splitting past, would stay divided and that the new and uncommitted regional groupings would never get their act together. It had expected to gain heavily from the confusion and even attract secular allies by watering down some of its more strident *Hindutwa* rhetoric on issues such as Article 370 of the Constitution (special status for Jammu and Kashmir) and a uniform civil code. But BJP's calculations went awry. Nothing of the kind happened. There was no accretion in its strength which stood at 194 (in the house of 534) on May 27 when Prime Minister Vajpayee formally moved the motion for vote of confidence. Ater two days' debate Vajpayee tendered his resignation losing all hopes of winning a simple majority for his government. His 13-day-old government was the "shortest-lived" in independent India.

Meanwhile, the Third Front, a coalition of 14 national and regional parties, was officially christened as "United Front". The President invited H.D. Deve Gowda, the newly-elected leader of the Front, to form a new government. With the support of 190 members belonging to 20 non-Congress and non-BJP parties and also of 135 Congress members, who pledged to support the UF government from outside, Deve Gowda formed his government on June 1, 1996 with the avowed object of keeping BJP out of power.

The motion for vote of confidence which Dev Gowda moved in the Lok Sabha on June 12, 1996 was just a formality as the government had the support of a comfortable majority of 325 members. The United Front adopted a Common Minimum Programme (CMP) which included among other things, an amendment of the Official Secrets Act "keeping in tune with the need for openness and transparency in governance" and introduction of a bill for freedom of Information to give the people access to information at all levels. A salient feature of the coalition government was the participation of the Communist Party of India, for the first time since independence, in the Government at the Centre although other partners of the Left Front—CPIM, RSP and Forward Block — preferred to remain outside. Uncertainty, doubtless, loomed over the future of such a coalition cobbled after the election. Yet, it was for the first time India had a government in which regional parties had a say in running the country and the concept of "federalism" was brought into full play.

However, Deve Gowda Government did not last long. Serious differences developed between the Congress and the United Front over the style of functioning of the Prime Minister. The relations between Deve Gowda and the Congress President Sitaram kesri deteriorated after the latter had demanded replacement of the former by a person who would be acceptable to the Congress. Kesri asked the United Front to elect a new leader as, in his opinion, Deve Gowda was "not only inefficient but communal as well". As the Front was dithering over the issue Kesri write a letter to the President Shankar Dayal Sharma on March 30, 1997 conveying his party's decision to withdraw support to the UF Government "which has failed to provide the leadership necessary to consolidate the forces of secularism and to confront the forces of communalism?".

Prime Minister Deve Gowda, as directed by the President, sought a vote of confidence in the Lok Sabha on April 11, 1997 and lost. The Government was voted out. Deve Gowda was suceeded by Indra Kumar Gujral who took over as the Prime Minister on April 21, 1997 promising to give the country "a clean and transparent" administration. Soon after, the Congress president retracted the letter he had earlier written to the President and extended unconditional support to the second UF Government headed by Gujral.

The Prime Minister maintained very cordial relations with the Press and, despite occasional outbursts of intolerance of the Press in certain quarters, the Fourth Estate commanded the respect it deserved and continued to perform its primary duties "to inform, educate and entertain" the people.

"As the history of Indian journalism is very much a part of the history of Indian emancipation, so also the history of the Press today and tomorrow will be an integral part of the history of Indian reconstruction."

Dr B.C. Roy (1962)

EPILOGUE

The Fourth Estate in India has, doubtless, become a force to reckon with. It has made rapid strides during the past four decades. When the first Press Commission was set up in 1952, there were 330 dailies, 1189 weeklies and 1733 journals and periodicals. The dailies had a combined circulation of a little over 25 lakhs. In 1979 when the Second Press Commission was surveying the Fourth Estate in India the dailies numbered 1173, weekly 5023 and other periodicals 10,972. In other words, the number of dailies increased by 250 per cent and of weeklies and periodicals by 300 percent and 530 per cent respectively during the period. The circulation of dailies in 1979 was approximately 132 lakhs, an increase of 423 per cent over the 1952 figure. In the case of weeklies, the circulation had gone up from 30.20 lakhs in 1956 (the earliest year for which circulation data are available) to 129.24 lakhs in 1979, a rise by 327.94 per cent. The circulation of other periodicals had also gone up from 50.24 lakhs in 1956 to 202.96 lakhs in 1979, an increase of 303.93 per cent.

In 1992, a decade after the Second Press Commission had submitted its report, the number of dailies was 3502, a rise of about 300 per cent over the 1979 figure.

Circulation-wise, the increase has been about 212 per ent from 132.29 lakhs in 1979 to 280 lakhs in 1992. Among the periodicals, weeklies had a share of about 192 lakh copies, fortnightlies about 57 lakhs, and monthlies 93 lakhs. Newspapers came out in 93 languages and dailects. In 1992, the highest number of newspapers were published in Hindi (11,638), followed by English (5,139), Urdu (2,120), Bengali (1,994), Marathi (1,510), Tamil (1,411), Malayalam (1,099), Kannada (1,045), Gujrati (945), Telegu (772), Punjabi (682), Oriya (478) and Assamesee (149), Besides, 2,051 newspapers were bilingual publications and 415 multilingual. This steady increase in the number of newspapers has been described by the Press Council of India as "a manifestation of power that the printed word exerts in influencing and moulding the public opinion".

Up to 1994, a total of about 38,800 newspapers, magazines etc. stood on the register of RNI. This mainly included 4155 daily newspapers, 12,250 weeklies, 5052 fortnightlies and 11,240 monthlies. About 2,026 newspapers were registered in 1994 only, which represented an increase of 5.3% over the previous year. The state of Uttar Pradesh took the lead in the matter of publication of newspapers and their circulation.

But in the overall context of Indian population of about 90 crores with a literary percentage of 48, the circulation of newspapers was anything but impressive. Evidently large areas still remained untapped by the Press.

"Newspapers today are working in a highly competitive environment. Revolutionary changes in the technology of information, communication and printing are taking place. The cost of various inputs of publication of newspaper is going up. These factors are having a severe effect on circulation, quality and financial viability of newspapers. To maintain their economic condition at the present level with expectations of growth at a reasonable rate, the newspapers have perforce to adopt

Epilogue

the most modern technology in communication and printing requiring huge investment. This factor operating in tandem with other forces, is leading to increased concentration of the ownership of newspapers in the hands of some big business houses or trading interests. As a result, the newspaper business in India is fast becoming a big money game. These monopolistic trends have brought in their wake a host of questions and apprehensions. Will the concentration of ownership and control of newspapers in the hands of big business, not exclusively belonging to the profession of journalism, subvert essential role of a free Press in the democracy? Will it not adversely affect the editorial freedom? Will the control of the Press by big business interests running it mainly or wholly for the purpose of maximising profits for their own benefit, not erode the utility of the Press as a medium serving the public with news and views in a truthful, accurate, objective and fearless manner on matters of public interest? These are difficult but important questions which do not admit of clear-cut simplistic answers .... However, the price-cut wars between newspapers have benefited those readers by way of increased pages, reduction in prices and introduction of more and more sophisticated reports with greater emphasis on qualitative reporting. The price-cut competition among newspapers has not yet assumed a predatory character to "kill rivals" (PCI Annual Reports, 1989-1990) and 1993-1994).

The move by some Indian newspapers for tie-ups with foreign newspapers continued to be a subject of intense controversy. The move envisaged Indian editions of leading international dailies, including the *Wall-Street Journal, The Guardian, International Herald Tribune* and *the Time* magazine. The Indian participants were believed to be *Business Standard, the Deccan Herald, the Hindu* and *the Living Media Limited.*

The Central Government referred the matter to the Press Council. The council did not favour publication of foreign newspapers/news journals in India involving equity and management participants, but suggested that present arrangements could be reconsidered or reviewed after three to five years. The Government constituted a cabinet Sub-Committee to make recommendations for modification in the policy decisions of 1955-56. This rekindled a sharp debate and concern over the projected entry of foreign newspapers in India and gave rise to a spate of writ petitions in High Courts all over the country. Six such writ petitions were dismissed by Delhi High Court on March 2, 1994 on the ground that petitions are based not on any violation of any right of petitioners, but are speculative in nature and a product of some misapprehension in the minds of the petitioners. The matter lay in limbo till July 8 1996 when the controversy was again raked up by the Foreign Investment Promotion Board's approval of the proposed tie-up between Business Standard and Financial Times of London. There was hue and cry all over the country. All the political parties, including the constituents of the United Front Government, made it clear in no uncertain terms that they were totally opposed to the entry of foreign print media into the country as "this would lead to unprecedented degeneration of Indian culture and loss of national identity which, in turn, would pose a serious threat to national unity and sovereignty". They asked the Government to cancel the FIPB clearance given to *Business Standard - Financial Times* tie-up.

The government yielded to their pressure; The Cabinet Committee on Foreign Investment (CCFI) on August 14, 1996 rejected the recommendation of the FIPB. However, while rejecting the proposal CCFI asked the FIPB to prepare a status paper on the present media scenario, particularly the changes that had taken place since 1955 when the then Government, headed by Nehru, had adopted a resolution prohibiting foreign participation in Indian print media. The CCFI also directed the board to suggest policy changes regarding foreign investment proposals in the media sector, particularly the print media.

Epilogue

But at the same time a disconcerting feature was the sudden spurt in the closure of newspapers all over India. The major contributing factors, according to a Press Council study, were lack of advertisement support, rising price of newsprint and other inputs.

"The council noted with great concern the unparalleled and unprecedented increase in the price of newsprint, the main raw material for the production of newspapers which accounts for 60% to 70% of the total cost of production of newspaper. The public and joint sctor mills producing newsprint had announced whooping increase in the prices 3-4 times, thereby making the newsprint costlier by about 26%. There was no essential commodity where the prices had gone up more than 150% during the last five years other than the newsprint where the increase had been to the extent of about 158% — the sole reason being the monopolistic market situation arising out of Government policies ensuring sale of the newspapers manufactured by these mills irrespective of the cost and the quality they supply. The Government's contention that it had no control over the mills in the matter of fixation of prices was considered illogical and without any basis. The situation further worsened with an increase in the price of the imported newsprint which had more than doubled during the period.

"It was further noted that these mills were exploiting the situation by informally rationing supplies of the newsprint to newspapers and artificial scareity was being created. As a result thereof, the newspaper establishments were not getting the required quantity of newsprints. The council felt that the existence of the newspapers was under threat and the fundamental right to freedom of speech and expression was being stiffled. In the light of the above, immediate indulgence of the Government was sought in the matters with the request that the newsprint be decontrolled whereby the newsprint manufacturing mills operated in a free market where the market forces decided the price and also requested for such actions as were necessary for building up the financial viability of newspaper establishments, particularly by the medium and small newspapers who were worse affected and were on the verge of closure". (Annual Report of Press Council of Media, 1994-1995).

The situation, however, eased with the decontrol of newsprint though the high price continued to affect the viablilty of the newspapapers.

However, the Press has generally shouldered its responsibility satisfactorily. It has, by and large, maintained reasonably good professional standard. Communal and separatist write-ups with inflamable tendencies have been generally avoided by the Indian Press except for a few aberrations here and there. Growth of specialised journals, targeted to a particular audience interested in a specified field, be it technical and technological, has been rather impressive. The second Press Commission listed nine such area covered by specialised journals. The areas have fast expanded since then. Economic and business journalism has out-distanced other kinds of specialised journalism by miles. Growth in this field is simply phenomenal.

The Press Council of India set up under the Central Act of 1978 has come of age. It has steadily gained in stature and worked towards achieving harmony and balance between the freedom of the Press on the one hand and improvement of standards of newspapers and news agencies on the other. The increasing number of complaints being made every year to the council, by the Press and against the Press, for adjudication speaks volumes of the peoples growing confidence in the council as the 'watch-dog of Press freedom'.

Rapid expansion of the electronic media, especially the television, has yet to come as a threat to the print media which will take years to reach the stage of saturation. But the threat to the profession of journalism has come from within. The Second Press Commission has observed, "If the Press is to play its role it should

Epilogue

be able to resist not only external pressure but also inducements which would undermine its independence from within. Journalists should be on guard against temptation to enjoy favours, whether from Government authorities, employers, advertisers or others".

Unfortunately, this caution seems to have fallen on deaf ears of a section of greedy journalists amenable to offer of bribes from politicians and businessmen. The allegations by the Uttar Pradesh Chief Minister Mayawati (June 1995) that her predecessar Mulayam singh Yadav distributed, out of the state exchequer, largesse ranging from Rs. 2000 to Rs. 10 lakh and more with a view to ensuring favourable media coverage for him and his Government and disclosure of a list of beneficiary journalists and media organisations shocked the country. It was further alleged that incredibly fabulous amounts of Rs. 27 lakh, Rs. 22 lakh and Rs. 20 lakh were given to some journalists holding key positions in newspapers in Lucknow and Delhi. It is quite possible that many of the news items and write-ups that came out in some newspapers at that time in support of Mulayam Singh Yadav's Government were inspired by financial considerations. This distressing trend is comparable to that prevailed during the reign of Aurangzeb when 'news-writers', on pecuniary considerations, used to send false reports to the court misleading the Emperor into disastrous misadventures. (see prologue). The noble profession of journalism must guard itself against what the second Press Commission called the "Enemy within", if only to protect its 'credibility' on which stands the edifice of the Fourth Estate in a democracy.

APPENDICES

APPENDICES

APPENDIX - I

"AEROPAGITICA OF INDIAN PRESS"

MEMORIAL TO THE SUPREME COURT IN DEFENCE OF FREEDOM OF THE PRESS SUBMITTED BY RAJA RAMMOHUN ROY AND FIVE OTHER DISTINGUISHED GENTLEMEN IN MARCH 1823.

To The Honourable Sir Francis Macnaghten, Sole Acting Judge of the Supreme Court of Judicature at Fort William in Bengal

My Lord,

In consequence of the late Rule and Ordinance passed by His Excellency the Governor General in Council, regarding the Publication of Periodical Works, your Memorialists consider themselves called upon with due submission, to represent to you their feelings and sentiments on the subject.

Your Memorialists beg leave, in the first place, to bring to the notice of your Lordship, various proofs given by the Natives of this country of their unshaken loyalty to, and unlimited confidence in the British

Government of India, which may remove from your mind any apprehension of the Government being brought into hatred and contempt; or of the peace, harmony, and good order of society in this country, being liable to be interrupted and destroyed, as implied in the preamble of the above Rule and Ordinance.

First, Your Lordship is well aware, that the Natives of Calcutta, and its vicinity, have voluntarily entrusted Government with millions of their wealth, without indicating the least suspicion of its stability and good faith, and reposing in the sanguine hope that their property being so secured, their interests will be as permanent as the British Power itself; while, on the contrary, their fathers were invariably compelled to conceal their treasures in the bowels of the earth, in order to preserve them from the insatiable cupidity of their oppressive Rulers.

Secondly, Placing entire reliance on the promises made by the British Government at the time of the Perpetual Settlement of the landed property in this part of India, in 1793, the Landholders have since, by constantly improving their estates, been able to increase their produce, in general, very considerably; whereas, prior to that period, and under former Governments, their forefathers were obliged to lay waste the greater part of their estates, in order to make them appear of inferior value, that they might not excite the cupidity of Government, and thus cause their rents to be increased or themselves to be dispossessed of their lands,— a pernicious practice which often incapacitated the landholders from discharging even their stipulated revenue to Government, and reduced their families to poverty.

Thirdly. During the last wars which the British Government were obliged to undertake against neighbouring Powers, it is well known that the great body of Natives of wealth and respectability, as well as the Landholders of consequence, offered up regular prayers to the objects of their worship for the success of the British arms from a deep conviction that under the sway of that nation, their improvement, both mental and social, would be promoted, and their lives, religion and property be secured. Actuated by such feelings, even in those critical times, which are the best test of the loyalty of the subject, they voluntarily came forward with a large portion of their property to enable the British Government to carry into effect the measures necessary for its own defence, considering the cause of the British as their own, firmly believing that on its success, their own happiness and property depended.

Fourthly. It is manifest as the light of day, that the general subects of observation and the constant and the familiar topic of discourse among the Hindu community of Bengal, are the literary and political improvements which are continually going on in the state of the country under the present system of government, and a comparison between their present auspicious prospects and their hopeless condition under their former Rulers.

Under these circumstances, your Lordship cannot fail to be impressed with a full conviction, that whoever charges the Natives of this country with disloyalty, or insinuates aught to the prejudice of their fidelity and attachment to the British Government, must either be totally ignorant of the affairs of this country and the feelings and sentiments of its inhabitants, as above stated, or, on the contrary, be desirous of misrepresenting the people and misleading the Government, both here and in England, for unworthy purpose of his own.

Your Memorialists must confess that these feelings of loyalty and attachment, of which the most unequivocal proofs stand on record, have been produced by the wisdom and liberality displayed by the British Government in the means adopted for the gradual improvement of their social and domestic condition, by the establishment of colleges, schools, and other beneficial institutions in this city, among which the creation of a British Court of Judicature for the more effectual administration of Justice, deserves to be gratefully remembered.

A proof of the Natives of India being more and more attached to the British Rule in proportion as they experience from it the blessings of just and liberal treatment, is that the inhabitants of Calcutta, who enjoy in many respects very superior privileges to those of their fellow-subjects in other parts of the country, are known to be in like measure more warmly devoted to the existing Government; nor is it at all wonderful they should in loyalty be not at all inferior to British-born subjects, since they feel assured of the possession of the same civil and religious liberty, which is enjoyed in England, without being subjected to such heavy taxation as presses upon the people there.

Hence the population of Calcutta, as well as the value of land in this city, have rapidly increased of late years, notwithstanding the high rents of houses and dearness of all the necessaries of life compared with other parts of the country, as well as the inhabitants being subjected to additional taxes, and also liable to the heavy costs necessarily incurred in case of suits before the Supreme Court.

Your Lordship may have learned from the works of the Christian Missionaries, and also from other sources, that ever since the art of printing has become generally known among the Natives of Calcutta, numerous publications have been circulated in the Bengalee language, which by introducing free discussion among the Natives and inducing them to reflect and inquire after knowledge, have already served greatly to improve their minds and ameliorate their condition. This desirable object has been chiefly promoted by the establishment of four Native newspapers, two in the Bengalee and two in the Perisan language, published for the purpose of communicating to those residing in the interior of the country, accounts of whatever occurs worthy of notice at the Presidency or in the country, and also the interesting and valuable intelligence of what is passing in England and in other parts of the world, conveyed through the English newspapers or other channels.

Your Memorialists are unable to discover any disturbance of the peace, harmony, and good order of society, that has arisen from the English Press, the influence of which must necessarily be confined to that part of the community who understand the language thoroughly; but they are quite confident that the publications in the Native languages, whether in the shape of a newspaper or any other work, have none of them been calculated to bring the Government of the country into hatred and contempt and that they have not proved, as far as can be ascertained by the strictest inquiry, in the slightest degree injurious; which has vey lately been acknowledged in one of the most respectable English Missionary works. So far from obtruding upon Government groundless representations, Native Authors and Editors have always restrained themselves from publishing even such facts respecting the judicial proceedings in the interior of the country as they thought were likely at first view to be obnoxious to Government.

While your Memorialists were indulging the hope that Government from a conviction of the manifold advantages of being put in possession of full and impartial information regarding what is passing in all parts of the country, would encourage the establishment of newspapers in the cities and districts under the special patronage and protection of Government, that they might furnish the supreme authorities in Calcutta with an accurate account of local occurrences and reports of Judicial proceedings,— they have the misfortune to observe, that on the contrary, His Excellency the Governor-General-in-Council has lately promulgated a Rule and Ordinance imposing severe restraints on the Press and prohibiting all periodical publications even at the Presidency and the Native languages, unless sanctioned by a Licence from Government, which is to be revocable at pleasure whenever it shall appear to Government that a publication has contained anything of an unsuitable character.

Those Natives, who are in more favourable circumstances and of respectable character, have such an invincible prejudice against making a voluntary affidavit, or undergoing the solemnities of an oath, that they will never think of establishing a publication which can only be supported by a series of oaths and affidavits, abhorrent to their feelings and derogatory to their reputation amongst their countrymen.

After this Rule and Ordinance shall have been carried into execution, your Memorialists are therefore extremely sorry to observe that a complete stop will be put to the diffusion of knowledge and the consequent mental improvement now going on, either by translations into the popular dialect of this country from the learned languages of the East, or by the circulation of literary intelligence drawn from foreign publications. And the same cause will also prevent those Natives who are better versed in the laws and customs of the Brirtish nation, from communicating to their fellow-subjects a knowledge of the admirable system of government established by the British, and the peculiar excellencies of the means they have adopted for the strict and impartial administration of jutice. Another evil of equal importance in the eyes of a just Ruler, is that it will also preclude the Natives from making the Government readily acquaintd with the errors and injustice that may be committed by its executive officers in the various parts of this extensive country; and it will also preclude the Natives from communicating frankly and honestly to their Gracious Sovereign in England and his Council, the real conditon of His Majesty's faithful subjects in this distant part of his dominions and the treatment they experience from the local Government: since such information cannot in future be conveyed to England, as it has heretofore been, either by the translations from the Native publications inserted in the English newspapers printed here and sent to Europe, or by the English publications which the Natives themselves had in contemplation to establish, before this Rule and Ordinance was proposed.

After this sudden deprivation of one of the most precious of their rights, which has been freely allowed them since the establishment of the British Power, a right which they are not, and cannot be charged with having ever abused, the inhabitants of Calcutta would be no longer justified in boasting, that they are fortunately placed by Providence under the protection of the whole British nation, or that the King of England and his Lords and Commons are their Legislators, and that they are secured in the enjoyment of the same civil and religious privileges that every Briton is entitled to in England.

Your Memorialists are persuaded that the British Government is not disposed to adopt the political maxim so often acted upon by Asiatic Princes, that the more a people are kept in darknes, their Rulers will derive the greater advantages from them; since by reference to history, it is found that this was but a short-sighted policy which did not ultimately answer the purpose of its authors. On the contrary, it rather proved disadvantageous to them; for we find that as often as an ignorant people, when an opportunity offered, have revolted against their Rulers, all sorts of barbarous excesses and cruelties have been the consequence: whereas a people naturally disposed to peace and ease, when placed under a good Government from which they experience just and liberal treatment, must become the more attached to it, in proportion as they become enlightened and the great body of the people are taught to appreciate the value of the blessings they enjoy under its Rule.

Every good Ruler, who is convinced of the imperfection of human nature, and reverences for the Eternal Governor of the world, must be conscious of the great liability to error in managing the affairs of a vast empire; and therefore he will be anxious to afford every individual the readiest means of bringing to his notice whatever may require his interference. To secure this important object, the unrestrained Liberty of Publication, is the only effectual means that can be employed. And should it ever be abused, the established Law of the Land is very properly armed with sufficient powers to punish those who may be found guilty of misrepresenting the conduct or character of Government, which are effectually guarded by the same laws to which individuals must look for protection of their reputation and good name.

Your Memorialists conclude by humbly entreating your Lordship to take this Memorial into your gracious consideration; and that you will be pleased by not registering the above Rule and Ordinance, to permit the Natives of this country to continue in possession of the rights and privileges which they and their fathers have so long enjoyed under the auspices of the British nation, whose kindness and confidence, they are not aware of having done anything to forfeit.

Chunder Coomer Tagore,

Dwarka Nauth Tagore,

Rammohun Roy,

Hurchunder Ghose,

Gowree Churn Bonnerjee,

Prossunno Coomar Tagore

… *Appendices*

APPENDIX - II

THE PRESS AND REGISTRATION OF BOOKS ACT, 1867 (25 OF 1867)
(Relevant Extracts)
[22nd March 1867]

An Act for the regulation of Printing-Presses and Newspapers, for the preservation of copies of books and newspapers printed in India, and for the registration of such books and newspapers

Preamble— Whereas it is expedient to provide for the regulation of printing presses and newspapers, for the preservation of copies of every book and newspaper printed in India and for the registration of such books and newspapers; it is hereby acted as follows:

PART I
PRELIMINARY

1. Interpretation-clause— (1) In this Act, unless there shall be something repugnant in the subject of context,

["editor" means the person who controls-the selection of the matter that is published in a newspaper;]

"Magistrate" means any person exercising the full powers of a Magistrate, and includes a Magistrate of police.

"newspaper" means any printed periodical work containing public news for comments of public news

"paper" means any document, including a newspaper, other than a book

5. Rules as to publication of newspaper—No newspaper shall be published in India, except in conformity with the rules hereinafter laid down.

(1) Without prejudice to the provisions of Sec. 3,

every copy of every such newspaper shall contain the names of the owner and editor thereof printed clearly on such copy and also the date of its publication.

(2) The printer and the publisher of every such newspaper shall appear in person or by agent authorised in his behalf in accordance with rules made under Sec. 20, before a District, Presidency or Sub-divisional Magistrate within whose local jurisdiction such newspaper shall be printed or published, and shall make and subscribe, in duplicate, the following declaration:

"I,A.B., declare, that I am the printer (or publisher, or printer and publisher) of the newspaper entitled— and to be printed or published, or to be printed and published, as the case may be at —".

And the last blank in this form of declaration shall be filled up with a true and precise account of the premises where the printing or publication is conducted.

(2-A) Every declaration under rule (2) shall specify the title of the newspaper, the language in which it is to be published and the periodicity of its publication and shall contain such particulars as may be prescribed.

(2-B) Where the printer or publisher of a newspaper making a declaration under rule (2) is not the owner thereof, the declaration shall specify the name of the owner and shall also be accompanied by an authority in writing from the owner authorising such person to make and subscribe such declaration.

(2-C) A declaration in respect of a newspaper made under rule (2) and authenticated under Sec. 6 shall be necessary before the newspaper can be published.

(2-D) Where the title of any newspaper or its language or the periodicity or its publication is changed, the declaration shall cease to have effect and a new declaration shall be necessary before the publication of the newspaper can be continued.

(2-E) As often as the ownership of a newspaper is changed, a new declaration shall be necessary.

(3) As often as the place of printing or publication is changed, a new declaration shall be necessary:

Provided that where the change is for a period not exceeding thirty days and the place of printing or publication after the change is within the local jurisdiction of the Magistrate referred to in rule (2), no new declaration shall be necessary—

(a) a statement relating to the change is furnished to the said Magistrate within twenty-four hours thereof; and

(b) the printer or publisher or the printer and publisher of the newspaper continues to be the same.

(4) As often as the printer or the publisher who shall have made such declaration as is aforesaid shall leave India for a period exceeding ninety days or where such printer or publisher is by infirmity or otherwise rendered incapable of carrying out his duties for a period exceeding ninety days in circumstances not involving the vacation of his appointment, a new declaration shall be necessary.

(5) Every declaration made in respect of newspaper shall be void, where the newspaper does not commence publication—

(a) within six weeks of the authentication of the declaration under Sec. 6, in the case of a newspaper to be published once a week or oftener, and

(b) within three months of the authentication of the declaration under Sec. 6, in the case of any other newspaper, and in every such case, a new declaration shall be necessary before the newspaper can be published.

(6) Where, in any period of three months, any daily, tri-weekly, bi-weekly, weekly or fortnightly newspaper publisher issues the number of which is less than half of what should have been published in accordance with the declaration made in respect thereof, the declaration shall cease to have effect and a new declaration shall be necessary before the publication of the newspaper can be continued.

A copy of the declaration attested by the official seal of the Magistrate, or a copy of the order refusing to authenticate the declaration, shall be forwarded as soon as possible to the person making and subscribing the declaration also to the Press Registrar ....

8. New declaration by persons who have signed a declaration and subsequently ceased to be printers or publishers— If any person has subscribed to any declaration in respect of a newspaper under Sec. 5 and the declaration has been authenticated by Magistrate under Sec. 6 and subsequently that person ceases to be the printer or publisher of the newspaper mentioned in such declaration, he shall appear before any District, Presidency or Sub-divisional Magistrate, and make and subscribe in duplicate the following declaration:

"IA.B., declare that I have ceased to be printer or publisher or printer and publisher of the newspaper entitled—

Authentication and filling— Each original of the latter declaration shall be authenticated by the signature and seal of the Magistrate before whom the said latter declaration shall have been made, and one original of the said latter declaration shall be filed along with each original of the former declaration.

Inspection and supply of copies.— The officer-in charge of each original of the latter declaration shall allow any person applying to inspect that original on payment of a fee of one rupee, and shall give to any person applying a copy of the said latter declaration, attested by the seal of the Court having custody of the original on payment of a fee of two rupees.

Puttng copy in evidence.— In all trials in which a copy, attested as is aforesaid, of the former declaration shall have been put in evidence, it shall be lawful to put in evidence a copy, attested as is aforesaid of the latter declaration, and the former declaration shall not be taken to be evidence that the declarant was, at any period subsequent to the date of the latter declaration, printer or publisher of the newspaper therein mentioned.

A copy of the latter declaration attested by the official seal of the Magistrate shall be forwarded to the Press Registrar.

8.A. Person whose name has been incorrectly published as editor may make a declaration before Magistrate.— If any person, whose name has appeared as editor on a copy of a newspaper, claims that he was not the editor of the issue on which his name has so appeared, he may, within two weeks of his becoming aware that his name has been so published, appear before a District, Presidency or Sub-divisional Magistrate and make a declaration that his name was incorrectly published in that issue as that causing such inquiry to be made as he may consider necessary is satisfied that such declaration is true, he shall certify accordingly, and on that certificate being given the provisions of Sec. 7 shall not apply to that person in respect of that issue of the newspaper.

The Magistrate may extend the period allowed by this section in any case where he is satisfied that such person was prevented by sufficient cause from appearing and making the declaration within that period.

(7) Where any other newspaper has ceased publication for a period, exceeding twelve months, every declaration made in respect thereof shall cease to have effect, and a new declaration shall be necessary before the newspaper can be re-published.

(8) Every existing declaration in respect of a newspaper shall be cancelled by the Magistrate before whom a new declaration is made and subscribed in respect of the same:

Provided that no person who does not ordinarily reside in India, or, who has not attained majority in accrodance with the provisions of the Indian Majority Act, 1875 (9 of 1875), or of the law to which he is subject in respect of the attainment of majority, shall be permitted to make the declaration prescribed by this section, nor shall any such person edit a newspaper.

5-A. Keepers of printing-presses and printers and publishers of newspapers in Jammu and Kashmir to make and subscribe fresh declaration within specified period— (1) No person who has made and subscribed a declaration in respect of any press under Sec. 4 of the Jammu and Kashmir State Press and Publication Act, Svt. 1989, shall keep the press in his possession for the printing of books or papers after the 31st day of December, 1968, unless before the expiry of the date he makes and subscribes a fresh declaration in respect of that press under Sec. 4 of this Act.

(2) Every person who has subscribed to any declaration in respect of a newspaper under Sec. 5 of the Jammu and Kashmir State Press and Publication Act. Svt. 1989, shall cease to be the editor, printer or publisher of the newspaper mentioned in such declaration after the 31st day of December, 1968 unless before the expiry of that date he makes and subscribes a fresh declaration in respect of that newspaper under rule (2) of the rules laid down in Sec. 5 of this Act.

6. Authentication of declaration— Each of the two originals of every declaration so made and subscribed as is aforesaid, shall be authenticated by the signature and official seal of the Magistrate before whom the said declaration shall have been made.

Provided that where any declaration is made and subscribed under Sec. 5 in respect of a newspaper, the declaration shall not, save in the case of newspapers owned by the same person be so authenticated unless the Magistrate is, on inquiry from the Press Registrar, satisfied that the newspaper proposed to be published does not bear a title which the same as, or similar to, that of any other newspaper published either in same language or in the same State.

Deposit.—One of the said originals shall be deposited among the records of the office of the Magistrate and the other shall be deposited among the records of the High Court of Judicature, or other principal Civil Court of original jurisdiction for the place where the said declaration shall have been made.

Inspection of supply of copies.— The officer-in-charge of each original shall allow any person to inspect that original on payment of a fee of one rupee, and shall give to any person applying a copy of the said declaration, attested, and seal of Court which has the custody of the original, on payment of a fee of two rupees.

8.B. Cancellation of declaration.— If, on an application made to him by the Press Registrar or any other person or otherwise, the Magistrate empowered to authenticate a declaration under this Act, is of opinion that any declaration made in respect of a newspaper should be cancelled, he may, after giving the person concerned an opportunity of showing cause-against the action proposed to be taken, hold an inquiry into the matter and if, after considering the cause, if any, shown by such person and after giving him an opportunity of being heard, he is satisfied that —

(i) the newspaper, in respect of which the declaration has been made is being published in contravention of the provisions of this Act or rules made thereunder; or

(ii) the newspaper mentioned in the declaration bears a title which is the same as, or similar to, that of any other newspaper published either in the same language or in the same State; or

(iii) the printer or publisher has ceased to be printer or publisher of the newspaper mentioned in such declaration; or

(iv) the declaration was made on false representation or on the concealment of any material fact or in respect of a periodical work which is not a newspaper;

the Magistrate may, by order, cancel the declaration and shall forward as soon as possible a copy of the order to the person making or subscribing the declaration and also to the Press Registrar.

8-C. Appeal.— (1) Any person aggrieved by an order of a Magistrate refusing to authenticate a declaration under Sec. 6 or cancelling a declaration under Sec. 8-B may, within sixty days from the date on which such order is communicated to him, prefer an appeal to the Appellate Board to be called the Press and Registration Appellate Board[1] [consisting of a chairman and another member to be nominated by the Press Council of India, established under Sec. 4 of the Press Council Act, 1978, from among its members:

Provided that the Appellate Board may entertain an appeal after the expiry of the said period, if it is satisfied that the appellant was prevented by sufficient cause from preferring the appeal in time.

(2) On receipt of an appeal under this section, the Appellate Board may, after calling for the records from the Magistrate and after making such further inquiries as it thinks fit, confirm, modify or set aside the order appealed against.

(3) Subject to the provisions contained in sub-section (2) the Appellate Board may, by order, regualte its practice and procedure.

(4) The decision of the Appellate Board shall be final.

APPENDIX - III
NEWS AGENCIES IN INDIA

The communication system in the nineteenth centruy was revolutionised by the development of the electric telegraph. The British Post Office purchased the private telegraph companies and established its control over telegraphic communication. The cost of transmission was substantially cut down. Press telegrams were charged at the rate of only a shilling for a hundred words. Rapid means of communication lead, among other things, to the development of news agencies. This was welcomed by the mercantile community all over the world who were looking for some means of speedy exchange of commercial intelligence.

In those days the bankers and merchants of Germany were dependent on the slow mail coach which brought the Paris Bourse prices everyday from Brussels, because the French telegraph system ended at Brussels and the German telegraph system began at Aachen. Realising the problem Julius Reuter, a young jewish bank clerk of Cassel, in Germany, started a pegion service between Brussels and Aachen in the middle of the nineteenth century beating all competitors in transmitting the Paris Bourse prices to the German towns.

Originally, *Reuter's* service covered only commecial and financial prices. Later, he conceived the idea of starting a news service after gaining experience as a courier to several courts of Europe. Since the British Press was more organised than the German Julius went to London with the hope of finding better opportunities there.

Until 1858 there existed nothing like systematic telegraphic communication from the continent to Great Britain. That was the year when Julius Reuter met with James Grant, Editor of the *Morning Advertiser*, and suggested that he might be able to feed the daily Press of London with earlier and more accurate intelligence of importance by telegraph as a result of his experience and personal contacts with most of the European Governments. The cost, he estimated, would be less than the payments the papers were then making for their telegraphic news. After a detailed discussion Reuter offered to supply his telegraphic information from the continent daily for a fortnight without any charge. This was to enable Grant to compare the news service with that of his special correspondents. Reuter proved the superiority of his news organisation in no time. His proposals were accepted not only by Grant but also by managers of other journals. Thus the "*Reuter's Agency*" had come into being. Soon Reuter established a telegraphic news service between India and Great Britain.

The history of the origin and growth of news agencies in India has to be traced back to the year 1866 when Henry Collins, Reuter's represetnative in India and Far East, started his office in Bombay. Essentially a colonial venture, its purpose was to supply to the newspapers commercial news about the eastern as well as foreign markets. Herbert Reuter, the eldest son of Julius remarked at the outbreak of Anglo-Afghan war in 1878, "this war has created such an interest in India that we cannot afford to let Indian politics drop." The output initially was 77 words a day from India, and the rate was one pound sterling per word. *Bombay Times* was the first Anglo-Indian newspaper in India to subscribe to *Reuter's* wire service. Other Anglo-Indian papers followed. But the first Indian journal to buy Reuter's service was the *Bengali* when it was converted from a weekly into daily paper in February, 1900.

The concept of an Indian news agency developed gradually along with the growing national experiences in the later nineteenth century which culminated in the birth of the Indian National Congress in 1885. The first Indian news agency was the *Associated Press of India* (API) floated in 1910 by Keshab Chandra Roy (popularly known as K.C. Roy) in collaboration with Everard

Coates, a correspondent of the London *Daily Mail* the Statesman and the *Madras Mail* and Edward Buck, the political correspondent of *Reuters* in India who also functioned as a stringer for the Englishman. The *API* had offices in Bombay, Madras, Calcutta while K.C. Roy operated from Simla, the summer capital of the empire. After the capital has been shifted from Calcutta to Delhi in 1911 news was relayed from Delhi to other centres. With the exit of Roy from the management over certain proprietorial issues, the *API* passed into the hands of *Reuters* in 1919. Roy formed a rival agency, the *Press Bureau*, together with Usha Nath Sen. Roy's genius threatented to develop the Press Bureau into a serious rival of *API*. Having failed to withstand the opposition of the *Press Bureau* the directors of the Associated Press capitulated on the conditions imposed by Roy, who, they had to acknowledge, was the "mainspring of the comprehensive machine" as Pat Lovett described in his 'Journalism in India'.

The third news agency, the *Free Press of India* (*FPI*) was established in 1927 by S. Sadanand. Like the *API* at its inception, the FPI had its roots in the persisting awareness of the inability of an externally-controlled news agency to reflect the Indian viewpoint. Sadanand's venture received unqualified support from some of the foremost personalities in Indian industry and public life like Walchand Hirachand, G.D. Birla, Pheroze Sethna, Purushottamdas Thakurdas and M.R. Jayakar who were directors of the agency along with the founder. This was not to the liking of the colonial rulers. Pressure was put on the directors and four of them resigned in 1929 and the fifth left the organisation in 1930.

The Press Ordinance of 1930 came down with a heavy hand on all newspapers publishing *Free Press* news, *Free Press* telegrams were subjected to a strict censorship and newspapers became reluctant to carry news supplied by the agency for the fear of being victimised by the government. The *FPI* also faced direct hostility from its competitor, the *Associated Press*, which also exerted pressure by insisting that its service would not be available to newspapers subscribing to any other news agency.

Finding that his news agency was in danger of extinction Sadanand started the *Free Press Journal* as an English morning daily in June 1930. This newspaper and other associated newspapers he started published *Free Press* news exclusively. For quite some time all the *Free Press* publications did well. But this was resented by other newspapers. They protested against a news agency running newspapers in competition with customers and discontinued their subscription to *Free Press* of India.

Sadanand went bankrupt through the forfeiture of Rs 70,000 he had to pay as securities for the violation of the imperial code. Penalty had to be paid for an editorial entitled" Swaraj is the Only Remedy" in the *Free Press Journal* and for publishing extracts from an article by Gandhi and a report of Vithalbhai Patel's speech in New York. The agency was shut down in 1935 because of acute financial difficulties. Publication of *Free Press Journal* was also suspended.

In 1933, two years before the closure of FPI, Bidhu Bhusan Sen Gupta, its Calcutta representative, started *United Press of India* with the support from locally influential circles. Prominent among the patrons was Dr Bidhan Chandra Roy who was the Chairman of the Board of Directors while Bidhu Bhusan Sen Gupta was the Managing Director. This agency too weathered many crises through its efforts and resilience.

The introduction of the teleprinter system in 1937 by the General Manager of Reuters in India, W.J. Moloney, was the most significant development at this stage. It radically changed the system of news transmission and made it possible to provide agency service at reasonable rates to small newspapers throughout the country. The era of pegion post, the telegram and mail as the transmitters of news came to an end. In 1940 another news agency, the Orient, was started by some prominent Muslim League leaders with official encouragement. It enjoyed the patronage of Nizam of Hyderabad.

PRESS TRUST OF INDIA (PTI)

The transfer of political power in 1947 was followed by transfer of power in the sphere of news. However, this transfer was not without tension. The idea of the take-over of *API* from *Reuters* was mooted in 1946 at a meeting of the Indian and Eastern Newspaper Society (IENS) in Lahore. Among those who supported the scheme was Devdas Gandhi, Kasturba Srinivasan and Tushar Kanti Ghosh. Meanwhile, the Labour Government in the U.K. had sounded Reuters to come to terms with Indian newspapers about the transfer of its interests. *Reuters* agreed to hand over the business of internal agency, *API*, to the national news agency but wanted to retain control over the foreign news service. The deadlock was finally resolved through the intervention of Sardar Vallabhbhai Patel, the then member for Home and Information of the Government of India. He insisted on the total transfer of *Reuter's* Indian interests to Indian agency, failing which the *Reuter's* teleprinter line licence due for renewal in July 1947, would not be renewed. This clinched the issue. Thus *the Press Trust of India (PTI)*, registered as a company in August 1947, went into operation on February 1, 1949.

The *PTI* began as a non-profit venture. Shareholding was restricted to newspapers regularly published in India which subscribed to its services. The shareholders could not be paid any dividends with the income being invested solely on the promotion of professional activities. Its constitution had also provided that " control shall at no time pass into the hands of any interests, group or section." Administration was the responsibility of a General Manager and Board of fourteen directors, of whom ten were from the newspapers and four were public men. A chairman was elected annually.

In 1959 PTI's exclusive partnership with Reuters for the purchase of Reuter news ended. PTI kept its windows on the world scene open through arrangements for exchange with more than a dozen foreign news agencies.

UNITED NEWS OF INDIA (UNI)

The *United Press of India (UPI)* had collapsed in 1958. But the void had to be filled. The first Press Commission report (1952-54) had spoken of the need to have "at least two news agencies each competing with the other and also acting as a corrective to the other." The newspapers were in agreement with this recommendation. The *UNI* was sponsored by eight newspapers — *Hindu, The Times of India, Statesman, Amrita Bazar Patrika, Hindustan Times, Hindusthan Standard, Deccan Herald* and *Aryavarta*.

The agency for some time had to manage with old *UPI* teleprinter machines, rusted through disuse. But the *UNI* grew into an important rival agency within a decade. Though its pace of growth was rapid its coverage is still inadequate in absolute terms and in relation to the country's requirements.

The *UNI* has started a number of specialised services like a weekly Backgrounder Service of well-documented, in-depth backgrounders on current topics; the Agricultural News and Feature Service, Airmail News Service etc. *UNI* is also the first to venture into the field of science reportage with a full-time science correspondent. For world news the *UNI* has tie-up with a number of foreign news agencies.

HINDUSTAN SAMACHAR

Soon after independence small news agencies with slender resources were started with the object of filling in the many gaps in domestic news coverage. One such was the *Hindustan Samachar*, India's first multi-lingual agency set up as a private limited company in 1948 by

S.S. Apte. Its avowed aim was to educate and to strive for material integration through the promotion of all Indian languages. This early effort was limited to the distribution of news among local newspapers through Devnagri telegrams. The situation improved somewhat with the advent of Devnagri teleprinters. But the heavy transmission costs forced Apte to hand over the agency to a cooperative society of workers. Being a workers cooperative, it remained free from the control of both the government as well as big newspapers.

The agency supplied news to its subscribers in ten languages—Hindi, Gujrati, Marathi, Punjabi, Urdu, Bengali, Oriya, Assamese, Telegu and Malayalam.

SAMACHAR BHARATI

Samachar Bharati, the second language agency, came into being on October 2, 1966 and started operations in 1967. Four years later the agency was converted almost into a Government company with the State Governments of Bihar, Gujrat, Rajasthan and Karnataka holding more than fifty per cent of the company's shares. Sri Prakasa, the then Governor of Bombay, was its first Chairman. Jayaprakash Narayan also served as its Chairman for several years.

The agency rendered valuable services in supplying news to small and medium language papers, not only in Hindi but also in Marathi, Gujrati, Kannada, Urdu and Punjabi. In 1973 it started an annual reference manual in Hindi called" *Desh aur Duniya*". It also had a feature service — "*Bharati*". The agency had at various times organised seminars and workshops to give professional training to language journalists.

The four agencies merged their separate identities into what came to be known as "Samachar" in February 1976. It was for a brief period. They got back their separate identities after the Janata Party had captured power at the Centre in 1977. However, *Hindustan Samachar* and *Samachar Bharati* did not survive. They merged into the two language agencies started by PTI and UNI and named PTI Bhasa and Univarta respectively.

This apart, there are about eight non-wire agencies accredited to Government of India. These agencies broadly deal features, films, cartography, news analyses etc.

Sources: The Indian Press by Margarita Barns, History of Indian Journalism by J. Natarajan and report of the committee on news agencies.

> "A second drama in which contemporary journalists are involved, consists in the conflict between their pursuit of the truth and their need and their desire to be on good terms with the powerful. For the powerful are perhaps the chief source of the news. They are also the dispensers of many kinds of favour."
>
> Walter Lippman

APPENDIX - IV
GUIDELINES FOR JOURNALISTS
(Framed By Press Council Of India)

The fundamental objective of journalism is to serve the people with news, views, comments and information on matters of public interest in a fair, accurate, unbiased, sober and decent manner. Towards this end, the Press is expected to conduct itself in keeping with certain norms of professionalism universally recognised. The norms enunciated below and other specific guidelines appended thereafter, when applied with due discernment and adaptation to the varying circumstances of each case, will help the journalist to self-regulate his or her conduct.

ACCURACY AND FAIRNESS:

1) The Press shall eschew publication of inaccurate, baseless, graceless, misleading or distorted material. All sides of the core issue or subject should be reported. Unjustified rumours and surmises should not be set forth as facts.

PRE-PUBLICATION VERIFICATION:

2) On receipt of a report or article of public interest and benefit containing imputations or comments against a citizen, the editor should check with due care and attention its factual accuracy- apart from other authentic sources with the person or the organization concerned to elicit his/her or its version, comments or reaction and publish the same with due amendments in the report where necessary. In the event of lack or absence of response, a footnote to that effect should be appended to the report.

CAUTION AGAINST DEFAMATORY WRITINGS:

3) Newspaper should not publish anything which is manifestly defamatory or libellous against any individual

or organization unless after due care and checking, they have sufficient reason to believe that it is true and its publication will be for public good.

4) Truth is no defence for publishing derogatory, scurrilous and defamatory material against a private citizen where no public interest is involved.

5) No personal remarks which may be considered or construed to be derogatory in nature against a dead person should be published except in rare cases of public interest, as the dead person cannot possibly contradict or deny those remarks.

6) The Press shall not rely on objectionable past behaviour of a citizen for basing the scathing comments with reference to fresh action of that person. If public good requires such reference, the Press should make prepublication inquiries from the authorities concerned about the follow up action, if any, in regard to those adverse actions.

7) The Press has a duty, discretion and right to serve the public interest by drawing reader's attention to citizens of doubtful antecedents and of questionable character but as responsible journalists they should observe due restraint and caution in hazarding their own opinion or conclusion in branding these persons as 'cheats' or 'killers' etc. The cardinal principle being that the guilt of a person should be established by proof of facts alleged and not by proof of the bad character of the accused. In its zest to expose, the Press should not exceed the limits of ethical caution and fair comments.

8) Where the impugned publications are mainfestly injurious to the reputation of the complainant, the onus shall on the respondent to show that they were true or to establish that they constituted fair comment made in good faith and for public good.

ACTS AND CONDUCT OF PUBLIC OFFICIALS:

9) So far as the government, local authority and

other organs institutions exercising governmental power are concerned they cannot maintain a suit for damages for acts and conduct relevant to the discharge of their official duties unless the official establishes that the publication was made with reckless disregard for truth. However, judiciary which is protected by the power to punish for contempt of court and the Parliament and Legislatures, protected as their privileges are by Articles 105 and 194 respectively, of the Constitution of India, represent exception to this rule.

10) Publication of news or comments/information on public officials conducting investigations should not have a tendency to help the commission of offences or to impede the prevention or detection of offences or prosecution of the guilty. The investigating agency is also under a corresponding obligation not to leak out or disclose such information or indulge in disinformation.

11) The Official Secrets Act, 1923 or any similar enactment or provision having the force of law equally bind the Press or media though there is no law empowering the state or its officials to prohibit, or to impose a prior restraint upon the Press/ media.

12) Cartoons and caricatures in depicting good humour are to be placed in a special category of news that enjoy more liberal attitude.

RIGHT TO PRIVACY:

13) The Press shall not intrude upon or invade the privacy of an individual unless outweighed by genuine overriding public interest, not being a prurient or morbid curiousity. So, however, that once a matter becomes a matter of public record, the right to privacy no longer subsists and it becomes a legitimate subject for comment by Press and media among others.

Explanation: Things concerning a person's home, family, religion, health, sexuality, personal life and private affairs are covered by the concept of PRIVACY excepting where any of these impinges upon the public or public interest.

14) Caution against identification: While reporting crime involving rape, abduction or kidnap of women/females or sexual assault on children, or raising doubts and questions touching the chastity, personal character and privacy of women, the names, photographs of the victims or other particulars leading to their identity shall not be published.

15) Minor children and infants who are the offspring of sexual abuse or 'forcible marriage' or illicit sexual union shall not be identified or photographed.

INTERVIEWS AND PHONE CONVERSATION:

16) The Press shall not tape-record anyone's conversation without that person's knowledge or consent, except where the recording is necessary to protect the journalist in a legal action, or for other compelling good reason.

17) The Press shall, prior to publication, delete offensive epithets used by an interviewee in conversation with the Press person.

18) Intrusion through photography into moments of personal grief shall be avoided. However, photography of victims of accidents or natural calamity may be in larger public interest.

CONJECTURE, COMMENT AND FACT:

19) Newspapers should not pass on or elevate conjecture, speculation or comment as a statement of fact. All these categories should be distinctly stated.

SUGGESTIVE GUILT:

20) Newspapers should eschew suggestive guilt by association. They should not name or identify the family or relatives or associates of a person convicted

or accused of a crime, when they are totally innocent and a reference to them is not relevant to the matter reported.

21) It is contrary to the norms of journalism for a paper to identify itself with and project the case of any one party in the case of any controversy/ dispute.

CORRECTIONS:

22) When any factual error or mistake is detected or confirmed, the newspaper should publish the correction promptly with due prominence and with apology or expression of regrets in a case of serious lapse.

RIGHT OF REPLY:

23) The newspaper should promptly and with due prominence, publish, either in full or with due editing, free of cost, at the instance of the person affected or feeling aggrieved/or concerned by the impugned publication, a contradiction/reply/clarification or rejoinder sent to the editor in the form of a letter or note. If the editor doubts the truth or factual accuracy of the contradiction/ reply/ clarification or rejoinder, he shall be at liberty to add separately at the end a brief editorial comment doubting its veracity, but only when this doubt is reasonably founded on unimpeachable documentary or other evidential material in his/her possession. This is a concession which has to be availed of sparingly with due discretion and caution in appropriate cases.

24) However, where the reply/ contradiction or rejoinder is being published in compliance with the discretion of the Press Council, it is permissible to append a brief editorial note to that effect.

25) Right of rejoinder cannot be claimed through the medium of Press Conference, as publication of a news of a conference is within the discretionary powers of an editor.

26) Freedom of the Press involves the readers' right

to know all sides of an issue of public interest. An editor, therefore, shall not refuse to publish the reply or rejoinder merely on the ground that in his opinion the story published in the newspaper was true. That is an issue to be left to the judgment of the readers. It also does not behave an editor to show contempt towards a reader.

LETTERS TO EDITOR:

27) An editor who decides to open his columns for letters on a controversial subject, is not obliged to publish all the letters received in regard to that subject. He is entitled to select and publish only some of them either in entirety or the gist thereof. However, in exercising this discretion, he must make an honest endeavour to ensure that what is published is not onesided but represents a fair balance between the views for and against with respect to the principal issue in controversy.

28) In the event of rejoinder upon rejoinder being sent by two parties on a controversial subject, the editor has the discretion to decide at which stage to close the continuing column.

OBSCENITY AND VULGARITY

29) Newspapers/journalists shall not publish anything which is obscene, vulgar or offensive to public good taste.

30) Newspapers shall not display advertisements which are vulgar or which, through depiction of a woman in nude or lewd posture, provoke lecherous attention of males as if she herself was a commercial commodity for sale.

31) Whether a picture is obscene or not, is to be judged in relation to three tests: namely

    i) Is it vulgar and indecent?

    ii) Is it a piece of mere pornography?

Appendices

iii) Is its publication meant merely to make money by titallating the sex feelings of adolescents and among whom it is intended to circulate? In other words, does it constitute an unwholesome exploitation for commercial gain.

Other relevant considerations are whether the picture is relevant to the subject matter of the magazine. That is to say, whether its publication serves any preponderating social or public purpose, in relation to art, painting, medicine, research or reform of sex.

VIOLENCE

32) Newspapers/ journalists shall avoid presenting acts of violence, armed robberies and terrorist activities in a manner that glorifies the perpetrators' acts, declarations or death in the eyes of the public.

SOCIAL EVILS:

33) Newspapers shall not allow their columns to be misused for writings which have a tendency to encourage or glorify social evils like Sati Pratha or ostentatious celebrations.

COMMUNAL DISPUTES/CLASHES:

34) News, views or comments relating to communal or religious disputes/clashes shall be published after proper verification of facts and presented with due caution and restraint in a manner which is conducive to the creation of an atmosphere congenial to communal harmony, amity and peace. Sensational, provocative and alarming headlines are to be avoided. Acts of communal violence or vandalism shall be reported in a manner as may not undermine the people's confidence in the law and order machinery of the State. Giving community-wise figures of the victims of communal riot, or writing about the incident in a style which is likely to inflame passions, aggravate the tension, or accentuate the strained relations between the communities/

religious groups concerned, or which has a potential to exacerbate the trouble, shall be avoided.

HEADINGS

35) In general and particularly in the context of communal disputes or clashes—

a. Provocative and sensational headlines are to be avoided;

b. Headings must reflect and justify the matter printed under them;

c. Headlines containing allegations made in statements should either identify the body or the source making it or at least carry quotation marks.

CASTE, RELIGION OR COMMUNITY

36) In general, the caste identification of a person or a particular class should be avoided, particularly when in the context it conveys a sense or attributes a conduct or practice derogatory to that caste.

37) Newspapers are advised against the use of word 'Scheduled Caste' or 'harijan' which has been objected to by some persons.

38) An accused or a victim shall not be described by his caste or community when the same does not have anything to do with the offence or the crime and plays no part either in the identification of any accused or proceeding, if there be any.

39) Newspapers should not publish any fictional literature distorting and protraying the religious characters in an adverse light transgression of the norms of literary taste and offending the religious susceptibities of large sections of society who hold those characters in high esteem, invested with attributes of the virtuous and lofty.

40) Commercial exploitation of the name of prophets, seers or deities is repugnant to journalistic ethics and good taste.

NATURAL CALAMITIES:

41) Facts and data relating to spread of epidemics or natural calamities shall be checked up thoroughly from authentic sources and then published with due restraint in a manner bereft of sensationalism, exaggeration, surmises or unverified facts.

NATIONAL INTERESTS:

42) Newspapers shall, as a matter of self-regulation, exercise due restraint and caution in presenting any news comment or information which is likely to jeopardise, endanger or harm the paramount interests of the State and society, or the rights of individuals with respect to which reasonable restrictions may be imposed by law on the right to freedom of speech and expression under clause (2) of Article 19 of the Constitution of India.

43) Publication of wrong/incorrect map is a very serious offence, whatever the reason, as it adversely affects the territorial integrity of the country and warrants prompt and prominent retraction with regrets.

MISUSE OF DIPLOMATIC IMMUNITY:

44) The media shall make every possible effort to build bridges of co-operation, friendly relations and better understanding between India and foreign States. At the same time, it is the duty of a newspaper to expose any misuse or undue advantage of the diplomatic immunities.

INVESTIGATIVE JOURNALISM

45) Investigative reporting has three basic elements.

a. It has to be the work of the reporter, not of others he is reporting;

b. The subject should be of public importance for the reader to know;

c. An attempt is being made to hide the truth from the people.

(i) The first norm follows as a necessary corollary from

(a) that the investigative reporter should, as a rule, base his story on facts investigated, detected and verified by himself and not on hearsay or on derivative evidence collected by a third party, not checked up from direct, authentic sources by the reporter himself.

(ii) There being a conflict between the factors which require openness and those which necessitate secrecy, the investigative journalist should strike and maintain in his report a proper balance between openness on the one hand and secrecy on the other, placing the public good above everything.

(iii) The investigative journalist should resist the temptation of quickies or quick gains conjured up from half-baked, incomplete, doubtful facts, not fully checked up and verified from authentic sources by the reporter himself.

(iv) Imaginary facts, or ferreting out or conjecturing the non-existent should be scrupulously avoided. Facts, facts and yet more facts are vital and they should be checked and corss- checked whenever possible until the moment the paper goes to Press.

(v) The newspapers must adopt strict standards of fairness and accuracy of facts. Findings should be presented in an objective manner, without exaggerating or distorting, that would stand up in a court of law, if necessary.

(vi) The reporter must not approach the matter or the issue under investigation, in a manner as though he were the prosecutor or counsel for the prosecution. The reporter's approach should be fair, accurate and balanced. All facts properly checked up, both for and against the core issues, should be distinctly and separately stated, free from any onesided inferences or unfair comments. The tone and tenor of the report and its language should be sober, decent and dignified, and not needlessly offensive, barbed, derisive or castigatory, particularly while commenting on the version of the person whose alleged activity or misconduct is being investigated. Nor should the investigative reporter conduct the proceedings and pronounce his verdict of guilt or innocence against the person whose alleged criminal acts and conduct were investigated, in a manner as if he were a court trying the accused.

(vii) In all proceedings including the investigation, presentation and publication of the report, the investigative journalist/newspaper should be guided by the paramount principle of criminal jurisprudence, that a person is innocent unless the offence alleged against him is proved beyond doubt by independent, reliable evidence.

(viii) The private life, even of a public figure, is his own. Exposition or invasion of his personal privacy or private life is not permissible unless there is clear evidence that the wrong doings in question have a reasonable nexus with the misuse of his public position or power and has an adverse impact on public interest.

(ix) Though the legal provisions of Criminal Procedure do not in terms, apply to investigating proceedings by a journalist, the fundamental principles underlying them can be adopted as a guide on grounds of equity, ethics and good conscience.

CONFIDENCE TO BE RESPECTED:

46) If information is received from a confidential source, the confidence should be respected. The journalist cannot be compelled by the Press Council to disclose such source; but it shall not be regarded as a breach of journalistic ethics if the source is voluntarily disclosed in proceedings before the Council by the journalist who

considers it necessary to repel effectively a charge against him/her. This rule requiring a newspaper not to publish matters disclosed to it in confidence, is not applicable where

(a) consent of the source is subsequently obtained; or

(b) the editor clarified by way of an appropriate footnote that since the publication of certain matters were in the public interest, the information in question was being published although it had been made 'off the record'.

CRITICIZING JUDICIAL ACTS:

47) Excepting where the court sits 'in-camera' or directs otherwise, it is open to a newspaper to report pending judicial proceedings, in a fair, accurate and reasonable manner. But it shall not publish anything:—

- which, in its direct and immediate effect, creates a substantial risk of obstructing, impeding or prejudicing seriously the due administration of justice; or

- is in the nature of a running commentary or debate, or records the paper's own findings, conjectures, reflection or comments on issues, sub judice and which may amount to arrogation to the newspaper the functions of the court; or

- regarding the personal character of the accused standing trial on a charge of committing a crime.

Newspapers shall not as a matter of caution, publish or comment on evidence collected as a result of investigative journalism, when, after the accused is arrested and charged, the court becomes seized of the case: Nor should they reveal, comment upon or evaluate a confession allegedly made by the accused.

48) While newspapers may, in the public interest, make reasonable criticism of a judicial act or the

judgment of a court for public good; they shall not cast scurrilous aspersions on, or impute improper motives, or personal bias to the judge.

Nor shall they scandalise the court or the judiciary as a whole, or make personal allegations of lack of ability or integrity against a judge.

49) Newspapers shall, as a matter of caution, avoid unfair and unwarranted criticism which, by innuendo, attributes to a judge extraneous consideration for performing an act in due course of his/her judicial functions, even if such criticism does not strictly amount to criminal Contempt of Court.

CRASS COMMERCIALISM:

50) While newspapers are entitled to ensure, improve or strengthen their financial viability by all legitimate means, the Press shall not engage in crass commercialism or unseemly cut-throat commercial competition with their rivals in a manner repugnant to high professional standards and good taste.

51) Predatory price wars/trade competition among newspapers, laced with tones disparaging the products of each other, initiated and carried on in print, assume the colour of unfair 'trade' practice, repugnant to journalistic ethics. The question as to when it assumes such an unethical character, is one of fact depending on the circumstances of each case.

PLAGIARISM:

520 Using or passing off the writings or ideas of another as one's own, without crediting the source, is an offence against the ethics of journalism.

UNAUTHORISED LIFTING OF NEWS:

53) The practice of lifting news from other newspapers and publishing them subsequently as their own, ill-comports with the high standards of journalism. To

remove its unethicality, the 'lifting' newspaper must duly acknowledge the source of the report. The position of features articles is different from 'news' : Feature articles shall not be lifted without permission/proper acknowledgement.

54) The Press shall not reproduce in any form offending portions or excerpts from a proscribed book.

NON-RETURN OF UNSOLICITED MATERIAL:

55) A paper is not bound to return unsolicited material sent for consideration of publication. However, when the same is accompanied by stamped envelope, the paper should make all efforts to return it.

ADVERTISEMENTS:

56) Commercial advertisements are information as much as social, economic or political information. What is more, advertisements shape attitude and ways of life at least as much as other kinds of information and comment. Journalistic propriety demands that advertisements must be clearly distinguishable from editorial matters carried in the newspaper.

57) Newspaper shall not publish anything which has a tendency to malign wholesale or hurt the religious sentiments of any community or section of society.

58) Advertisements which offend the provisions of the Drugs and Magical Remedies (Objectionable Advertisement) Act, 1954, should be rejected.

59) Newpapers should not publish an advertisement containing anything which is unlawful or illegal, or is contrary to good taste or to journalistic ethics or proprieties.

60) Newspapers while publishing advertisements, shall specify the amount received by them. The rationale behind this is that advertisements should be charged

at rates usually chargeable by a newspaper since payment of more than the normal rates would amount to a subsidy to the paper.

61) Publication of dummy advertisements that have neither been paid for, nor authorised by the advertisers, constitute breach of journalistic ethics.

62) Deliberate failure to publish an advertisement in all the copies of a newspaper offends against the standards of journalistic ethics and constitutes gross professional misconduct.

63) There should be no lack of vigilance or a communication gap between the advertisement department and the editorial department of a newspaper in the matter of considering the propriety or otherwise of an advertisement received for publication.

(64) The editors should insist on their right to have the final say in the acceptance or rejection of advertisements, specially those which border on or cross the line between decency and obscenity.

65) An editor shall be responsible for all matters, including advertisements published in the newspaper. If responsibility is disclaimed, this shall be explicitly stated beforehand.

COMMUNAL DISTURBANCES

Recognising that the press which enjoys the utmost freedom of expression has a great and vital role to play in educating and moulding public opinion on correct lines in regard to the need for friendly and harmonious relations between the various communities and religious groups forming the fabric of Indian political life and in mirroring the conscience of the best minds of the country to achieve national solidarity, the Press Council of India considers that this object would be defeated, communal peace and harmony disturbed and national unity disrupted if the Press does not strictly adhere to proper norms and standards in reporting on or commenting on matters which bear on communal relations. Without attempting to be exhaustive, the Council considers the following as offending against journalistic proprieties and ethics:

66) Distortion or exaggeration of facts or incidents in relation to communal matters or giving currency to unverified rumours, suspicions or inferences as if they were facts and base their comments on them.

67) Employment of intemperate or unrestrained language in the presentation of news or views, even as a piece of literary flourish or for the purpose of rhetoric or emphasis.

68) Encouraging or condoning violence even in the face of provocation as a means of obtaining redress of grievances whether the same be genuine or not.

69) While it is the legitimate function of the Press to draw attention to the genuine and legitimate grievances of any community with a view to having the same redressed by all peaceful, legal and legitimate means, it is improper and a breach of journalistic ethics to invent grievances, or to exggerate real grievances, as these tend to promote communal ill-feeling and accentuate discord.

70) Scurrilous and untrue attacks on communities, or individuals, particularly when this is accompanied by charges attributing misconduct to them as due to their being members of a particular community, or caste.

71) Falsely giving a communal colour to incidents which might occur in which members of different communities happen to be involved.

72) Emphasising matters that are not to produce communal hatred or illwill, or fostering feelings of distrust between communities.

73) Publishing alarming news which are in substance untrue or make provocative comments on such news or even otherwise calculated to embitter relations between different communities or regional or linguistic groups.

74) Exaggerating actual happenings to achieve sensationlism and publication of news which adversely affect communal harmony with banner headlines or in distinctive types.

75) Making disrespectful, derogatory or insulting remarks on or reference to the different religions or faiths or their founders.

76) The state Government should take upon themselves the responsibility of keeping a close watch on the communal writings that might spark off tension, destruction and death, and bring them to the notice of the Council.

77) The Government may have occasion to take action against erring papers or editors. But it must do so within the bounds of law. If newsmen are arrested, or search and seizure operations become necessary, it would be healthy convention if such developments could be reported to the Press Council within 24 to 48 hours followed by a detailed note within a week;

78) Under circumstances must the authorities resort to vindictive measures like cut in advertisements, cancellation of accreditation, cut in newsprint quota and other facilities;

79) Provocative and sensational headlines should be avoided by the Press;

80) Headings must reflect and justify the matter printed under them;

81) Figures of casualities given in headlines should preferably be on the lower side in case or doubt about their exactness and where the numbers reported by various sources differ widely;

82) Headings containing allegations made in statements should either identify the person/body making the allegation or, at least, should carry quotation marks;

83) News reports should be devoid of comments and value judgement;

84) Presentation of news should not be motivated or guided by partisan feelings, nor should it appear to be so;

85) Language employed in writing the news should be temperate and such as may foster feelings or amity among communities and group;

86) Corrections should be promptly published with due prominence and regrets expressed in serious cases; and

87) It will help a great deal if in-service training is given to journalists for inculcation of all these principles.

REPORTING AIDS

From sporadic news, AIDS must become a compaign target for our mass media with the following components of Do's and Don'ts:

88) Media must inform and educate the people, not alarm or scare them. The emphasis must be on HIV (Human Immunodeficiency Virus) can be prevented from going into unaffected humans. AIDS takes around 10 years to develop and HIV is a virus which does not survive for long outside a body.

Thus it is not spread by casual contact, hugging or kissing through food or water or through insects.

89) Media must hammer home the point that AIDS through sexual transmission or blood infection can be prevented. Minimum precaution of use of condoms in sex, and sterilisation of skin-piercing instruments and their prompt disposal after use.

90) Media must report every case pertaining to AIDS be it positive or negative. There must be constant liaison between the media and the medical profession to report on latest developments and research findings.

91) Media must highlight and crusade against such practice as quarantine, isolation and ostracism of AIDS patients.

Besides being an affront to human dignity, those

practices will not help minimise AIDS infection, and are injurious to public health as: "they give a false sense of security to people outside the stigmatised group that the treat of infection has been removed and the need for precaution minimised. Also, such practices will drive the AIDS problem underground and make the campaign against the scourge more difficult.

Community education, using all the latest expertise of mass education and behavioural scientists and media experts, has to play a crucial role in spreading the message about preventing this dreaded infection. Opinion builders of the society (political and religious leaders, movie and sports personalities, other famous persons) must take the leadership in educating the public about AIDS and how to avoid contracting this infection. Innovative use of media and a positive reporting attitude of media will go a long way in making AIDS awareness campaign a success.

92) Media must force the authorities to impose rigorous bloodtesting norms on prostitutes and professional women and issue periodical warning to the public about areas where the incidence of AIDS had high probability.

93) Media must help the authorities in eliminating commercial blood collection and pre-testing of all blood donors for HIV and other diseases.

94) Media must as a role respect the right to privacy of AIDS patients and must not subject them to needless exposure and social stigma.

95) Every mass medium must observe the terms of the final document of the international Consultation of AIDS and human rights, and promptly report the violation of such rights protecting the basic human rights to life and liberty, privacy and freedom of movement.

GUIDELINES FOR FINANCIAL JOURNALISTS

96) The financial journalist should not accept gifts,

loans, trips, discount, preferential shares or other consideration which compromise or are likely to compromise his position.

97) It should be mentioned prominently in the report about any company that the report is based on information given by the company or the financial sponsors of the company.

98) When the trips are sponsored for visiting establishments of a company, the author of the report who has availed of the trip must state invariably that the visit was sponsored by the company concerned and that it had also extended the hospitality as the case may be.

99) No matter related to the company should be published without verifying the facts from the company and the source of such report should also be disclosed. 5) A reporter who exposes a scam or brings out a report for promotion of a good project, should be encouraged and awarded.

100) A journalist who has financial interests such as share holdings, stock holdings, etc., in a company, should not report on that company.

101) The journalist should not use for his own benefit or for the benefit of his relations and friends, information received by him in advance for publication.

102) No newspaper owner, editor or anybody connected with a newspaper should use his relations with the newspaper to promote his other business interests.

103) Whenever there is an indictment of a Particular advertising agency or advertiser by the Advertising Council of India, the newspaper in which the advertisement was published must publish the news of indictment prominently.

ELECTION COVERAGE

104) It will be the duty of the Press to give objective

reports about elections and the candidates. The newspapers are not expected to indulge in unhealthy election campaigns, exaggerated reports about any candidate/party or incident during the elections. In practice, two or three closely contesting candidates attract all the media attention. While reporting on the actual campaign, a newspaper may not leave out any important point raised by a candidate and make an attack on his or her opponent.

105) Election campaign along communal or caste lines is banned under the electionrules. Hence, the Press should eschew reports which tend to promote feelings of enmity or hatred between people on the ground of religion, race, caste, community or language. 3. The Press should refrain from publishing false or critical statements in regard to the personal character and conduct of any candidate or in relation to the candidature or withdrawal of any candidate or his candidature, to prejudice the prospects of that candidate in the elections. The Press shall not publish unverified allegations against any candidate/party.

106) The Press shall not accept any kind of inducement, financial or otherwise, to project a candidate/party. It shall not accept hospitality or other facilities offered to them by or on behalf of any candidate/party.

107) The Press is not expected to indulge in canvassing of a particular candidate/party. If it does, it shall allow the right of reply to the other candidate/party.

108) The Press shall not accept/publish any advertisement at the cost of public exchequer regarding achievements of a party/government in power.

109) The Press shall observe all the directions/orders/instructions of the Election Commission/ Returning Officers or Chief Electoral Officer issued from time to time.

110) No newspaper shall publish exit-poll surveys, however genuine they may be, till the last of the polls is over.

APPENDIX - V
CHRONOLOGY OF EVENTS

1780 *Bengal Gazette* started by James Augustus Hicky; *India Gazette* established by B. Messink and Peter Reed;

1784 *Calcutta Gazette* started by the Government; Pitts's India Bill;

1785 *Bengal Journal* appears; *Oriental Magazine* or *Calcutta Amusement* comes out; *Madras Courier* founded;

1786 *Calcutta Chronicle*;

1789 *Bombay Herald*; French Revolution;

1790 *Bombay Courier*;

1791 *Bombay Gazette*;

1794 William Duane deported from India to England, *Calcutta Courier*;

1795 *Madras Gazette*; *India Herald*

1798 Charles Maclean, surgeon, deported for writing in newspapers; Lord Wellesly Governor-General; *Bengal Harkaru*

1799 Wellesly's Regulations for the control and Guidance of newspaper publishers in Calcutta ;

1801 First Bengali book published by Serampore missioneries;

1806 First Hindi printing Press in Calcutta

1807 Ban of public meetings without Government consent;

1812 First Gujerati Printing Press in Bombay;

1813 Charter Act;

1816 *Vangal Gazette*, first Bengali newspaper;

1818 Serampore missioneries start Bengali *Dig Darshan*,

Samachar Darpan and English *Friend of India*; Lord Hastings Regulation for the Press; James Silk Buckingham's *Calcutta Journal*;

1821 Buckingham warned; *John Bull in the East, Sambad Kaumudi, Samachar Chandrika*, First Hindi weekly *Udant Martand*;

1822 *Mumbaina Samachar* (oldest surviving newspaper);

1823 John Adam Acting Governor-General; Buckingham's licence revoked; new Regulations for the Press promulgated; Lord Amherst Governor-General; Sandford Arnot deported;

1824 C.J. Fair deported from Bombay; Buckingham's appeal to Privy Council:

1825 Press Regulation promulgated in Bombay;

1828 William Butterworth Bayley Acting Governor-General; Lord William Bentinck Governor General; Buckingham founds Athenaeum;

1829 "*Suttee*" abolished in Bengal; *Bengal Herald*;

1830 Growth of Bengali and Persian Press; Enforcement of "half bhatta" order; Charles Matcalfe's independent views; "Suttee" abolished in Bombay and Madras; Semaphoric system of communication used in Calcutta; *Mumbai Vartamam*, second Gujerati weekly from Bombay;

1831 *Sambad Prabhakar, Indian Reformer*;

1833 Company's Charter renewed; Growth of Press in various languages;

1835 Macaulay's Minute urging the use of the English in preference to Sanskrit and Arabic. Lord Bentinck concurs; Calcutta journalists petition for abolition of Press laws; press restrictions abolished; *Friend of India* becomes a weekly;

1836 Lord Auckland Governor-General; Court of Directors condemns Metcalfe's liberation of the Press; *Bombay Times* and *Journal of Commerce*:

1837 Victoria Queen of England;

1838 Metcalfe leaves for England;

1840 Carriages introduced in India; Telegraph used in England;

1842 Lord Ellenborough Governor General;

1843 Conquest of Sind;

1844 *Calcutta Review*; Henry Hardinge Governor General;

1846 *Hindu Intelligencer*; *Lahore-Chronicle*;

1848 Lord Dalhousie Governor General;

1849 Annexation of the Punjab;

1851 Telegraph line used in Calcutta;

1856 Lord Canning Governor-General

1857 Great rebellion ; 274 miles of railway opened; Promulgation of Press Act;

1858 Crown takes over Government of India from East India Company; Lord Canning becomes Viceroy; Julius Reuter starts his world news service; *Som Prakash*;

1860 Completion of submarine telegraph line between England and India;

1861 India Councils Act; *Bombay Times, Standard* and *Telegraph* merge to become *Times of India*; *Indian Mirror*; *Mukherji's Magazine*;

1862 Lord Elgin becomes Viceroy; *Bengali*;

1863 *Indian Daily News*;

1864 Sir John Lawrence Viceroy;

1865 Completion of overland telegraph line between India and England; *Pioneer* of Allahabad;

1867 Press and Registration of Books Act;

1868 *Amrita Bazar Patrika*; *Madras Mail*;

Appendices

1869 Lord Mayo Viceroy; *Amrita Bazar Patrika* becomes bilingual; opening of Suez Canal;

1870 Indian Penal Code amended; *Sulav Samachar*;

1872 Lord Northbrook Viceroy; *Banga Darshan*;

1873 Enquiry into Indian-owned Press in Bengal;

1875 *Statesman* of Calcutta;

1876 Lord Lytton Viceroy; *Civil and Military Gazette* of Lahore;

1877 Victoria proclaimed Empress of India; *Tribune* of Lahore;

1878 Vernacular Press Act; *Hindu* of Madras founded; *Amrita Bazar Patrika* becomes English weekly;

1881 Vernacular Press Act repealed by Lord Ripon;

1884 Lord Dufferin Viceroy;

1885 Indian National Congress established;

1888 Lord Lansdowne Viceroy;

1890 Indian Official Secrets Act;

1891 *Amrita Bazar Patrika* becomes a daily;

1894 Ninth Earl of Elgin Viceroy; *Bihar Times*;

1896 Marconi invents wireless telegraphy;

1898 Indian Penal Code amended;

1899 Lord Curzon Viceroy;

1900 *Indian Review*;

1901 Edward VII King of England

1903 Indian Official Secrets Act amended;

1905 Partition of Bengal; *Associated Press of India* founded; Lord Minto Viceroy; Bengali daily *Sandhya*;

1906 *Vande Mataram* published;

1907 *Modern Review*;

1908 Newspapers (Incitement to Offences) Act;

1909 Morely-Minto Reforms; *The Leader* of Allahabad; Surendra Nath Banerjee represents Indian press in Imperial press Conference in London;

1910 Act to provide for the better control of the press; Lord Hardinge Viceroy; George V King of England;

1911 Delhi Durbar; Capital shifted from Calcutta to Delhi; First English eveninger *Empire*, Calcutta; *Comrade*;

1912 Urdu daily *Al-Helal* founded by Maulana Abdul Kalam Azad;

1913 *Bombay Chronicle* established.

1914 World War I; Defence of India Act; Bengali daily *Basumati*;

1915 Gandhi returns to India from South Africa; *New India*; *Justice*;

1916 Lord Chelmsford Viceroy; Home Rule League established;

1918 Central Publicity Bureau organised at Simla; Indian Press delegation visits theatre of war; *Servant of India*; War ends;

1919 Rowlatt Act passed; Gandhi launched Passive Resistance Movement; B.G. Horniman deported to England; *The Independent* of Allahabad founded; Montague-Chelmsford Reforms; *Young India* edited by Gandhi;

1920 *The Servant*; *Swarajya*;

1921 Prince of Wales visits India ; Lord Reading Viceroy;

1922 Gandhi arrested; Press Act of 1910 repealed; Newspaper (Incitement to offences) Act of 1908 repealed; Princes Protection Act certified by Viceroy. *Ananda Bazar Patrika* of Calcutta founded; *Forward*; *Hindustan Times*

1924 First Labour Government in Great Britain; Indian efforts at political and communal unity; *Calcutta Municipal Gazatte*;

1927 Indian Statutory Commission appointed; *Free Press of India* started;

1929 Second Labour Government in Great Britain; Round Table Conference proposed; Daily *Advance*;

1930 Gandhi launches Civil Disobedience Movement; Indian Press Ordinance promulgated; *Free Press Journal*; First R.T.C;

1931 Gandhi-Irwin Pact; Lord Willingdon Viceroy; second R.T.C; Indian Press (Emergency Powers) Act; *Indian Nation*;

1932 Foreign Relations Act; Bengal ordinance; Arrests of Gandhi and other leaders; Third R.T.C; *Free Press of India* begins world news service;

1933 White paper on Indian Constitutional Reforms; *United Press of India* founded;

1934 Indian States (Protection) Act; Congress adopts Council entry programme; Gujerati daily *Janmabhoomi*;

1935 Government of India Act passed; Congress opposes new constitution; *Hindustan* (Hindi); *Lokmanya* (Marathi); *Nav Bharat* (Hindi);

1936 Lord Linlithgo Viceroy; *Jagriti* and *Azad* (Bengali);

1937 Congress majority in six legislatures; Congress Governments in eight provinces; *Hindusthan standard*, Calcutta; *Jugantar* (Bengali); *Independent India*;

1938 *National Herald*, Lucknow; Daily *Krishak* (Bengali);

1939 Daily *Bharat* (Bengali); *Navshakti* (Marathi); *Free Press Journal*, Bombay; First session of AINEC; World War II;

1941 Weekly *Forward Bloc*; Daily *Navajug* (Bengali) Daily *Vande Mataram* (Gujerathi): *Aryavarta* (Hindi);

1942 *Morning News*, Calcutta; *People's War*, Bombay; Quit India Movement;

1944 *Nationalist*; *Dinsari* (Tamil); *Keral Bhusanam* (Keralese);

1945 *Eastern Express*, Calcutta;

1946 *Swadhinata* (Bengali); *Sanmarg* (Hindi); *Swaraj* (Bengali); *Ahome* (Assamese); *Jai Hind* (English);

1947 India wins freedom; *Indian News Chronicle*; *Nav Bharat*; *Ittehad* (Bengali); Committee on Press Laws in India; *Prajatantra* (Oriya);

1948 Inter-Dominion Conference on Press;

1951 Constitution amended to impose "reasonable restrictions" on freedom of speech and expression; AINEC protests Constitutional amendment; Newspapers suspend publication for one day. The press (Objectionable Matters) Act amended;

1952 First press Commission set up;

1954 Press Commission submits report;

1956 Press (Objectionable Matters) Act lapses; Newspaper (price and page) Act; Parliamentary Proceedings Act;

1961 Criminal Law (Amendment) Act;

1962 Newspaper (price and page) Act annulled; Chinese aggression; Emergency proclaimed;

1965 Press Council Act;

1966 First press Council set up;

1968 Civil Defence Act;

1969 Criminal and Election Laws (Amendment) Act; Indian Penal Code (Amendment) Act;

1975 Promulgation of Internal Emergency by Indira Gandhi Government; Prevention of publication of objectionable Matters ordinance;

1976 Press Council Act and Parliamentary Proceedings Act replaced;

1977 Janata Government at the Centre; prevention of publication of objectionable Matters Act repealed; Parlimentary proceedings Act re-enacted : Press Council Act passed and Press Council revived ; White paper on abuse of mass media; Report of the Committee on news agencies;

1978 Second Press Commission;

1980 Congress returns to power; Press Commission reconstituted; Assam Press Bill;

1981 Tamilnadu Press Bill; Assam Press Bill struck down by High Court.

1982 Press Commission submits report; Agitation over Bihar Press Bill and Andhra Pradesh Bill;

1984 'Blue Star' operation in Amritsar Golden Temple; Assassination of Prime Minister Indira Gandhi by her own guards. Rajiv Gandhi succeeds Indira Gandhi.

1987 Storm over Bofors Gun purchase;

1988 Agitation against Defamation Bill; Bill to amend PRB Act introduced and later abandoned.

1989 J & K Press Bill withdrawn, Congress defeated in Lok Sabha Poll; Viswanath Pratap Singh leads National Front Government;

1990 National Front Government falls; Chandrasekhar new Prime Minister;

1991 Chandrasekhar Government collapses; Assassination of Rajiv Gandhi; Mid-term poll, Congress emerges victorious . Narashimha Rao forms Government, Economic liberalisation;

1992 'Babri Mosque' demolished ; BJP Ministries in four states dismissed;

1993 Share Market scam; Bombay blasts;

1995 Congress split; Sugar scam and resignation of three central Ministers; Major Train disaster near Faizabad in U.P.; Disclosure of political largessse to select journalists; Sensational Tandoor murder case and probe into nexus between politicians and criminals; Decontrol of newsprint;

1996 Another Congress split; Lok Sabha elections; Congress routed; 'hung parliament', Atal Behari Vajpayee heads BJP Government; Vajpayee Government falls; H.D. Deve Gowda froms united Front Government supported by the Congress.

1997 (upto April): Deve Gowda Government falls as Congress withdraws its support. Indra Kumar Gujral forms second UF Government. Congress extends unconditional support to Gujral Government.

* This is not exhaustive. Many of the newspapers mentioned are now defunct.

APPENDIX - VI
SELECT BIBLIOGRAPHY

The Indian Press, Margarita Barns, George Allan & Unwin Ltd, London, 1940

Journalism in India, Pat Lovett, Banna publishing Co, Calcutta;

The First Press in India and its printers, Rev. J.B. Primrose, The Bibliographic Society, London, 1940

The Indian Press, Viswanath Iyar, Padma publications Ltd, Bombay, 1945;

History of Indian Journalism, J. Natarajan, Publications Division, Government of India, 1955;

Famous Indian Journalists and Journalism, P.G. Rao, Kanara Book and News Agency, Bombay;

Journalism, C.L.R. Shastri, Thacker and Co Ltd. Bombay, 1944;

The spirit of the Anglo-Bengali Magazine, M.N. Sharma, Thackar Spink & Co. Calcutta, 1873

Letters to the Marquis of Hastings on the Indian Press in British India, Captain Francis Romeo, J.M. Richardson, London, 1884;

Sketch of the History and Influence of the Press in British India, Leicester Stanhope, Chapple Royal Library, London, 1823;

Selections from the papers of Lord Metcalfe, J.W. Kaye, Smith Elder & Co. London;

The Great Contempt Case, R.C. Palit, B.C. Majumdar, Calcutta 1883;

Report of the proceedings of a public meeting on the Vernacular Press Act, S.N. Banerjee, Englishman Press, Calcutta;

The Newspapers in India, H.P. Ghosh, University of Calcutta;

Echoes from old Calcutta, H.E. Busteed. Thacker Spink and Co. Calcutta, 1888:

Memoirs of Raja Rammohun Roy, D.N. Ganguly. The people's press, Calcutta, 1884:

The Father of Modern India, Satish Chandra Chakravarty.

Rammohun Roy Centenary Committee, Calcutta, 1935.

Rammohun Roy, U.N. Ball, U. Roy and sons. Calcutta, 1933.

Rammohun Roy as a Journalist, Brajendra Nath Banerji.

Modern Review, April, May and August, 1931.

The English Works of Raja Rammohun Roy (Centenary edition) Sadharan Brahmo Samaj, Calcutta 1931.

RamMohun to Ramkrishna, F Max Muller, Sushil Gupta (India Ltd) Calcutta, 1952.

Selection from Gandhi, N.K. Bose, Navjivan publishing House, Calcutta 1947.

My Experiment with Truth, M.K. Gandhi, Navjivan Publishing House, Ahmedabad, 1940;

Life of Aurobindo Ghose, R. Palit, 1911'

Memories of Motilal Ghose, P. Dutt, Amrita Bazar Patrika, Calcutta, 1935;

Life of Sisir Kumar Ghose, Wayfarer, Amrita Bazar Patrika, Calcutta, 1946.

Memories of my life and time, Bepin Chandra Pal. Modern Book Agency, Calcutta, 1932.

Bal Gangadhar Tilak, Ganesh & Co, Madras.

Life and Times of C.R. Das, P.C. Roy, Oxford University Press, Calcutta, 1925

Calcutta Review, article by S.C. Sanyal. Vols CXXIV to CXXX, 1907-12

Private Journal, Marquess of Hastings

Letters from India, Emily Eden, 1834

British Government in India, Lord Curzon, 1925

Areopagitica, J. Milton

Travels, John Fryer, 1698

A Nation in the Making, Sir S.N. Banerji, Oxford University Press, Calcutta, 1925.

Press and Press Laws in India, H.P. Ghosh, D.K. Mitra, Calcutta 1930.

Freedom of the Press in India, Nikhil Ranjan Roy, General printers and Publishers Ltd, Calcutta, 1950.

Law of the Press in India, D.D. Basu, Prentice Hall of India Pvt. Ltd, N. Delhi.

A History of Indian Journalism, Mohit Moitra, National book Agency Pvt Ltd, Calcutta.

The Press Under Pressure, D.R. Mankekar. Indian Book Company, New Delhi

Mass Communication, R.K. Chatterjee, NBT, India.

Indian Politics since the Mutiny, C. Y. Chintamani, Andhra University, Waltair. 1937.

India, A Nation, Annie Besant, Theosophical publishing House, Madras, 1930.

The Saga of a Newspaper, fifty years of *Free Press Journal*;

India and the Aggressors- The trend of Indian Opinion between 1935-40, Compiled by the Bureau of Public information, Government of India, New Delhi;

Guide to selected newspapers and periodicals in India— Government of India, PIB, New Delhi;

The Provincial Press in India, Press Institute of India, New Delhi, 1966;

Press Laws in India, D.K. Maitra;

The Good old Days of John Company, W.H. Cary;

History of Indian National Congress, B.P. Sitaramayya;

Modern India, 1885-1947, Sumit Sarkar, Macmillan India Ltd, 1983

The political History of India, Sir John Malcalm, 1826

'Reminiscences of a Reporter', An article by Kedar Ghosh, IFWJ Sovrenir, 1962

James Silk Buekingham, Dr. Ralph E. Turner, 1934

Memoirs of a Journalist, J.H. Stocqueler, Bombay, 1934

Lives of Indian Officers, Sir J.W. Kaye, 1854

Lord Metcalfe, Edward Thompson, 1937

The Good Old Days of Honourable John Company, W.H. Carey, 1906

The Competition Wallah, Sir George Trevelyan, 1866
Urdu Journalism in Punjab, Bool Chang, Punjab University Historical Society, Lahore, 1933

Autobiography, Jawaharlal Nehru, 1936

India today and Tomorrow, Margarita Barns, 1937

Modern India, Perciral Stear, Oxford University Press, 1965

Journalism and Politics by M. Chalapathi Rao, Vikas, 1984

A Free and Responsible Press ed. By Robert D. Leigh, University of Chicago Press, Midway Reprint, 1974

Free Press/Free people by John Holenberg (Columbia University press)

Challenge and Stagnation by Chanchal Sarkar, Vikas Publications, 1969.

Annual Reports of Press Council of India;

Freedom of the Press in India, Martinus Nijhoff, The 1961

The changing Press, Chanchal Sarkar, Popular Prakashan, Bombay, 1967

The Pen as my sword, K. Rama Rao, Bharatiya Vidya Bhawan, 1965.

The Press in India, M. Chalapathi Rao, Allied Publishers, Bombay, 1968

Rambles and Recollections, William Sleeman, 1858

Dwarkanath Tagore: A Forgotten Pioneer, National Book Trust

A Hundred years of the Hindu by Rangaswami Parthasarathy, Kasturi & Sons, Madras, 1978

The Nativa Press in India, Sir George Birdwood, Society of Arts, March 1877

India: Bond or Free, Dr Annie Besant

India under Morley and Minto by M.N. Das, Allen and Unwin, 1964

The Press in India, M. Chalapati Rao, Allied Publishers: The Press, M. Chalapathi Rao, National Book Trust, New Delhi, 1974

Journalism in India by Pat Lovett, Banna Publishing Co.; Calcutta

Reuters' Century: 1851-1951 by Graham Storey, Max Parrish, 1951

A History of the Press in India S. Natarajan, Asia Publishing House, 1962

Kasturi Srinivasan by V.K. Narsimhan, Popular Prakashan, 1969

Press Trust of India, Story: Origin and Growth of the Indian Press and the News Agency, G.N.S Raghavan

Press in Chains by Zamir Niazi, Ajanta Publications, 1987

Pothan Joseff's India by T.J.S. George, Sanchar Publishing House, 1992

Selections from the Calcutta Gazettes, Seton-Karr, 1784-97.

Speeches and writings, M.K. Gandhi, Madras, 1917

The Provincial Press in India, Press Institute of India, New Delhi 1966

Emerging Estate, Press Institute of India, New Delhi, 1966

The Press and the Law, Press Institute of India, New Delhi,

The Newspaper and the community, press Institute of India, New Delhi, 1966

Press Councils and their role, Chanchal Sarkar, Press Institute of India

The Press in India, A New History, G.N.S Raghavan, Gyan Publishing House, N. Delhi, 1994

Crisis and Credibility, The Press Council of India, Lancer International, N. Delhi- 1991

White paper on Misuse of Media during internal Emergency, Government of India, 1977

Report of the Enquiry committee on small Newspapers;

Reports of the First and Second Press Commission

Report of the committee on News Agencies,

Ministry of Information and Broadcasting, 1977

Report of the Fact-finding Committee on Newspaper Economics;

'Press in India' — Annual reports of the Registrar of Newspapers, Government of India.

Proceedings of AINEC. 1940-1949

Annual reports of Press Council of India, 1979-1994)

> "I count it a high honour to belong to a trade in which the good men write each piece, each paragraph, each sentence as any Addison, and do so in the full knowledge that by noon the next day it will have been used to light a fire or saved, if at all, to line a shelf".
>
> *Alexander Woollcott*

INDEX

Adam, Frederick 102
   John 49-52, 69
   his regulations 71, 80, 123
Addison, J. 23
Afghanistan 107
AICC 243
AINEC 235, 236, 239, 243, 255, 256, 264, 270, 276, 277, 279, 284
Akhbar (in Persian) 77
Akhbar - E - Kabiseh 85
All Parties' Report 211
Alphonso VI 19
Ambedkar Dr. 252
Amrita Prabahini 131
Amrit Bazar Patrika 131, 132, 134, 135, 146, 153-156, 248, 249, 251

A petition jointly Indian and European journalists 92
Anglo - Indian Press 113
Army 30
Arnot, Mr. 30
Ashburner, Luke 19
Asiatic Mirror 29, 34, 43
"Athenacum" 53
Auckland, Lord 102 - 104
Azad, Maulana Abul Kalam 190
Bailey, William Butterworth 56, 57
Bande Mataram 165
Bangabhashi 157
'Banias' 4
Bangala Samayik Patro 65
Baptist Missionaries 63
Barlow's temporary rule 31

Barns 4, 16, 20, 43, 143
Barwell, Richard 5
Bayley, William Butterworth 68, 90
Bengal Gazette 9
   Harkorw 28, 59, 82, 85
   Herald 84
   journal 15, 21, 22
   Zamindars 15, 21, 22
   Famine (1943) 247, 250
Bentinck, William 32, 78, 80, 87, 90, 100-102
Besant, Annie. 185
Bhattacharya, Ganga Kishore 64
Bhawanicharan, role of 66
BJP (Bharatiya Janata Party) 311
Bolts, William 3-5
Bombay Chronicle 59, 85
   Commercial Advertiser 85
   Courier 19, 21, 85
   Gazette 6, 16, 19, 59, 85, 124
   Herald 19
   Merchants 40
   Samachar 72
   Times 124
Bose, Subhash Chandra 238
Brahminical Magazine 65
Bribes 8
British administration 21
   Government 59, 123
   Newspapers 18
   Parliament 32, 87
   Raj 125
Bryce, James 34, 43
Buckingham, Silk Jones 39, 45, 47, 49, 50, 53-55, 57-59
Columbio Press Gazette 76

Communists, influence of 209
Contemporary Urdu newspapers coming out from Delhi 112
Cooper, Kent 255
Cornwallis, Lord 21, 22, 24, 31
Cripps, Staford 241
Curzon, Lord 20
Daily Courier 72
   Gazette 72
Dalhousie, Lord 110, 111
Danish East India Company 17
Das, C.R. 203
Day in 1966 for Calcuttans 3
Defence of India Rules 228, 233, 234, 251
Delhi Akhbar 105
Depressed Classes 222
Dig Darshan 63
Dominion Status 229
Droz, Simeon
Drunkenness 8
Duane, William 22, 23, 24, 25
Dundas, Henry 25, 32
Duff, Alexander 121
Dufferin, Lord 153
Dutt, Aluree Hur 74, 76
East India Company 22
Ebtal - E - Kabiseh 85
Egypt 39
Ellenborough 107, 108
Elliot, Hugh 42, 43, 44
Englishman 85
English newpapers 112
Press 21
European dress 41
Europeans & sepoys raided Hicky's press 10

Index

Farrlie, Williem 29
Fawai - Nazarin 105
Ferriss, Paul 28
Financial Constraints 29
Firoz, Dastur Mullah 84
First Press Commission 280
Five contemporary Persian Newspapers 104
   Thegwere Jami - Johan - Nima 104
     Aina - i - Sikander 104
     Sultan - ul - Akbar 104
     Mah - Alam Afroz 104
     Mihr - i - Munir 104
Fort William 19, 24, 27, 44, 103
Fourth Estate in India 318
Francis, Philip 7
French Republic 25
Friend of India 63, 124, 135
Fumeron, M 23
Gambling 8
Gandhi, Devdas 265, 269, 271
Gandhi, Indira 288
Gandhi, Mahatma non-cooperation policies 185, 187
Gandhi, Papers 189
Gandhi, arrest 198
General Advertiser of the Interior 57
General Post Office 9
Geneva Conference 272
Ghosh, Aurobindo 170, 171
   ManMohan 129
Gokhale, Gopal Krishna 166
Golden Era 108
Government Gazette 72
   Gazetter 82
   hostility 9

newspaper from Bengal 20
Greenway, Morley 28
Guillin, Henry 31
Gujarati journalism 113
Gujral, I.K. 289
Haider Ali's forces 7
Halder Neil Puttan 84
Halls, James Stuart 18
Hamilton, Lord 32
Hastings, Lord 32
Hastings, Mrs. 8, 44, 48, 53
Hastings, Warren 7, 8, 10, 34
   (impeachment of) 21
Hatley, James 16
Hay 23
Heatley 34
Hicky, James Augustus, 5, 8, 9, 19
   Gazette 5, 6
   both a failure and a sucess 15
   his impri-sonment & fine 10
   the trader printer - turned journal list 10
   to be remembered as the- pioneer of the Indian Press 11
Hindoo Patriot 130
Hindu - Muslim feelings 207
Hitavada 191, 251
His majesty's Naval Force in Indian Seas 30
Hobhouse, Arthur 140
Hollingberry, Thomas 28
House of Commons 20
"Humayoon Shah" 40
Hume 152
Hunter, William 28
Hurkaru 17
Ilbert Bill Controversy 157

Imhoff, Russian painter 8
Impey, Elijah 9
INA 253
India Gazette 9
   Economist 134
   Herald 18
   Mirror 130
Indian Civil Service (1849 - 1882) 152
Indian National Congress 88, 159, 171
India-Pakistan Agreement 273
Internal Emergency 288
Jambhekar, Bal Shastri 113
Jamson, Dr. 49
Jan - i - Jahan - Numa (Persian Newspaper) 68, 74, 75, 76, 77, 83
Jinnah 261
John, Adam 46
   Bull 46, 73, 82, 85
Johnson, Richard 17, 19
Jones, Thomas 16
   William 85
J & K Government 307
Kashmir 154
Kelaidoscope 76
Kesri 172
Khan, Syed Mohammed 105
King George V 177
Kipling, Rudyard 141
Kishore, Jugal 73
Knight, Robert 139, 140, 152
Kumar, Nand (Maharaja) 8
Landon, Mr. 18
Landsdowne, Lord 157
Letters of Junius 7, 17

London 20, 21
London Daily 7
Long, J. (Rev.) 109, 128, 129, 136
Lord North's Regulating Act of 1773 6
Lytton, Lord 139, 141, 143
   Government 31
Majumdar, J.K. 64
Malaviya, Madan Mohan 175
Malcom, John 125
Marshman, J.C. 78, 79
   John 41
Martin, Robert Montgomery 84
Mckenly, Holt 25, 28
Meerut-ul-Akhbar 65, 68, 69, 70
Mehta, Firoz Shah 175
Metcalf, Charles. T. 88, 90, 92, 97, 100, 101, 102, 103
Milton's Aeropagitica 6
Macaulay 97
   his Act 97, 98, 99
Mac Donald, Ramsay 222
Machenzie, Holt 88
Maclean, Charles 25,26
MacNaghten, Francis 69, 71
Madras Courier 17, 18, 19. 72
Madras Gazette 18
Minto, Lord 31, 33
Mirror of the Press 85
Moitra, Mohit 81
Morning Post 28, 34
Morris, John 19
Morris, William 29
Moombai Samachar 84
   Vartaman 84
Montague - Chelmsford Reforms 195

Index

Montague-Chelmsford Report 195, 197
Motiwala Pestonji Maneqji 84
Mumbaina Samachar 72
Murzeban, Fardoonji 72
Muslim League 183, 261
Mustan, Mr. 58, 59
Mutsuddis 4
Natrajan, J. 113
"Navab Barwell" 5
Nehru, Jawahar Lal 203, 212, 213, 216
    Motilal 203
    Motilal his views 257
Newspaper Economics 286
New Weekly Register 57
"Old Tories" 108
Oodant Martand 73
Oriental Herald 53, 56, 57
    Chirstian Spectator 85
Oriental Magazine 16
Oriental Star 29
Palmer, John 40
Parker, Henry Meredith 41
Parliamentary reports 20
Pakistan 261
Partition of India 264
Patna Times 252
Pearce, R.R. 26, 28,
"Poet's Corner" 20
Political and Literary Register 85
Postal System 17
Pressure on the Press 299
Press in Bombay 18
Prinsep, H.T. 100
Privy Council 71
PTI (Press Trust of India) 347

Puja Holidays 154
Queen's Proclamation 125
Queen Victoria 142
Quit India (1942) 24, 242
Quran - ul - Saadin 105
Registration of Books Act, 1867 214
Ripon, Lord 149
Robison, Col. 47, 48, 49
Role of the Press 298
Round Table Conference 218
Rowalatt Committee 197
Roy, Raja Rammohan 39, 64, 65, 66, 68, 69, 70, 71, 81, 86, 88, 100
Rule by Ordinance 220
Russians are coming to India 112
Salisbury, Lord 143
Samachar Chandrika 66, 67, 73
Samachar Darpan 63, 64, 65, 73, 74, 75, 76,
Sambad Kaumudi 65, 66, 67, 73, 89
Sandfort, Mr. 55
Sandys, Mr. 53, 54, 55
Sangbad Timir Nashak 73
Sayyad - ul - Akhbar 105
Scotsman in the East 76
Sen, Keshab Chandra 129, 130
Serampore missionaries 31
Shams-ul-Akhbar (Persian news paper) 68
Shore, John 24, 25
Srinivasan, K. 244
Stocquelar, J.H. 107
Sulav Samachar 130
Sunday Mirror 130

Supreme Court 10, 285
"*Sutti*" issue 66, 85
   abolition of 81
   abolition of by Lord Bentinck 67
Swadeshi Movement 164
Tagore, Dwarakanath 69, 73, 84, 129, 86
   Prassna Kumar 84, 86, 87
   Rabindranath 65, 129
   Sunder Kumar 69
Tatvabodhini Patrika 129
Telegraph 25, 28
The Bombay Herald 19
   Civil and Military Gazettee 141
   Hindu Patriot 143 - 145
   Times 106
The Hindu 150
The Pioneer 141
The Statesman 129, 135, 152, 249, 257
The Times of India 160
Thomson, Archibald 28
Thomson, Edward 103
Tilak, Bal Gangadhar 159
Tipoo Sultan 26, 27
Tory 46
Tradesmen 24
Travelyan, Charles 106, 107

Tribune 142
Turton, Thomas 33
Ukhbara Seerampore 75
Unwarranted Restrictions 235
Urdu Journals 127
Vangal Gazette 63, 64, 65
Vellore Mutiny 31
Vernacular Press 1878 71
Vicar of Wakefield 48
Vidyasagar, Iswar Chandra 109, 27, 128
Weekly Gleaner 76
Wellesley, Lord 26, 28, 29
William, R. 18
Williams, J.D. 29
Whig Ministry 102
Wilson, John 85
Wilson, H.D. 28
World War I (1914) 183
World War II (Sep. 3, 1939) 227
Year 1835, a landmark in Indian Journalism 100